Graphic Design & Reading

Graphic Design

&READING

explorations of an uneasy relationship

edited by Gunnar Swanson

Park Library
University of Gloucestershire
Park Campus, The Park
Cheltenham
Gloucestershire
GL50 2RH

Allworth Press, New York

Cover design by
Gunnar Swanson
Ventura, California

05 04 03 02 01 00   5 4 3 2 1

Page composition
and typography by
Gunnar Swanson
Ventura, California

www.gunnarswanson.com

Library of Congress Cataloging-in-Publication Data:
Graphic design & reading: explorations of an uneasy
relationship / edited by Gunnar Swanson
p. cm.
includes bibliographical references and index.
ISBN: 1-58115-063-6
1. Graphic Design (Typography) 2. Legibility (Printing) 3.
Books—Format 4. Book design I. Swanson, Gunnar.

Z246 .G68 2000
686.2'2—dc21
                                    00-038993

Published by Allworth Press
An imprint of Allworth Communications
10 East 23rd Street, New York, NY 10010   Printed in Canada

*for Ray and Deedie
and for Rosemary.*

Thank you.

Graphic Design &Reading

Gunnar Swanson

re:word

HIS BOOK BEGAN WHEN I WAS ASKED to curate a show about graphic design for the Tweed Museum of Art at the University of Minnesota Duluth (UMD). The specifics were left up to me. It's an interesting problem—how do you avoid an amorphous theme like "Stuff Gunnar Swanson Happens to Like" but also avoid the sort of specificity that would defeat the purpose of introducing graphic design to a nondesigner audience? I hoped that people would leave with design issues in mind, but esoterica such as "The Origins of the Arbitrary Shape in 1987-1992 Cranbrook/CalArts Poster Design" wouldn't have been of much interest to the bulk of northern Minnesota museum-goers.

The several broadly thematic approaches I considered centered on graphic design's relationship with other subjects. I rejected a look at how graphic design has been shaped by the twin forces of client needs and design technology when I admitted to myself that it was as much for my number-one choice for the potential title ("Capitalist Tools") as for the potential of the exhibition. Another theme— looking at the relationships of graphic design and reading—won out.

One of the most difficult parts of putting together a medium-profile exhibition is financing the catalog. A significant publication is in order, but such limited-run books are rarely supported by sales. Short-run color printing is expensive, despite advances in technologies such as direct-to-plate printing, and many grant-funders don't like the idea of donating a lot of money to subsidize people's book-buying. My way around the problem was instead to create a book that could stand on its own and be commercially viable. If such a book were to be available for the show's opening, it would have to precede much of the shaping of the exhibition. A series of articles by various authors, I thought, could provide various points of view that I could incorporate into the show, enriching what I already hoped would be an eclectic look at graphic design.

The exhibition disappeared from the Tweed's calendar after I resigned my position as head of the graphic design program at UMD. The book already had a life of its own by that time, but freedom from functioning as a show catalog (and from a publication schedule based on the planned exhibition dates) allowed a very different and, I hope, richer book.

Like the bad old joke—"It's the same axe, but it's had five new handles and a new head"—the name also went through revision. The original title was *re:word,* and "Graphic Design and Reading" was to be the subtitle. Although I agree that there are many good reasons for a straightforward, descriptive title, I must admit some fondness for my original exhibition and book title. The name *re:word* doesn't do the explanatory work needed to sell an already somewhat esoteric book, but it speaks to the relationship of graphic design and reading, if by no other means than complexity and ambiguity.

Is graphic design *about words*—focusing on the writer's work—or *rewording* —a process of both restructuring and editing meaning? The answer, I believe, is neither and both. The sentiment in Beatrice Warde's famous "crystal goblet" simile —the idea that type should contain but not detract from or obscure a writer's ideas just as a wine glass should neither detract from nor obscure the wine—is in many ways a noble one. Whether it is also a naïve one (as I imply in "Clarety") or an exclusionary one (as Katie Salen indicates in "Surrogate Multiplicities: In Search of the Visual Voice-Over"), transparent typography is hardly the reason that most clients engage graphic designers. It would seem that most of the world fails to share Warde's disdain for the ornate chalice and preference for a metaphorical invisible bubble.

In "Seen and Not Seen," Kenneth FitzGerald quotes William Golden regarding clients' desire to have the designer "help create an attitude." Warde was, of course, talking largely about book typography, but I believe that most designers see their primary role as attitude creators for every medium, including the book (although the book's "attitude" might be more subtle). Robert Bringhurst, generally identified with restrained book design, notes that, "In a world rife with unsolicited messages, typography must often draw attention to itself before it will be read." He does clarify by stating that "in order to be read, it must relinquish the attention it has drawn,"[1] but since I'm already guilty of playing the bull in the china shop regarding the reference to Warde's simile in my essay, I won't further mix my metaphors by attempting to identify the alchemy that allows that glass's transformation.

[1] Robert Bringhurst, *The Elements of Typographic Style* (Vancouver, B.C.: Hartley and Marks, 1992) 17

While I was still in Duluth, Stephen Doyle was in town to speak at UMD, and we had a long conversation that centered on transformations. I told him about a 1970s L.A. band that recorded the lyrics of the Gilligan's Island theme song to the tune of "Stairway to Heaven" (much to the dismay of Robert Plant and his lawyers). I sang him my version of the Petticoat Junction theme to the tune of "The Banana Boat Song"; a.k.a., "Day-O." (The man is a tolerant dinner companion.) He told me about hearing a punk-rock version of Barney's "I Love You, You Love Me" song and let me in on the secret that any Emily Dickinson poem can be sung to the tune of "I'd Like to Buy the World a Coke." If you're old enough to remember those commercials, sing along:

> *Because I could not stop for Death*
> *Death kindly stopped for me.*
> *And in the carriage just ourselves*
> *And all eternity.*
> *It's the Real Thing, Death is . . .*

As Stephen pointed out to the students the next day, that's what we as graphic designers do—we put stuff in a new context. With all due respect to Ms. Warde and her aspirations, we do that whether we want to or not. We recontextualize the words and images we use in our design and, thus, in some sense, reword them. We may have a large amount of control over the new context and the new meaning, but the design (and the designer) will no more disappear than the host of a dinner party will suspend the wine in the air for the unobscured appreciation of the guests.

James Souttar dismisses the thought of wine without bottle or glass in his "The Myth of Content and the Encyclopedestrianization of Communication" and sees the attempt as not merely naïve but as regressive. In "The Written Word: The Designer as Mediator," William Drenttel quotes novelist Paul Auster on the individual nature of the reading experience. Kenneth FitzGerald's "Seen and Not Seen" notes how design can invite or discourage reading by certain groups of individuals, Michael Schmidt looks for a magazine for his demographic in "Two Days in Limbo," and Katie Salen's "Surrogate Multiplicities" considers groups' attempts at gaining a typographic voice and typographic depictions of various groups. None of this is in direct contradiction to Souttar's argument for a return to the communally understood narrative, but rejecting the notion of disembodied "content" leads many to question the believability of communal experience itself. Once you lobby for your demographic, the next logical step is to wonder whether anyone else really joins you in it.

None of the authors in this book resorts to the claim of complete individuality, where shared experience is seen as minimal and insignificant. This radically personal approach justifies[2] any weakness in clarity or legibility of type by dismissing the possibility of communication. While not intellectually untenable, this line of reasoning leads inevitably to the question of why anyone would then bother with design or designers; perhaps the pragmatic nature of designers is the cause for this line of argument having largely gone out of style.

[2] Pun not intended.

A parallel but more moderate argument doesn't reject the possibility of communication but does emphasize that language, including visible language, is typically what semioticians call "unmotivated." Just as words are arbitrary social convention[3]—the word "book" has no inevitable connection with the object you are reading and is no more a perfect description than is "libro" or, for that matter, "aardvark"—letterforms are legible because of familiarity rather than inherent nature. Zuzana Licko of *Emigre* has said that:

> *typefaces are not intrinsically legible, rather, it is the reader's familiarity with faces that accounts for their legibility. Studies have shown that readers read best what they read most. Legibility is also a dynamic process, as readers' habits are everchanging. It seems curious that blackletter typestyles, which we find illegible today, were actually preferred over more humanistic designs during the eleventh and fifteenth centuries. Similarly, typestyles that we perceive as illegible today may well become tomorrow's classic choices.[4]*

[3] Not arbitrary in the sense that any word can be replaced with another in a random fashion and still be understood, but in the sense that social agreement rather than natural connections between sound or shape and the definitions in a lexicon give words meaning.

While blackletter was the stuff of German newspapers within the past fifty years and was, by all accounts, easier to read for its audience than the

[4] Zuzana Licko, *Emigre* 15 (1990) 12

unfamiliar roman type-
faces, it would be hard to
make a similar case for
the Fraktur faces of the
fifteenth century. It would even be hard to make a case that there was such a
thing as immersive reading in the sense that Warde speaks of her encounters

Roman with *The Three Musketeers* in "The Crystal Goblet,
or Printing Should Be Invisible." The implication
that Gutenberg's customers might have read their bibles like we would read a Sue
Grafton novel runs counter to everything we know about their religious practices.

Whether the rules of legibility that Rolf Rehe brings us in his succinctly
titled "Legibility" are eternal or based on familiarity is perhaps arguable, but many
of the studies he notes seem to be based on physiological rather than cultural considerations. I must admit to doubts about some studies. How does someone testing
Times Roman versus Helvetica conclude that serifs are the factor being tested

rather than evenness of weight, angle of stress,
or x-height? Isolating factors in design is usu-
ally difficult and often impossible. A pharma-
cologist friend of mine slices brains and keeps
the parts alive to examine the effects of drugs
without the effects of those drugs on bodily
functions; anyone who has read *Cliff's Notes* can tell you that we have yet to find
out how to slice a book and keep the parts alive.

Factors such as line length and leading may be the subject of fashion and
familiarity, but hardly infinitely so. Some of Rehe's rules clearly apply to more than
passing cultural agreement. Interestingly, Licko's claim that familiarity breeds readability seems to be regarding the inherent legibility of a given typeface rather than
of the typeface's use, while many of the studies Rehe cites discuss the arrangement
and sizing of type.

What gets lost in many discussions of "the rules" is that reading is hardly
one activity. The assumption that what we know about reading a novel is applicable
to reading a medicine label, a billboard, the type on a TV commercial, the financials
section of a corporate annual report, and a comic book seems unwarranted.

These questions regarding different kinds of reading will continue to be
very important as we move even more into alternatives to ink on paper. Jessica
Helfand takes us through a few things we need to think about as type becomes
"virtual" in "Electronic Typography: The New Visual Language." In "Rethinking
the Book," David Small considers some particulars of use of books. In this excerpt
from his MIT Media Lab Ph.D. thesis, he looks by implication at the promise of
the electronic linking of all knowledge as he considers a possible digital version of
Talmudic study, an exercise in limited hypertext. Now that graphic designers have
the power to arrange type in four dimensions rather than two, can we improve upon
the time-tested ways of doing things? And what will our new rules of legibility be?

Graphic Design & Reading

Type designers—those who create new typefaces—make stuff for others to arrange rather than arranging existing elements as most graphic designers do. Although it may sometimes seem that typefaces are available in infinite variety, Hrant Papazian makes the case for a new sort[5] in "Improving the Tool." Graphic designers may be the greatest culprits in the obscuring of Warde's goblet, but Papazian makes a case for type designers' rethinking of the basic shapes of letters' "skeletons." His reconsideration of the conceptual structure of the alphabet represents something rare in design thinking—consideration of the "essence" without tending toward minimalism.

[5] Pun intended.

When I called and e-mailed my favorite design writers asking them to participate in what I was then calling *re:word*, I expected a bit more commentary on the designer's role in the mechanics of reading and *much* more polemic rejecting traditional standards of readability. Strangely enough, the only clear rejection of legibility (other than Kenneth FitzGerald's explanation of its usefulness) came from calligraphy, a field often assumed to be conservative to the point of being stodgy. Steven Skaggs's "The New Calligraphic Renaissance" talks about writing that values its own formal and expressionistic traits but not necessarily legibility. Like graffiti "writers," the calligraphers Skaggs introduces us to prefer the ornate chalice Warde rejects. They recognize wine drinking as an activity that often has little to do with an oenophile's concentration on the qualities of the drink.

There is a power of writing that goes beyond reading. One of the Norse Eddas is an ironic poem from the point of view of Odin, who, in wandering Earth, found himself sacrificed to himself. One of the few clear things in the murky story is that learning the runes[6] was an experience with cosmic importance for this dying god. When one considers the power of eternal memory that writing represented to heretofore illiterate peoples and the changes in economic and governmental structures possible with the advent of a written record, it is not

[6] Although runes have been used as a fortune-telling device, they were actually a Viking writing system based on a range of influences, including the Greek alphabet.

surprising that writing and reading take on mystic aspects. Paul Elliman's ode to the letter e is a case in point. (It is disturbing, however, that his catalog of e's glories fails to recognize its importance in the key of B flat, and thus the blues.) Ellen Lupton's "Visual Syntax" ostensibly deals with attempts to see abstract graphic form as language. Absent denotative meaning in these "languages," one could argue that the design exercises she shows are every bit as mystic as Odin's poetic cries from the hanging tree.

While Lupton calls for something more than a personalized and stylistically updated version of what some may dismiss as purely formal abstraction, Stephanie Zelman looks to the PoMo verso of the modernist recto and tries to find meaning in the way graphic design invites us to look and see. Zelman joins Marshall McLuhan and James Souttar in a critique of the Enlightenment model of dualism that separates vision from the body and/or self. It would be easy to see Neville Brody's typographic experimentation as part of the Emil Ruder–Cranbrook continuum shown in Lupton's "Visual Syntax" but Zelman claims that there is more going on in that post modern design opposes the assumption of an uninterrupted object/eye flow and that designing digitally made such a shift almost inevitable.

If Zelman is right, we are in the middle of a transition of how we read and, for that matter, what the act of reading entails. I think it best to avoid the assumption that reading ever was or ever will be a single activity, however. Nor would it be wise to assume the contrary—that different modes of reading are, were, or will be completely unrelated. The mystic fascination with letterforms and image has, I believe, more of a role in Warde's supposedly-invisible style of reading than "The Crystal Goblet" might lead us to believe and the type-as-image of Neville Brody and others does not need to completely preclude the efficiencies of "legibility." (Some of the assumptions of Rehe's article of that name may, in fact, be incompatible with the work Zelman talks about.)

Beatrice Warde makes the claim that advertising falls into the realm of her required invisibility, but Steve Heller gives us a case to the contrary. His tale of Lucian Berhard and the German one-word poster is clearly not about immersion in the sense that Papazian and Warde discuss. It did start to bring about a quite different immersion, however, one chronicled indirectly in Johanna Drucker's "Signs of Life/Spaces of Art: From Standard Brands to Integrated Circuits." Using signage depicted within art as a gauge, Drucker brings us through a consideration of the changing commercial (and private) landscape. Drucker raises some of the same questions about reading that we find in Colette Gaiter's annotated photos of her youth. The interaction of word and image is perhaps one of the most interesting topics of graphic design, and our claims that we "read" a photograph or other image raise many more questions than they answer.

Just as photography brought a ubiquity of images to our lives and thus changed the notion of how communication works, will electronic technologies change the definition of "reading"? There has been considerable talk about the end of the book and/or the rise of the e-book. The hardware part of e-book systems now available are, not surprisingly, a lot like books (if books had small LCD screens, that is). Maybe they'll become even more booklike. Much has been written about "electronic paper"—thin white material that can locally blacken with electronic impulses, acting like paper with ever-changeable ink. David Small's work reinforces my conviction that, no matter what the fate of book simulacra, we will soon face new reading situations and new ways to read.

One of the cliché examples of design development is the "horseless carriage." Early automobiles were designed by people who had no reference for what a car could or should be, so inventors placed engines in something much like the horse-drawn wagons the autos were meant to replace. Only later did cars take on a form of their own, a specifically automotive one. The Talmud project may be the Model T of books.[7]

An e-book and Small's Talmudic mechanism differ not just in form, but in nature. The LCD-screened books are meant to be essentially passive. A dictionary linking words in the text to their definitions may add functionality, but we're still talking about paperless books. The Talmud project

[7] Thanks, as always, to Lou Danziger for insights and good conversation.

may not have an electric starter, fuel injection, and automatic transmission, but it's a step away from a wagon with an engine bolted on. The project was not just a tool for display, but one for broad interactivity.

Books are richly interactive. We sense our place by the thickness of pages passed and pages yet to come. We navigate with our hands and eyes, with continuous feedback on several levels. At first glance, an e-book or an article on a Web site seems like nothing more than an impoverished book, but Small gives us a glance at possibilities of future form. But what would the electric starter for hyperlinked reference material be? Perhaps Hrant Papazian gave us a hint in his discussion of the mechanics of reading. Certain eye fixations can indicate a disruption of understanding. If fairly inexpensive cameras can track our eye movements to decide where to focus a photograph, why can't "books" determine our trouble with a particular word and provide the definition automatically or note our problem with a phrase and deliver us an explanatory link?

What innovations of communication would come of an automatically expanding book? Steven Johnson, editor-in-chief of the Web's *Feed*[8] magazine, makes a case in his book *Interface Culture*[9] that Web-based writing has just begun to deal with hyperlinks as more than footnotes and the Web as more than a transportable magazine. His example of a breakthrough was *Suck* magazine's use of self-referential hyperlinks where a link for "sell-out" brings the reader back to the same page of the *Suck* article. *Suck* made ironic comment on its own sold-out status by foiling the expectation that a link takes the reader someplace else. What at first seemed like a technical error became a new literary trope. If we are just starting to find the uses of the Web's engine-bolted-to-a-wagon mechanisms, who knows what we might do with an advanced automobile (and what will one look like)?

[8] www.feedmagazine.com

[9] Steven Johnson *Interface Culture: How New Technology Transforms the Way We Create and Communicate* (San Francisco: Harper Edge, 1997) 132–135

re:word

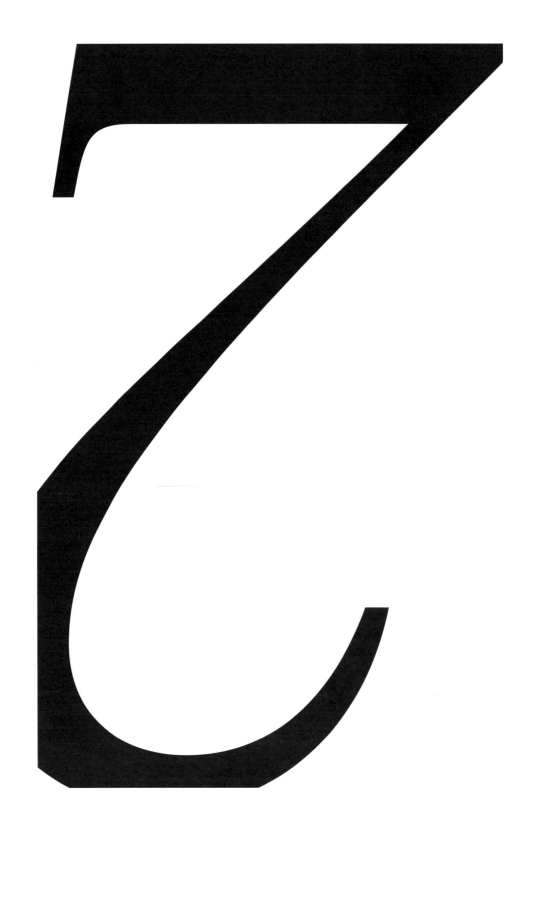

Two Days in Limbo

Michael Schmidt

Scene One: The Waiting Room

I have yet to walk into a doctor's office and find a magazine meant for me. It's always the same thing: a pile of two-year-old journalistic debris, none of which has any bearing on my life or interests. It's disquieting, unsettling even. How can I trust a physician that doesn't even acknowledge my demographic? I feel like asking for a referral to a specialist, one with *Emigre, ArtByte, 2Wice,* and *Critique* strewn across the waiting room. I would be comfortable then, content in the knowledge that the specialist has insight into my particular concerns and, therefore, possesses the unique ability to accurately diagnose all that ails the common graphic designer.

I'm a foreigner in the waiting room, a stranger seeking the familiar in whatever bit and scrap of reading material is left unclaimed. Dismayed by the only thing left, an issue of *Seventeen*—which may as well be typeset in Cyrillic, for all I care—I turn ever so casually to look over the shoulders of my ailing companions to catch a glimpse of what they find interesting, or at least palatable. I see their intent gazes, I imagine their minds at work, and I wonder what they're learning—or maybe they're not; maybe their eyes are moving across the words in the same manner television images flicker before a blank gaze. Maybe the context is wrong. This is all just some escape from anxiety, facilitated by the reading material. Yes! Of course, that's why the doctors place these publications here. I bet they don't even consider what they're subscribing to; it's just material for distraction. This realization doesn't do anything to help my trust issues. Horrified, I sit quietly reading my issue of *Seventeen*.

Now I'm floating in a reading limbo. I see myself from above as I bump against the ceiling. More perplexing than bumping against something (I'm out-of-body, after all) is how Kate Moss could stand up long enough for the photo I see myself staring at. I know how this is going to end. I die. Yep, I'm dead. It's funny how this waiting room looks about the same as the other. Damn, *Seventeen* again, and this time it is in Cyrillic!

Cut to: Gratuitous Explanation

What you have just witnessed is the death of the reader. All electrical impulses are cut: no neurons firing and no synapses forming. The current is still, knowledge is dormant, mental connections are irrelevant. But I'm still writing—how is this possible? I'm a dead reader, but a live writer. Boy, I bet this script is going to be boring. Just stop reading. I don't want to be rude, but I just don't have anything relevant to offer. Please forgive me; I'm dead, after all.

Deep metaphorical pause; pregnant pause. Hmm, is there something familiar about this story? Could I be a dead reader, like all those distracted sick people in the waiting room, while still being a live designer? I guess so, but what kind of professional life would this be? Little growth, a few paltry connections buzzing about in my brain, limited input to stimulate the dearth of output—not an appealing proposition; this point forms the springboard for my concerns regarding the connections between reading and graphic design. When reading is considered a key player in constituting one's knowledge of the world, the implication is that it has a great deal to do with the formation of an ideological base for decision making. Hence, creativity, problem solving, design practice, and pedagogical theory come to the foreground as manifestations of one's ideological beliefs, which reading helps constitute.[1] For clarity, I want to define "ideology" in relation to my statement of thesis: 1) Ideal or abstract speculation and visionary theorizing, and 2) A way of thinking or system of attitudes—the manner in which an individual or group views reality.[2]

In the process of investigating reading's impact on ideological formation, it appears the problem isn't so much with what we read as with how we read. Do we read for awareness? Inventive inspiration? Affirmation? Sleep? To put it simply, people who read are prone to inventing connections. This behavior is termed "creativity." And these people are extolled as "creative." Hence, this discussion articulates the value of knowledge in its dynamic states of acquisition, connection, and use. Furthermore, reading activity that engages thought and questioning (reading for awareness and inventive inspiration) is the greater aid to a unique and responsible understanding of one's ideological biases at work.[3]

The drawback to my thesis is that it contains a supposition: Reading actually has a constitutive effect on the common designer's knowledge base. Given the overwhelming number of reader responses to journals such as *Emigre* and the proliferation of design texts, anthologies, and bibliog-

[1] In the worst sense of the word, "ideology" connotes a static, rigid doctrine. This essay, however, espouses another meaning: The dynamic interplay of ideas and experiences that inform decision making.

[2] For a wonderful explanation of the meanings of "ideology," see Henry D. Aiken, ed., *The Age of Ideology* (New York: The New American Library, 1956) 13–14

raphies, my supposition may be closer to a truth. Designers prove to be just as concerned with what they read as with what they make. Simple enough. But when the discussion turns to how we read—and how this discussion reveals information about decision making, cognition, and creativity—the problems present themselves in a weblike fashion rather than a linear path of reasoning. As is often the case, realization seeks expression in symbolic form.[4]

[3] My argument is dialectic because it seeks to reconcile the individual with the collective. Ideology itself straddles the boundary between individual intention and public interaction, and, conversely, societal influence and personal decision making.

Hovering between thinking and making, research and production, this inquiry places me in a kind of limbo. In my version of limbo I can actually walk around inside my brain; I can see and touch the experiences that inform my decision making. Shorn of all religious reference in my model, limbo is a concept for an interactive exhibition where learning takes place laterally and diachronically as filmed images play out in response to my presence and thoughts. In the process, statements explicating my thesis are revealed.

[4] I owe this transition to Joseph Campbell. (See Joseph Campbell interview by Bill Moyers in Betty Sue Flowers, ed., *The Power of Myth* [New York: Doubleday, 1988] 41)

Scene Two: Day One in Limbo

Oh, the irony. There I was in the waiting room. The last thing I was worried about was being a writer. I would have felt self-actualized and engaged with a simple, decent bit of reading material—something that would have enriched my knowledge base, fed my brain, created new insights. I would have felt like a thinker, an alive and fully conscious participant in that microcosmic society encamped in my doctor's waiting room. Hell, I might have even struck up a conversation with someone, voicing my agency and intention. Yeah, I could have participated in an actual discourse (or maybe just a simple dialogue).

I exist now between the material and the immaterial: This position serves to help me better grasp the dual nature of reading. First, as reading material, reading deepens the pool of knowledge—collectively and individually—while helping to form opinions, convictions, and ideological beliefs. For this reason such material is both valued and shunned. Labeled as anti-American, anti-Christian, anti-Semitic, anti-Islamic, anti-German, anti-Napoleon, the ideological biases of what we read bubble to the surface like molten lead; cast into type, they press against our very conscience. Throughout modern history, reading and ideology carry the connotations of power and threat, respectively.

In the ether of my new immaterial environment, all I have left are my thoughts—reminding me of the cognitive function of reading. Strategy, technique, conceptions regarding the operation of the mind, creativity, and even ontological awareness are all engaged, developed, and utilized during the process of reading, or afterwards, upon reflection.

Now the images of my past are rolling faster. (For some reason, limbo doesn't have an audio system. Figures.) I see the moments when reading most affected me. There were the times that reading reconfigured my conceptions, creating awareness of everything from propagandistic persuasion to genuine academic or artistic provocation. Then there were the more intimate moments, further back in my youth, when I used to go to church (that might have something to do with the holdup here). Those moments employed reading as ceremony, as reaffirmation of existing structures/beliefs. The steady repetition of The Apostles' Creed week after week formed the basis of a faith I forgot to question. The ideological package was so neatly wrapped, it was easy to accept.

As I watch my life's film, I become another type of reader: a mind reader uncovering the millions of thoughts written out in invisible ink across a thousand strands of memories. It's impossible to escape my training as I look for patterns or any other identifiable structural form to my knowledge base and how I used it. I'm looking first for some dominant hierarchical element, an anchor that might be holding this complex composition together. An anchor for my thoughts would have to be something of great importance, something that was recurrent in my readings or at least in my interpretation of readings, something influential enough to affect the very products of my craft.

Memory Sequence
(Insert cheesy Video Toaster and fade to memory sound effects here.)
Never in all my life have I seen so many bagpipers and cops in one place. The St. Patrick's Day parade in New York City is hard to escape, unless you manage to push your way into the Met, another overwhelming public institution.

The Met is a wonderful and yet difficult place to bring young kids. There's so much to see, and one young man I saw wanted to tug his parents around to every last thing that caught his eye. His annoyed mother finally said, "We only have time to see the important things."

Suddenly I remembered all the "important" books I was told to read as a kid. Why? Because they're important, damn it. I remembered the school field trips to supposedly important places or important exhibitions. I felt privileged, but I didn't fully understand why. It was a neat package again, one as easy to accept as any other. In any case, my teachers provided guidance but little encouragement to think for one's self.

What disturbed me about the exchange I overheard between the parent and child was that this boy's curiosity was trampled. He was clearly born with the desire to seek information out and make it his own. In return he was offered a McArt lesson. Importance, he may later realize, is culturally understood and artificially constructed: a McIdeology.

I think it's fair to say we all want to be genuine, and some of us go to great lengths to prove our uniqueness. It stands to reason then that intellectual growth and critical-thinking skills are valuable assets to the designer in terms of personal identity and professional performance. But how much of our decision making is based on a unique sense of self—a critical ideological base from which to work—

instead of from the many McIdeologies pervasive in society?[5] As my memory reveals, we're taught from an early age to be McThinkers, McViewers, and even McReaders.

Memory Sequence Two
(Insert more cheesy sound effects.)

One of the things I enjoy about exhibitions is that I feel like I'm walking around inside a story. The text and images of the tale surround me in three-dimensional space, inviting me to navigate through the environment in a linear sequence akin to turning pages in a book. Rarely, however, do I read one book at a time or move through the chapters in order. So sometimes I piss people off and walk backward through the space just to see how the narrative reads in reverse. This requires an act of defiance when there's a tape-recorded docent talking into my ear. "Now please move into the next room, where you will find . . ." It's bad enough that I'm being directed to all the "important" things just like the kid in the Met, but Martin Sheen is ruining all the surprises by telling me what I will see next.

Click—Silence—Pregnant pause—(I just like that term). Ah, reading material. Silk-screened type on plex: signs, labels, didactic panels—mmm, heaven.

No?

Sorry, still limbo.

Damn.

What did you say?

Nothing. This is a really great issue of *Seventeen*.

Peer pressure gets the better of me. Click—Martin's soothing voice again fills my ears. "In the display case to your left you will see an accounting device used by the ancestors of the Incas. Called a "quipu" (kee-poo), this tool was used around A.D. 1200 as a record-keeping device for debts owed the king. You will notice the dozens of long strands radiating out from the central leather loop. Numerous knots were tied into each strand. The purpose of the strands and the meaning of all the different knots remain unknown. Only the king's special accounting staff could read the quipu."[6]

The object in the case is remarkable. Even though I don't understand how it was used, I have the overwhelming impression that this thing is the perfect graphic representation of accounts and debts for a culture with no system of writing.

The well-crafted presentation of the object makes a further impression. Each strand radiating out from the object's central leather loop is pinned, perfectly straight, into position. All the strands are equidistant and,

[5] Designers who clearly have an ideological base for their work—those who employ abstract speculation and visionary theorizing or who simply operate from a critically developed system of attitudes/beliefs—inform their practice with information outside the taxonomies of design. Listening to designers speak about their process, whether Fred Woodward of *Rolling Stone* or April Greiman, reveals a consistent but evolving base of inspiration, thought, and investigation. Even so, I know equally intelligent and successful designers who do not manifest aspects of their belief system in any discernable way in their client work, which, by the way, is not required to acknowledge the influence of ideology in our personal and professional lives. It is the prerogative of each designer to decide where her identity fits or doesn't fit, where self should be evident or kept private.

[6] This story is based on an actual exhibition I attended called "Ancestors of the Incas," part of the Wonders Series, which was displayed at the Memphis, Tennessee, Pyramid in 1998. While Martin Sheen was the narrator, his quote is very loosely paraphrased. The physical description of the quipu and speculation regarding its original function are factual.

Two Days in Limbo

together, form a perfect arc. The refined museum lighting in the case is concentrated on the central loop; gradually it tapers off along the strands.

The presentation is exacting. Despite the best efforts of the narrator, the quipu is so at home in its glass case that I cannot imagine the object in its original environment. Through its survival the quipu transcends time and place, but through its presentation it transcends historical documentation. The object resonates at a symbolic level: metaphor. It therefore strikes me that the quipu could become a graphic representation of one's knowledge base. The more diverse one's knowledge, the more strands on the quipu. The greater the depth of one's knowledge, the more knots on the strands. Something is missing, though. Like the object itself, my cognitive model is static because knowledge is, up to this point in the discussion, stored and not yet used. Despite diversity and depth of knowledge, there is no described thought process.

Reading is a process, writing is a process, designing is a process. Ideas form during each of these activities, connections are found, and a countless number of decisions are made. How?

Fade to Black. Cut to: Limbo

My life's film plays on, but now I'm looking at multiple projections as the waiting room slowly fills with one illuminated image after another. Along the walls and ceiling I can see the diversity of my knowledge base pictured in numerous long columns, and I see the depth of my knowledge as images hit these surfaces in a rapid-fire sequence.

Situated in the center of the room is one of those little projection screens upon which my grandparents presented slides from their trips out West. (I'm getting the impression limbo is under-funded.) Images start to move off the walls and ceiling, colliding in brilliant juxtaposition on this humble central screen. I am witnessing all the connections I ever made pictured before me like a family vacation. The commingling of images form in meaningful sequence, gradually revealing the guidance of my belief system. Both the things I questioned and the beliefs I once took for granted determine the pace and pairing of images and ideas I see before me now.

Still unable to escape my training, I think of this experience in graphic terms. I picture the quipu once more; illuminated and pristine, it is the ideal model for the human intellect, yet it remains incomplete. Each strand, pinned perfectly in position, does not touch any of its neighboring strands. No two knots—representative of specific nodes of knowledge—ever meet. But what if I added string? Then I could tie the different strands of knowledge together. I could tie one knot to another: one notion to another to form some third, greater idea. In so doing I would be representing the very sensation I feel when I read. Reading, in my experience, catalyzes the dynamic interplay of nodes of knowledge, creating connections between bits of information that were present in my head all the while as well as confronting old notions with new information.

The process of making connections through reading, or through other forms of knowledge acquisition and questioning, is not random. Results may be unexpected and unpredictable, and chance certainly plays a role. It is likely, though, that the connection of one idea with another is guided. Because ideology is constituted by our beliefs, it follows that our ideological base has a lot to do with our expectations. Therefore, many connections may occur, but the ones we "see" correlate with what we hope to find. Ideology is the navigator. Then there's the problem of use: Because our ideological beliefs are intimate statements about ourselves, they affect the choices of ideas we share with the outside world.[7]

The quipu serves as a graphic representation of the reading process but more generally as a representation of an informed decision-making system guided by ideological beliefs. Fundamentally, though, it's just a sketch of a process. Could the process of design be sketched similarly? Would such a drawing, with its contours shaped largely by the designer's knowledge base, place too much emphasis on the individual designer at the expense of the client, audience, and surrounding societal context? Strangely enough, I found a couple of statements from legendary Beat author Jack Kerouac that poignantly respond to such a dilemma:

> Bear well in mind what Sinclair Lewis told Thomas Wolf: "If Thomas Hardy had been given a contract to write stories for the Saturday Evening Post, do you think he would have written like Zane Grey or like Thomas Hardy? I can tell you the answer to that one. He would have written like Thomas Hardy. He couldn't have written like anyone else but Thomas Hardy. He would have kept on writing like Thomas Hardy, whether he wrote for the Saturday Evening Post or Captain Billy's Whiz-Bang."[8]

No fear or shame in the dignity of your experience, language and knowledge.[9]

Kerouac wrote these statements for fellow writers, but his insights are significant for anyone involved in the creative process of communication. There is reason for caution when comparing designers to authors, however. I am not espousing selfishness or inconsideration for client, message, or audience. Kerouac's words simply serve as a reminder that all you can ever

[7] My concepts regarding the structure of knowledge, catalysts for connections, and ideological navigation arose largely from empirical research. To provide analytical support for my assertions, I referred to writings on perceptual psychology, cognitive psychology, and cognitive science. Specific correlations were uncovered. Components of creativity described by Hans and Shulamith Kreitler of Tel Aviv University provided a larger formula to house my observations while providing a springboard for the notion of ideology as a navigator. (Hans Kreitler and Shulamith Kreitler, "Psychosemantic Foundations of Creativity," *Lines of Thinking: Reflections on the Psychology of Thought*, vol. 2, K. J. Gilhooly et al., eds. [Chichester, NY: John Wiley and Sons, 1990] 191–202.) Diagrams of neural connections look strikingly similar to the quipu itself: There is actually a physical correlation to what I metaphorically described. Moreover, learning creates new synaptic connections between neurons in the same manner the quipu's knots—representing ideas—became connected: not with string, but with string-like axons and dendrites. (Pierce J. Howard, *The Owner's Manual for the Brain: Everyday Applications from Mind-Brain Research* [Austin, TX.: Bard Press, 1996] 37) It was haunting to discover that this eight-hundred-year-old accounting device could serve as both diagram of and concept for the operation of the mind.

[8] Ann Charters, ed., *The Portable Jack Kerouac* (New York: Penguin Books, 1996) 489

[9] From Kerouac's "Belief and Technique For Modern Prose," Charters, 483

Two Days in Limbo

really be is one person—one designer. If you're not right for a certain job, then someone else will be. The wheels of capitalism will continue to turn. But this isn't as simple as pride in a signature style. It involves the desire to learn more about the vast complex of experiences and contexts that surround you. Whether you write or design doesn't matter. Notwithstanding client meetings, research, marketing professionals, behavioral psychologists, and applied anthropologists, you will respond to whatever context you ultimately find yourself in by using what you know. And you will take the information you are given and do with it only what you can.

Scene Three: Day Two in Limbo

I'm glad that limbo doesn't have an IMAX theater. The only thing worse than seeing my intellectual inadequacies play out before me would be to view them four stories high and fifty feet across with THX surround sound blasting me through the bottom of my seat.

IMAX—which stands for "image maximum," the largest motion-picture format—is the monster-truck pull of visual media. By its very scale the two-dimensional screen becomes a quasi three-dimensional experience. It is the perfect medium for an image-dominated, convenience-oriented society.

The IMAX images surround me. It's impossible to become distracted or to lose focus. The images come to me, no effort involved. The sound pours down over my head so I never have to strain to listen. The whole experience just rolls over my body and seeps into my visual receptors through some perceptual form of osmosis. Is this a product of a culture that really understands the value of reading or that encourages the active acquisition of knowledge? It appears that the very structure of this visual medium is inimical to both verbal and visual literacy. Maybe I'm overreacting. IMAX is just entertainment, after all—or is it more? Is it perhaps a four-story-high manifestation of what our culture values as important? If size is still any indication of importance, IMAX certainly qualifies.

The irony of the IMAX medium is that it purports to bring the world to your hometown. Everything from the Grand Canyon to the rain forests of South America is available for the price of admission. But how much of the world can really be exposed through a medium that replaces discovery with physical sensation? And it is unlikely that knowledge can be gained empirically when the senses are flooded. Such ironies become the stock and trade of another medium closer to the purview of graphic design: advertising. The trade wisdom of successful advertisers reveals the primacy of the physical/visual experience of reading over its ideological content.

"'Most readers," the advertising guru Bill Bernbach has observed, 'come away from their reading not with a clear, precise, detailed registration of its contents on their minds, but rather with a vague, misty idea which was formed as much by the pace, the proportions, the music of the writings as by the literal words themselves.'"[10]

This statement certainly gives those of us involved in typeface

[10] Ann Marie Seward Barry, *Visual Intelligence: Perception, Image, and Manipulation in Visual Communication* (Albany, NY: State University of New York Press, 1997) 254

design and typography something to think about. As designers, we tend to pride ourselves on using typography to communicate both the denotative and connotative meanings of words. We employ type as simile and metaphor, and we quote the great designers who stated that typography represents its era. I'm certainly in no position to take anything away from these ideas; I value and use them. And I certainly believe visual media can catalyze thought just as much as verbal communications. Yet it is no secret that our typographic solutions can often create the effect Bernbach describes, leading the consumer to an incomplete, or even false, understanding of the reading material.

Bernbach describes a closed text with a fixed purpose under the guise of open-ended interpretation, but his form of reading is no more open to interpretation than an IMAX movie. So much of the difficulty of establishing a unique and responsible ideological base lies in the multitude of texts that seek to program rather than educate the mind. McIdeology and McReading promoted once more.[11]

So, where does this leave graphic designers? Well, as Bill Moyers states of Joseph Campbell, ". . . he continued to remind others that one sure path into the world runs along the printed page."[12] This statement, in contradistinction to Bernbach's, regards an erudite scholar, someone with the capacity to comprehend all sorts of reading material and who possesses the ability to channel his comprehension towards transforming the immaterial—ideas—into cogent discussions. This, I believe, is truer to the aims of effective graphic design and echoes the belief of Anton Stankowski that graphic form can represent invisible processes. Attention to reading —in design research and audience reception—can help wed the immaterial with the material: the subject with a responsible communication of its essence, and the word with its typographic presentation.

Scene Four: Nightfall in Limbo

As the sun sets on my time in limbo, I only have a moment for a few last thoughts. Since this whole story centers around reading, it seems appropriate to mention at least one book. Tim McCreight's text *Design Language* is amazingly useful for graphic designers and students.[13] McCreight's book is so availing because of its structure. Composed of definitions, etymologies, brief discussions, and quotes—all presented in juxtaposition over double-page spreads—*Design Language* serves as an incredible tool for ideating through reading. (Reading becomes strategy.)

I appreciate McCreight's tactic because it strikes to the core of this reading. Whether discussing reading's contribution to the formation of an ideological base for decision making or how we read versus what we read, I'm presenting reading and, by extension, ideology as strategies for attaining expertise.[14] The trickle-down implication for creativity is that it is more than just some outward manifestation of a keen idea; it is instead

[11] For a complete and brilliant discussion of open and closed texts, see Umberto Eco, *The Role of The Reader: Explorations in the Semiotics of Texts* (Bloomington, IN: Indiana University Press, 1979)

[12] Bill Moyers in Joseph Campbell, *The Power of Myth,* Betty Sue Flowers, ed. (New York: Doubleday, 1988) xiv

[13] Tim McCreight, *Design Language* (Cape Elizabeth, ME: Brynmorgan Press, 1996)

[14] "Strategy," like "ideology," is a loaded term. In the context of this discussion, "strategy" should not be interpreted as a fixed set of ideas that never alter or evolve. Instead, flexibility and change are key aspects of strategic ideological development and creative growth, and they must be accounted for when describing cognitive processes.

a richer journey that melds the outside world with the interior processes of the intellect. Reading, therefore, exposes and contributes to the ideological proclivities guiding our thoughts and craft.[15]

[15] While this essay focuses heavily on the analytical side of cognition, empiricism is given equal weight in the fuller description of my theory (not yet published). There are obviously plenty of ways to acquire, catalyze, and use knowledge besides reading. But because of reading's potent effect on the mind, it merits exclusive attention.

Scene Five: Leaving Limbo

My perspective from limbo was certainly ideal, unlike the messy world where we actually have to function. In the "real world" context I've read and heard far more customary theories than mine: Designers don't read. Designers make decisions based on what David Carson's doing. Clients suck the life out of good design. Students don't want to think too hard; they just want to play in Photoshop. On and on it goes. Call it pessimism or call it realism. In any case, this field needs a place like limbo: an area where designers can suspend their current restrictions for as long as it takes to propose new approaches. This is what is meant by "visionary theorizing," the true value of which lies in both application and general enrichment, even if the design world appears, at times, to be one big waiting room.

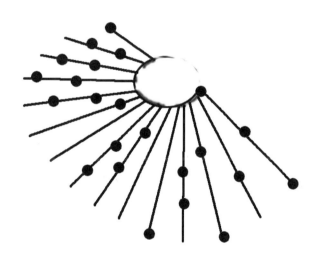

Kenneth FitzGerald

Seen and Not Seen

The over-largely lettered signs and placards of the street, escape observation by dint of being excessively obvious; and here the physical oversight is precisely analogous with the moral inapprehension by which the intellect suffers to pass unnoticed those considerations which are too obtrusively and too palpably self-evident.
—Edgar Allan Poe, "The Purloined Letter"

Business wants him [the designer] to help create an attitude about the facts, not to communicate them. And only about some of the facts.
—William Golden

Graphic design as a project of legibility of the world little by little extends to all aspects of the environment.
—Abraham A. Moles, "The Legibility of the World: A Project of Graphic Design"

*L*et's agree for a time that all histories are conspiracy theories. Today, that isn't asking much. It isn't even necessary to be paranoid. Histories are commonly presented as narratives, so we're merely concluding logically. Briefly, all developments are provoked by various individuals acting in concert to achieve desired ends. Events are set into motion that culminate in the present—the plot's culmination. Argued in reverse, there's a sense of inevitability. And why not? It all happened.

Design history works the same way—as visual scheming on a vast scale. Our particular history is a series of successful graphic intrigues upon the culture. These schemes are also considered, by most, benign—Bauhaus to Basel to Yale to Cranbrook and beyond. All are members of a cabal of clarity.[1]

Going against type, design's conspiracies supposedly seek to reveal. Like a free-market CIA, design deciphers the world and sells its encoding and decoding talents to the highest bidder.

Of course, design has debates about the efficacy of some fellow conspirators' plots. Certain practitioners and theorists will occasionally be accused of counter-insurgency. However, it is generally accepted that a clarity is the core mission. To obscure (or be obscure) is merely a sign of poor contrivance.

But the larger conspiracies in our visual culture are silent and undirected. They evolve from inertia. They're the unintended consequences of innumerable actions in the clarity conspiracy. The extract from Poe illustrates one of these outcomes. Individually, each sign is clarion. As a group, they're cacophony.

One hundred and fifty years after Poe's description, matters obviously haven't improved. Along with articulating the world on its own terms, design is also locked in a struggle against itself. It's now a truism that the contemporary designer's challenge is cutting through the media noise. Always ignored is the fact that any counteraction generates *more* furious sound. The strategy of choice is pumping up the volume—same tools, same outcome. Is it possible to overcome the conspiracy with its own weapons?

Before cranking the amp to twelve, we might examine the operation of (in)visibility more closely. Is graphic visibility solely a product of novelty and invisibility inevitable when that novelty wears off? Is invisibility hastened by ubiquity? Are there strategies of low visibility (small scale, limited distribution) that may prove more effective for longevity? Is longevity desirable if possible? Are many claimed strategies of graphic efficiency actually camouflage?

Poe's "palpable self-evidence" could be more simply described as *familiarity breeds invisibility*. Or, to restate another cliché: *in sight, out of mind*. As attaining high visibility, then maintaining it, is design's traditional goal, these are disturbing realities. However, a need has arisen for a design that selectively obscures and reveals. This design is responding to a multiplicity of new texts created for the overabundance of products churned out by consumer society. It may be that design essentializes itself modernistically not so much to have the ultimate clarity but to be able to squeeze more new languages onto artifacts.

These new texts are specialized and arcane: inventory numbers, catalog numbers, indicia, ingredients, legal notices, copyrights, and so on. As more artifacts are brought into being, the more texts we need to situate and describe them. A

[1] In this context, I am using "clarity" to indicate a stated intent to *reveal* a complex of ideas, as opposed to a deliberate obscuring of relevant information. We may, of course, debate the viability of a particular strategy or its ultimate functionality—as this essay does. Here, however, I am taking all designers' claims at face value. In my interpretation, all of the design theories expressed across this spectrum ultimately desire to generate—rather than withhold or direct attention away from—significant awareness.

location within the language must be established. These languages are specialized, a kind of ambient code: ever-present but ignorable.

Chief amongst these new texts is the UPC symbol—the bar code. The bar code is the most prominent and omnipresent example of an essential language that is meant to be invisible—to humans. While created by humans, the UPC is text for machines to read. However, as the bar code has multiplied and been disseminated in our culture, it has acquired meanings for humans. And for designers, the bar code is possibly the most visible—and maddening—language they must deal with.

Karrie Jacobs's 1989 *Metropolis* article, "The Code,"[2] presents a thorough and entertaining history of the UPC symbol. In her essay, Jacobs immediately notes the UPC's ubiquity and invisibility, and how the two aspects intertwine. She recognizes that bar codes are now "read" by people. Simply, the presence of a bar code signifies that something is for sale. It's a stamp of authority. The UPC is the elementary signifier of commerce. Many designers utilize the bar code rhetorically to trade on this.

2 Karrie Jacobs, "The Code' *Metropolis* vol. 8 #8, April 1989

To claim the bar code as also having invisibility, Jacobs suggests it is willed out of existence by the public. But is this really the case? To drive something from your consciousness, you must first acknowledge its presence. Perhaps Jacobs is only partially right. The bar code likely exists in a kind of public quasi-existence where it is more *sensed* than seen. For the public, the UPC is of a kind with the rest of the designed environment: natural. It's just there—no more or less than the type and imagery seen elsewhere on the box.

Of course, the UPC's designers (or, more appropriately, engineers) never considered human response to their artifact and its final impact. And (also, *of course*) this is the precise reason designers object to it.

As visual sophisticates, Jacobs and designers overall understandably obsess over the formal import of bar codes. If anyone is determinedly trying to will UPCs out of existence, it's designers. After providing background on the code, the majority of Jacobs's article is given over to various designers' statements of loathing for the symbol and their attempts to circumvent or conceal it. For designers, the lesson of the UPC is an old one: Nondesigners always impose restrictions that prevent us from doing good design.

In this way, the bar code is the designer's ultimate nightmare. Created by a committee of nondesigners, it requires prominent placement at oppressive scale on everything and—most of all—is impervious to aesthetic manipulation. Imagine musicians being forced to include a monotone voice bellowing a string of numbers in all their tunes. Unless you're Philip Glass, it's an intolerable requirement.

We might, though, measure a designer's true acceptance of her material role by her level of comfort with bar codes. A willing embrace of commerce is frequently cited by designers as what distinguishes their practical activity from art. The quality of designers is regularly determined by their facility in ameliorating aesthetic and commercial demands. Welcoming the UPC may be the greatest demand commerce has placed upon designers. Following this rationale, it's The Designers Republic that emerges as exemplars. Their designs make a fetish of all of the unseen languages of our commercial culture, so it is ironic that The Designers Republic is regarded as a group of avant-garde and artistic designers.

The desire to have unbroken vistas of formal space likens designs to fine artwork. "Artwork" is popularly regarded as artifacts born out of and generative of emotion. Bar codes are frequently accused of being soulless and mechanical. Their precise, rigid vertical lines are devoid of any feeling. It may be, though, that such criticism is looking in the wrong way for feeling in formalism.

In the abstract art that was created after World War II, profound emotion was invested in straight lines. For Barnett Newman, deep meaning was contained within works such as his *Stations of the Cross* series—all vertical stripes of white within a black background. In the shadow of extermination camps and potential nuclear holocaust, figure drawing seemed precious and incapable of expressing disturbing new realities. Artists could only turn to the stark abstractions and contrasts of light and dark and elemental form. Their works emphasized the collapse of old methods of expression and the artists' struggle for a language to communicate the enormity of contemporary fears.

Formally portraying profound moral concerns will always be problematic. But it is worth noting that minimal linearity has been the resort of artists seeking to engage society's ills after both world wars. The early modernists also turned to elemental, abstract forms in the early decades of the twentieth century. While we continue to debate the validity of these creative programs, we must also credit the impulse to transcend art's insularity from immediate social concerns. And rather than being regarded as soulless, straight lines were the formal weapons of choice to assert responsibility.

The legacy of these formal movements is highly questionable. The repetitive grids of artists such as Sol LeWitt derive all their significance within the boundaries of art theory. In design, the bar code might be the elemental symbol of Modernism's failure and colonization by commerce. Societal good has been defined as transmitting the broadest, most persuasive commercial message—and ignoring the source and impact of that message.

In the clarity conspiracy, the central tenet has been the greatest visibility for the greatest numbers. The audience for design was regarded as a singularity. Increasingly, the public has become a true plurality, at least in becoming an array of target audiences. The directive to know your audience implies a multiplicity. Design has more than allowed directed visibility; it has demanded and trumpeted strategies of directed *in*visibility as a virtue.

The strategy of creating visibility for a product is long-recognized in design. Passed over is a corollary *invisibility* that is generated. A novel aspect claimed for design works like the David Carson–designed *Ray Gun* was that they attracted one audience by repelling another. Youths identified with and desired artifacts adults refused to or couldn't see. This supposedly turned the clarity conspiracy on its head: a willing unseeability.

The designers of such artifacts claim this repulsion/attraction as a fortuitous consequence of their primary strategy: self-expressive, rebellious design. Theirs is an accidental genius of branding. Since then, strategic repulsion has been invoked many times and adjudged a viable tactic.

The truth is that this strategy has always been with us and is occurring more often at the "conservative" end of the spectrum. Once again, the rule of unintended consequences is more properly credited as a generator of invisibility. But if we indulge in our conspiracy theories, a different agenda may be outlined. In this formulation, "classic" or "outdated" design is kept in place to deter investigation by certain audiences.

Take the *Wall Street Journal*. An argument can be made that it is the central informational artifact of our capitalist society. Detailed here are the operations and movements of capital, from which all power derives. To know who controls wealth and the uses to which it is put is to have key information on how the world works and who's in charge.

The *Journal*'s design is hardly inviting, particularly to the average newspaper reader. *USA Today* it's not. (This is not to suggest that *U.S. Today* is any ideal of design or information delivery.) While arguably polished and refined, it is just as arguably dense and user–unfriendly. As much as any "cutting-edge" design, it requires a strong motivation to plumb its depths. What is probably considered "sober" may also be called unappealing.

The *Journal*'s rationale is that it is inviting to its audience and provides the desired information in the most efficient and appropriate manner. "Visually, the *Journal* has a unique trademark quality," said *Journal* publisher Peter Kann in a 1999 article. "It's a uniquely recognizable page. But the main reason we haven't changed is it's a very useful format. I think we fit more news in those two What's News columns than you get in a half-hour news program." According to Kann, text is content, visuals are entertainment. As it is, the *Journal*'s design signifies "high quality, high demographic."

For all the import claimed by and attributed to the *Journal,* no effort is made to make it any more accessible to a wider audience. It can make the argument that it is already widely popular, with 1.6 million subscribers. However, that audience is hardly mainstream or populist. To that audience, the paper's stolid grid of grey type acts like camouflage colors or a forcefield. *I'm boring and of no significance to you,* its pages say, *go on about your business elsewhere. Ideally, the mall.*

If one believes the activity of capital to be innocuous, a conspiracy of invisibility seems dubious. And as we venture further into a world of niche markets and target audiences, such theories will seem even more suspect. The conspiracy of clarity is still ascendant, and designers are just talking to their audiences in the languages they understand.

In Thomas Pynchon's short novel *The Crying of Lot 49,* heroine Oedipa Maas stumbles upon the vast Tristero conspiracy. Or, she may have been driven to delusion by a crazed culture and condensed a paranoia fantasy out of graffiti, misprinted postage stamps, and updated anthologies of Shakespearean-era plays.

Once she becomes sensitive to particular markings that previously blended into a background of signs, symbols, images, and texts, her view of the world shifts like a double-image postcard. Turned slightly askew, a new, sinister world is revealed where an alternative message-delivery system parallels our familiar one. Only this alternate system is reliable—conveying both the artifacts *and* their true meanings.

Pynchon's vision has been replicated *en mass media* for the past three decades since its publication. With conspiracy theories a prevalent mainstream theme of television, movies, and books, suspicion has been downgraded. The more fiction turns to it as subject, the more all conspiracy theories are likely to be regarded as more (mere) entertainment. Meanwhile, the true conspiracies are far more subtle and closer to the surface. In design, they *are* the surface. And the conspirators are unaware (or uncaring) of their involvement in and sustenance of the plot.

Frequently seeing themselves as victims, designers are more rightly perpetrators. Cursing the minor inconveniences of clients' stylistic demands—such as fouling their layouts with a bar code—they ignore the major machinations of capital. Having historically not seen beyond the surface, they distance themselves from their role as conspirators *against* clarity.

A wonderful conspiracy would be participating in a true, populist program of visibility. Designers might make themselves discernible as a group dedicated to social and cultural change. The machinations of power might be made apparent, and designers would refuse to be complicit. Such a program is, admittedly, utopian —though no more so than the modernist program. Designers also do not possess the capital to create and disseminate mass messages; however, it is undeniable that they are actively engaged in creating them. A mental reassessment from active to activist may make a world of difference.

We also know that small messages, multi-plied a thousandfold over time, may also have an impact. They may also be ideal for the best vis-ibility. Making a living need not equal papering over corporate interest or barring the question-ing of institutional prerogative. Design-ers with foresight and critical hindsight might make a life of res(v)olution. We might then see all there is to see.

John Sloan, *Hairdresser's Window,* 1907

Wadsworth Atheneum, Hartford, the Ella Gallup and Mary Catlin Sumner Collection Fund

Signs *of* Life/Spaces *of* Art:

From *Standard Brands* to *Integrated Circuits*
Johanna Drucker

dvertising signage has frequently served as the subject matter for works of fine art in the twentieth century. Such works are part of broader interactions among fine art, commercial work, and mass media aspects of culture, and they provide a useful insight into the variations in the rhetoric of twentieth-century signs as perceived through the editorial perspective of artists' imagery. From its initial role in serving to identify products and businesses in specific locations, signage has become an ageographical network of virtual relations. In the process, modes of persuasion as well as fundamental assumptions about the role of signage in articulating the public sphere have changed dramatically. Early rhetorical devices of attention-getting for goods and services have been replaced by signs that function almost autonomously in highly mediated systems of real and imagined value.

Each of the paintings or photographs discussed here contributes information that a simpler formal reading of decontextualized graphics does not. The history of sign production in terms of the style and material history of typographic, pictorial, and photographic elements is itself a part of the cultural production of meaning. But because artists' depictions embody *responses* to mass culture at a variety of historical moments, they reveal assumptions about the way signage is conceived to function through direct address, projection, visual seduction, or in circulation among a system of other signs. Even the idea of what kind of system a sign is conceived to be part of—a real space, a virtual community, a network of production and consumption—can be traced in the shifts that occur in the works

Lari Pittman, *Untitled #32 (A Decorated Chronology of Insistence and Resignation)*, 1907

Courtesy Regan Projects, Los Angeles

Graphic Design & Reading

considered here. The spaces of art change as much as the signs of life that they inscribe as both participate in reformulated conceptions of the public sphere in the course of the twentieth century.

John Sloan's 1907 painting of a scene in New York's Lower East Side, *A Hairdresser's Window,* and Lari Pittman's 1994 visually frenzied image of signs in a synthetic unreal design world, *A Decorated Chronology of Insistence and Resignation,* serve as chronological brackets for my discussion of the rhetoric of "signage" in American culture in the twentieth century. Both are fine-art representations of graphic art signs; both suggest explicit, if radically different, visions of the "public sphere" of shared communicative exchange; and both present the persuasive public language of graphic design within a fine-art tradition of personal expression and vision.

The history of American art is punctuated by numerous instances of interaction between the commercial arts of advertising, illustration, and sign painting and the "fine arts," narrowly defined. Throughout the twentieth century, the sign painters and commercial lithographers of earlier centuries were absorbed into the increasingly specialized realms of commercial art. Graphic designers frequently became fine-art practitioners. The higher stakes and celebrity markets of fine art held a promise of material reward in excess of those in graphic design (until the relatively recent celebrity designer phenomenon). Therefore, in every decade of the twentieth century there were artists who brought the skills and sensibilities of commercial art into the fine-art image, transforming its conceptual and visual language. This includes painters from the so-called Ashcan school in the group of American modernists around Robert Henri, American abstract artists of the 1920s, photographers of the American scene in the 1930s to pop artists of the 1960s, and post-Modern and contemporary appropriators of the forms of mass communication and design. These artists have served as the conduit through which the technologies of production associated with the design industry—lithography, airbrush, offset, photo-typography, and electronic manipulation—have often found legitimacy within art production. By the same token, fine artists have contributed to the development of graphic design languages by providing images for key advertising campaigns or by diffusing contemporary modes of visual style.[1]

My focus here is on one specific kind of exchange between fine art and design: between two modes of what I am terming "rhetoric." The first mode, associated with signage, is that of presumed public address; the other, associated with fine art, is that of a presumably private and personal mode of expression. In fact, paintings and signage both have a public aspect. It would be specious to suggest that painting is really a "private" form of imagery, but it addresses or construes a public as the sign of a "private" space; its "rhetoric" is that of an individual vision and statement. The space of fine art enframes the idealized myth of private, interior life to articulate the idea of personal expression and private viewing *in* the public domain. By contrast, the original impetus of signage presumes that there is a public

[1] Michele Bogart, *Artists, Advertising, and the Borders of Art* (Chicago: The University of Chicago Press, 1995); Richard Wightman Fox and T. Jackson Lears, eds., *The Culture of Consumption* (New York: Pantheon, 1983); Neil Harris, *Cultural Excursions* (Chicago and London: The University of Chicago Press, 1990); Victor Margolin, *Design Discourse* (Chicago, IL and London: The University of Chicago Press, 1984); Roland Marchand and Estelle Jussim, *Visual Communication and the Graphic Arts* (New York and London: R. R. Bowker Co., 1983)

space in which the sign will communicate. Both signage and its reflection in fine art changed throughout the twentieth century, as did the relation between them. This exchange is not merely constituted by a play of reflections or imitations of form but, rather, through a more complex mutual definition of roles and identities for the rhetorics of each domain. By concentrating on one very specific area of intersection —signage concerned with commercial product identity and brand-name advertising as it has been represented in the fine arts—I want to show the ways in which changes in representing this signage provides an insight into attitudes towards what constitutes the public sphere.

The term "public sphere" is defined in the writings of the German philosopher and social critic Jürgen Habermas as a domain in which informed discussion and argument serve as the basis for political action.[2] The public sphere is a conceptual space that may, but need not, overlap with the literal, geographically located idea of public *space*—as evidenced in recent debates that have extended the idea of the "public sphere" into the electronic environment. The ways in which the "signs of life" (signage created in a design context) show up within the "spaces of art" demonstrate the productive dialogue between the private spaces of art and the public rhetoric of design, alternatively contrasted (in an uneven analogy) as that between individual expression and mass production. The depiction of signage *in situ* contrasts with images that are direct "signs of a sign," underscoring the difference between the "reference function" (to something such as a product, event, or other consumable item) and "identity function" (in itself) of signage. In its reference function, signage serves as an indexical link to the systems of commerce, advertising, and exchange, of which it is a visible articulation, while in the identity function signage exists as an image or icon with aesthetic properties that are symptomatically indicative of their time, place, and historical circumstances of production.

John Sloan's *The Hairdresser's Window* depicts signage functioning in a public mode of direct address, *in situ*, where the signs function as an integral part of the street life and among a community of viewers. Such interconnections among signage, advertising, and the literal public spaces of urban life are amply documented in photographs of New York's denser commercial districts of the time with their conspicuous billboards, posted signs, and crowded hoardings.[3] In the specific geographical and sociological location of a Lower East Side New York neighborhood, life is not entirely given over to consumption, but consumerism is part of the activity of daily life. The signage here has a very basic rhetorical function: It announces the presence and location of various sites and services within the actual landscape. It speaks the "here it is, come and get it" rhetoric of street signs, mainly advertising local merchants, but inserting them within the larger networks of commerce and burgeoning markets in which product identity, packaging, and advertising imagery all participate. The public sphere is an arena of competitive exchange in which signage has a value for its own sake, using its promotional skills to lay claim to a certain share of the ter-

[2] Jürgen Habermas, *The Structural Transformation of the Public Sphere* (Cambridge, MA: MIT Press, 1991); Craig Calhoun, *Habermas and the Public Sphere* (Cambridge, MA and London: MIT Press, 1993)

[3] Bogart, "Posters versus Billboards," *Artists, Advertising, and the Borders of Art*, 79–123

ritory of advertising. In Sloan's work, we see certain basic structural features linking the "signs of life" with the "spaces of art" while also preserving fundamental distinctions between them. The links reiterate the social space as a physical, urban space that is lived, inhabited, and fundamentally literal in its existence even while the signage within it may suggest worlds and systems of commerce far beyond the immediate arena of the street outside the hairdresser's window.

The many subdivisions within painting help forge these links according to a familiar logic of conventional image making. The hairdresser's window, in which a woman is grooming another woman's thick mane of hair, is a painting within a painting. Though an interior space, it is visible to the street, thus theatricalizing the events enacted within the frame of the window. Separating these two spaces is the wall of the building, a plane parallel to the picture plane that is the pictorial representation of the surface that supports signs. The signs and the street, with all its bustling activity, presumably extend beyond the picture frame. Advertising appears *in* the image, but the signs reinforce the image of the street as a public space, so that as viewers of the painting we occupy the same position as those members of the public in the street who pass the hairdresser's window. The women in the window are clearly aware of their audience, the audience is a public free to come and go, and the signs vie for attention in the busy space of this public arena.

Sloan's painting mimics the rhetoric of graphic art signage, which can be characterized as big mouthed, broad based, and appeal oriented. The signs in Sloan's painting almost all appear to advertise local businesses. There are almost no "standard" signs or brand-name products advertised in this picture, with the possible exception of the sign for the hair product "Curline" in the middle of the image. But by 1907, when this picture was painted, mass production, distribution, and accompanying changes in marketing strategies had given a new impetus to brand names in product advertising. In the urban environment, posters had been replaced by the larger scale presence of billboards giving rise, as Michele Bogart has detailed, to many controversies.[4] Conflicts pitted members of the citizenry aligned with the turn-of-the-twentieth-century City Beautiful movements, who felt that public sensibility suffered an assault from the crassness of many billboards, against private-property owners who claimed it was up to them to either permit or deny use of their buildings as billboard supports according to their own self-interested adjudication. Commercial interests supported the view that public space should be free and open for all comers. The differences among these vested interests were frequently resolved by zoning billboards out of exclusive neighborhoods and into concentrated areas of commerce or entertainment. Such conflicts provide evidence of the ways in which literal public space and the concept of a public sphere can be distinguished even while they overlap. Sloan's signage literally links the place and service of commercial identity by staging its presence within the "public space" of the street; the "public sphere," however, remains constituted as a more diffuse network of contentions and consensual negotiations about the ways in which the discourses of advertising interact with the domain's social life.

[4] Ibid.

While Sloan's attention to signage remains painterly and generic, brand-name advertising as a feature of visual culture in the early twentieth century comes into focus in the early work of Stuart Davis. Davis's work shifts from mimetic repetition of street-sign rhetoric in the "come and get it *here*" linking of sign and place to a rhetoric of production of conspicuously *modern* design. In Davis's work, fine art provides a place in which to celebrate and legitimate the new forms of graphic design.

The late nineteenth and early twentieth centuries witnessed a new era in advertising graphics as changes in industrialization, communication, and transportation participated in a shift from a production economy to a consumption economy. Goods once largely produced and consumed locally in bulk form could now be packaged and shipped to compete in national markets. Tobacco was one industry that was radically transformed through these novel innovations. Davis made two *Lucky Strike* paintings (in 1921 and 1924): Both present the brand-name cigarette in its new guise, as a product with an identity. Cigarettes had been rolled by hand through the 1880s, at which point James Buchanan Duke introduced innovations in mass production. The slim, elongated form of the cigarette became a sign of "urban sophistication," in contradistinction to the "hick" identity of chewing tobacco.[5]

Cigarettes became a glamour industry associated with chic modernity. In such changed circumstances, the brand name "Lucky Strike" served a guarantor of quality, or at least of standardization, and its recognizable box was an integral feature of the selling strategy emerging in the move from bulk to packaged goods. In *The Making of Modern Advertising*,[6] Daniel Pope notes that the package and the ad became a substitute for the salesman in asserting the availability and identity of the product to the buying public.[7] The expansion of "national" and "international" markets thus opened the opportunity and perceived necessity for the advertising of product identity through graphic means.

Because it served the interests of American business, Stuart Davis considered advertising an attribute of "high civilization." So did Calvin Coolidge, whose 1926 address to the president of the Association of Advertising Agencies characterized their efforts as the "highest responsibility of inspiring and ennobling the commercial world" and "part of the great work of the regeneration and redemption of humankind."[8] These attitudes provided a moral and aesthetic justification for what had already been signaled as a fundamental need by President Wilson a decade earlier when he stated in 1912, "Our industries have expanded to the point where they will burst their jackets if they cannot find a free outlet to the markets of the world."[9] For such outlets to successfully serve

[5] Howard Zinn, *The People's History of the United States* (New York: Harper and Row, 1980) 248

[6] Daniel Pope, *The Making of Modern Advertising* (New York: Basic Books Publishers, 1983) 3–5

[7] In a striking example, Pope brings home the extent to which standard brands were a twentieth-century phenomenon by pointing to the fact that in 1833, when Abraham Lincoln was working as a store clerk in Old Salem, Illinois, the only brand name item in the store was "Walter Baker's chocolate." Everything else was bulk goods, locally produced and consumed. Ibid. 31

[8] Roland Marchand, *Advertising the American Dream* (Berkeley, CA and Los Angeles: University of California Press, 1985) 8

[9] Zinn, *The People's History of the United States*

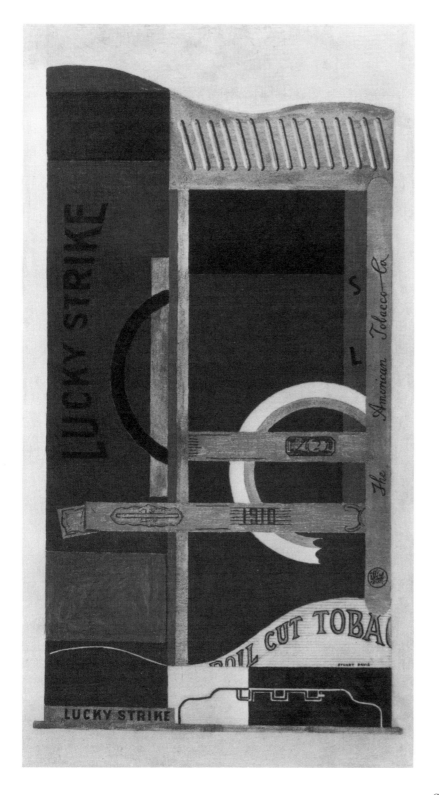

Stuart Davis,
Lucky Strike, 1921
The Museum of Modern Art,
New York, Gift of the
American Tobacco
Company, Inc.

the interests of individual businesses, such businesses needed to mark their market share with a distinct and graphically articulated identity. The functions of signage expanded from merely serving to facilitate recognition and points of purchase for goods and services to a competition of signs circulating in spaces that were not linked to specific geographies but rather evolved an independent network through that system of circulation of goods as consumable products.

Advertising graphics and the standardization of package design served the interests of expanding markets by fixing the "nonquantifiable attributes" of specific products in a consumer's mind. The essence of the Lucky Strike became an image and style choice. A side effect of this growth of standardization was that trademarks themselves became identified as a commodity, as something with value that could be bought, sold, and traded. In the words of an ad man as early as 1908, "At least fifty percent of the advertising being done today is for the purpose of creating property in trademarks."[10] Davis's 1921 painting replicates the iconography of Lucky Strike's package as its subject matter, thus giving the trademarked form a fine-art affirmation while demonstrating that such imagery constituted a subject, an identity, and an image value.

[10] Pope, *The Making of Modern Advertising*, 68

The 1921 *Lucky Strike* is not just a direct appropriation and celebration of the visual rhetoric of commercial design, it is a sign that modernity is a shared space of fine-art and graphic-art visual modes. The conventions of the painting are those of the flat, graphic surfaces endemic to the printing trade. There are no longer any of the discrete boundaries of the frames within the frame through which Sloan kept his image of signage clearly intact, as an element within a metonymically implied "real" public space. By contrast with the Sloan painting, this is *not* an image of popular public culture rendered in fine art's pictorial rhetoric but an image of a standard brand in terms of the very rhetoric that gives and guarantees its standardized identity: package design. Flat, unironic, celebratory, and modern, the 1921 painting embodies the exchange between the newly invented languages of "modern" graphics and the legitimating "space" of the enframed fine-art image. In short, the rhetoric of Davis's 1921 *Lucky Strike* is that of the modern design aesthetic elevated to the position of fine art, clearly hand painted, observed, and inflected by that private hand/eye of the artist. It would be difficult to assess which of the two rhetorics, of signage and of fine art, dominates the pictorial image, but the sign function of the image has clearly escaped the literal realm of lived spaces to operate on its own.

By contrast, the 1924 *Lucky Strike* follows the conventions of paintings done by turn-of-the-twentieth-century trompe l'oeil artists like William Harnett. In these so-called bachelor paintings, the signs of a masculine world of tobacco and newspapers create an image of discourse consumed in the sacred, private space of the study. The traditions of the still-life composition determine the structure of the work. The conjunction of package and newspaper, a primary site of print advertising, in the 1924 painting raises another interesting point about the debates on signage that began to command legal attention during that period. The concept of "truth in advertising" was an issue of public concern in which the common welfare was to be weighed against profit motives and the unregulated rhetoric of persuasion. In the early part of the twentieth century, these led to legal precedents in which the crucial terms of "truth" were determined by accountability to a referent. The premise was that there was a "real" to which the advertising and/or package claims had to be accountable.[11] Like the depiction of public space, this a feature that gets transformed later in the century when sign and referent are separated and the concept of the "real" is displaced by an emphasis on signs as significant in their own right.

[11] Sandra Braman, "Trigger: Law, Labeling, and the Hyperreal," *Freeing the First Amendment: Critical Perspectives on Freedom of Expression,* David S. Allen and Robert Jensen, eds. (New York: New York University Press, 1995)

Critical analysis of the distinction between the features of fantasy projections of commercial advertising and the realities of lived experience across a broad spectrum of the American public (that is, the sense that it was in this contradiction of advertised image and documented "reality" that a truth of contemporary conditions could be produced) is evident in the work of photographers in the 1920s and 1930s. Unlike Davis, whose work is largely uncritical and celebratory, Margaret Bourke-White and Walker Evans provide visual evidence of the ironies producible by juxtaposing advertising rhetoric with documentary imagery. Their photographs are not concerned with imitation or recording of brand-name design or style; they do address the sites of advertising graphics as spaces of evident contradiction between the imagined existence projected by sophisticated advertising in the 1920s and 1930s and the contexts in which they were received. In the 1920s, the glamour industries—automobiles, pharmaceuticals, movies, radios, and tobacco—had developed a vivid fantasy existence in the medium of photographic advertisements. These made extensive use of illustrations of lifestyles (rather than the rendering of products or packaging) in vignettes that depicted an "American way of life" that replaced claims for any individual product. Photography was an effective instrument in such advertising campaigns, where the referent of the ad became a vague, elusive scenario of existence rather than a set of qualities or ingredients that could be examined in terms of labeling or promotional promises for performance. Whatever the fate of these images in print media (that is, whatever their effect when encountered by readers of mass-circulation magazines), in outdoor public space, the placement of such advertising focused attention on the marked discrepancies between fantasies of consumption and the realities of the lives of most consumers. Such irony is readily communicated in photographic images.

Bourke-White's 1937 photograph *At the time of the Louisville Flood* shows a line of destitute and displaced people queued in front of a billboard for an automobile advertised as the center of a glamorously stable all-American life, effectively communicating a striking contrast between the projected and inhabited reality, but even more, between an established image of advertising as "false" and a place for documentary or fine-art photography as more "true." Bourke-White's photograph pits a fine-art rhetoric of disjunction, irony, and critical realism against the rhetoric of consumerism as if the two can or should be clearly demarcated, though in fact they act to reinforce each other's specificity. Evans's 1936 *Outdoor Advertising* shows a half-painted billboard and two artist-workmen on a scaffold. Here the perfect illusion of the "sign" is shown to be a product of labor, brought into being through artistic skill, rather than simply "appearing" seamlessly and effortlessly in the landscape. By undoing the familiar terms of encounter, Evans reinscribes the sign itself within relations of production, thus commenting on the way its finished form tends to conceal vital information about the industry of advertising. The rhetoric of design attempts to appear as a "natural" and readily consumable image, though here it is exposed as constructed so that the fine-art image can assume the "natural" role. Signs function within these images as representations of broken promises, false hopes, and unrealistic expectations. The familiar effect of the fine-art photograph engages in a dialogue with the consumable discourse of mainstream culture and, in fact, upstages it as equally consumable in its rhetoric of critique. The dream machine of signage exists to be deconstructed and its artifices laid bare; both fine art and design are obviously to be consumed.

Stuart Davis's 1961 *Standard Brand* shows how much the artistic dialogue, with the visual languages of design, has changed from that of the appreciation of its modernity as a sign. In the era of booming post–World War II consumerism, fine art flirts with media culture without any sense of threat. It is as if the "modernity" of advertising has been subsumed into a painterly style that has thoroughly absorbed the lessons of graphic excitement, jazzy design, and inventive, bold, innovative reduction in form but transformed them into a fine-art mode. The "signs of life" are well contained with the "signs of artness" in Davis's painting, demonstrating the extent to which signage has become its own language of contemporary visual culture. The rhetoric of the sign is safe, and Davis uses its forms as an excuse to exploit the painterliness of fine art. This is in distinct contrast to the 1921 *Lucky Strike* painting's celebration of the novelty of modern design as a visual vocabulary that could inform the activity of modern painting. Signage has become an excuse to display the painterliness of painting rather than offer a model for a modern painting practice, which has now fully absorbed its lessons, anyway.[12]

As the fascination with media culture and consumable imagery developed in the climate of the 1950s and 1960s boom economy, the sneaking conviction that signage is not merely a formal influence but a more profound cultural model of image behavior and identity began to shift the balance from fine art to graphic design as the power player in the dialogue of signage and visual art. A fascination with commercial signs became evident in the work of a number of artists associated with the more figurative aspects of abstract expressionism, such as Grace Hartigan (paintings with a billboard theme) and Larry Rivers (of a package of Camel cigarettes). Commenting on the work of his contemporaries, Harold Rosenberg observed the striking correspondence between identifiable painterly styles—the unique signature—and the idea of standard brand identity. In his 1952 essay, "The American Action Painters," Rosenberg says, ". . . the common phrase, 'I have bought an O—' (rather than a painting by O) becomes literally true. The painter who started to

[12] This "lesson" goes back to the influence of Japanese prints and graphics on the lithographic signage of the late nineteenth century and its subsequent effect on the visual forms of modern painting.

Stuart Davis, *Standard Brand,* 1961

[13] Harold Rosenberg, "The American Action Painters," *The Tradition of the New* (Chicago and London: The University of Chicago Press, 1960) 23–39

specific quote, 35

remake himself has made himself into a commodity with a trademark."[13] Rosenberg has identified a new paradigm of commercial identity that transcends individual work or its content, forging an analogy between the production methods of commercial art and the struggling identity of fine art in its increasingly disadvantaged position in contemporary visual culture. The idea that the very conceptual premise of artistic practice as linked to product, to the sign function of a standard brand, to images unleashed from singular content or effective, communicative, artistic vision, indicates a radical rethinking of the paradigm of fine art.

This rethinking takes mature form in the work of pop artists engaged directly with the rhetoric of signage. Here the distinction from earlier work by Stuart Davis has to be carefully nuanced. There is a similar celebratory engagement with the visual forms of advertising and commercial signage, but there is a marked disconnection from the forms of painterly handling evident in Davis's early-twentieth-century efforts, with their naïvely marked incorporation of commercial language into its fine-art tradition. Davis's appreciation has become overshadowed by the sheer force of the commercial industry of image and sign production. Even the hand-painted pop works of Warhol or Lichtenstein's first canvases, for all their apparent tentativeness, are not marked by a sense that commercial signage is an unknown rhetoric, rather the opposite—it is an overwhelmingly familiar and dominant rhetoric, and they are already its skilled practitioners. It is fine art that has become the outsider in the mainstream visual dialogue. The developed imagery of Pop Art in its slicker, more finished modes, such as Ed Ruscha's *Standard Station, Amarillo, Texas* (1963), contain a distinctly peculiar absence of actual public space (Andy Warhol's *Campbell's Soup Cans*, like Davis's *Lucky Strike*, foreclose this question through their iconographic collapse of image surface and image icon, but Ruscha's image suggests a landscape, thus making its absence conspicuous). The icon in the Ruscha image projects itself forward, as if from a brilliant light-source display. But its exaggerated, perspectival vanishing points eliminate all possibility of space as a real space. Like the images that promoted outdoor advertising to potential advertisers of the period, Ruscha's image is about the marketing of marketing. The high visibility of the Standard Station logo in the painting promotes the consumer industry product as an image that Pop Art's vocabulary embraces and enframes. But the conviction expressed is of a universe in which sign consumption has become considerably distanced from the streetscape in which Sloan had embedded his signage, or from the setting of individual or personal consumption marked in the Davis still life of 1924. Nor is signage able to be redeemed and wrest free from its commercial domain by mere painterliness, which looks to be ineffectual as a critical mark of transformation. The ironies of Evans and White, like the artistic optimism of Hartigan and Rivers, have been reduced to an impotent dimension. Fine art suffers from anemic aesthetic ennui practice in contrast with the synthetic and aggressive hubris by which sign language colonized the fine-art realm.

This argument gains even more momentum with the realization that

Edward Joseph Ruscha, *Standard Station, Amarillo, Texas,* 1963

Hood Museum of Art, Dartmouth College, Hanover, New Hampshire;

gift of James J. Meeker, Class of 1958, in memory of Lee English

Pop Art's relation to the visual tropes and graphic forms of consumable products extended beyond the mere celebration of the stylistic features of design's own visual language (already available in the Stuart Davis paintings of the 1920s) and into a rhetoric of fetishization. Warhol's Kellogg's and Brillo box sculptures defied distinction from the functional originals on which they are based. Identities had become conflated: The rhetoric of the Kellogg's box and logo have become signs in their own right, elements of a visual culture in which sign value need not have any referent at all outside the system of signs themselves. In their fetishized form, these commodities–cum–signs, stacks of Kellogg's boxes, reveal nothing of the relations of labor and capital that bring them into being. The critical interrogation of Sloan, Evans, and White are completely gone. Davis's prescient disjuncture of sign and context has been fulfilled in a myriad of images or art objects in which relations among people are concealed in the "things." These sign-images don't stand for themselves as signs in the conventional sense of a sign that stands for an object or referent, but they don't stand for anything else either, and thus they introduce a new confusion about the identity of art and commercial objects that Davis's paintings resisted in their essential existence as art objects.

  Pop Art iconography marks a total separation of image from context. Mel Ramos's paintings of women and brand-name products ("Miss Cornflakes," for instance) shifts the emphasis from that of a standard brand object to that of a sexually fetishized commodity. His paintings display all the classic elements of such fetishism in their vocabulary of phallic forms (the woman's nude body is comically and with great overdetermination elided with a banana) in an image in which consumption and eroticization are combined in imagery so heavy-handed it can't be saved from kitsch, even by its own irony. Ramos's work becomes indistinguishable from advertising, except by the institutional context in which it operates. The public discourse of communications, advertising, and media have been fully transformed from elements with a referent ("truth in labeling" would mean what in relation to Ramos's woman-peeled-banana-phallus?) to elements that conceal the absence of truth. Similarly the "truth" value of art—the nature of its identity—is here clearly upstaged by that of designed images. Media culture, it would seem, has triumphed over the fine-art domain, and art is playing out the signs of that fact through an act of concealment that passes as a flirtatious appropriation of signage into artistic imagery.

Richard Estes's hyperrealist paintings from the late 1960s, such as *Food City* (1967), offer a return to an *in situ* context. This should remind us of the theatrical situation of the public street in the Sloan painting of *Hairdresser's Window,* but in fact, it merely emphasizes the distance from that earlier work. The Estes paintings are much closer in sensibility to those of his Pop Art counterparts. The public space is a space of consumption, and the identity of the product-objects seems to be one of infinitude and potentially infinite substitution. The paintings show a world shaped according to the visual rhetoric of signage and consumption. There is no public activity or human audience in his works. They are dense with product information. Public space has completely been subsumed into the category (and functions) of consumer space. There are no exchanges, no comments, no dialogue of individuals with each other or in comment on the situation or circumstances. One enters the public sphere only as a consumer and only in order to distinguish among the choices offered in the rhetoric of spectacular display. In the words of Guy Debord, author of the 1962 *Society of the Spectacle,* "Everything which was formerly lived has moved into representation"—and a representation in terms of commercial transactions, promotions, displays.[14] Life in the domestic environment—so-called private life—shows up in the public arena as comparative shopping, options about laundry soap, cantaloupes, and bags of onions. There is no "truth" to Estes's images, in spite of their "photorealism," any more than there is a truth-value that can be assessed in the objects he depicts. They promise an endless variety of possibilities as our eyes are drawn from one to another in a ceaseless visual production that refuses closure or any return to real systemic relations of production. Consumption has become the condition of signs par excellence, and the fine-art depiction of this situation makes explicit the difficulties in breaking the cycle of consumer fascination.

In the 1980s, artists appropriated the methods of direct visual address central to the rhetoric of advertising in a move quite different from the depiction or mimicry of the visual forms of signage graphics. Barbara Kruger and Jenny Holzer made frequent use of the first person plural in their verbal language. Kruger combined these with Dick and Jane visuals familiar to a generation that learned to read before *Sesame Street* to pose a critique of received concepts of gender roles and power. The

14 Guy Debord, *The Society of the Spectacle* (Detroit, MI: The Red and the Black, 1983)

Richard Estes, *Food City,* 1967
Collection of the Akron Museum, Museum Acquisition Fund

visual rhetoric of advertising, Kruger seemed to be saying, has a much greater effect than the subtler means of persuasion available within the rhetorics of fine arts. A sense of urgency, of a compelling, pressing, immediacy, is thus infused into the fine-art frame. It is only the content/thematics of the image that distinguish it from other billboards. Hans Haacke, chameleon-like, copied the precise iconography, typography, layout, and design of various corporate campaigns in order to reveal the contradictions between the public face of corporate identity and the often abusive tactics in such less visible domains as labor relations. Haacke was well aware of the ways in which the effect of signage and the concentration of capital are interlinked within power relations that are most often concealed by the familiar rhetoric of the public face of advertising. Holzer and Kruger, meanwhile, put their work into public spaces as a means of directly confronting the engagement with the public sphere.

At the height of 1980s post-Modern appropriation, Richard Prince lifted the imagery of an ad campaign directly, letting go of the identifying trademarks, logos, and text. In his use of the photographic images of Marlborough ads, where the image itself unambiguously invokes a particular product by association, Prince depends upon the concept of public sphere to produce meaning with these images. Excised from their usual print media/billboard environment, they carry a chain of associations that leads us back to that domain, forcing an awareness of its existence —we know what this image "means" is not dependent on the visual information it contains, but on the network of interconnections that it immediately calls to mind, a network established in the public arena of visual culture. The idea that private life is completely produced by the imagery of mass media shows up in this ceding of the enframed space of art—the "sign" of the private discourse of individual expression or perception or commentary—to the terms, materials, "pictures" of the commercial realm. For Prince, the idea of art as individual expression is long outmoded —a mythic concept put to rest from the advent of Pop Art onward, now finalized by a gesture of "art making" that refuses any kind of transformation of the material it appropriates.

The notion of the "private" space of art may always have been fictive (in Habermas's discussion, domestic space is always considered an extension of the public sphere since the family serves as a primary place where the social relations of production are defined and replicated). But the structural distinction between public and private domains as an idea allows for some mobility of perception, such that a dialogue can be imagined that is largely foreclosed in the Prince image. In Prince's work, the earlier, enframing function of art vanishes, or is banished, so that there are no marks of any kind distinguishing the rhetoric of commercial media and advertising from that of fine art. When 1980s entrepreneurial-spirited artist Jeff Koons made a billboard of himself and Ciccolina (his then-wife and costar) to advertise his forthcoming movie, he demonstrated the extent to which the identity of the artist had elided with that of other products for promotion and consumption. Koons borrowed the particular images and promotional tropes peculiar to the entertainment industry. To be an artist, Koons seemed to be saying, was to be an ephemeral, consumable product, a diversion.

By contrast, in his piece *Three Wheaties Boxes* (1980s), David Hammons transformed the received imagery of product design. By making use of its familiarity he posed a clear critique of the concepts of standardization, consumerism, and packaging. The visual rhetoric is subverted through its own iconography and the insertion of new material obviously unexpected in the familiar context. The work performs as art through its argument, by intervening in the visual culture of signs and signage to disrupt them. The gesture is significant because it registers an unknown imagery (of fine art) within the known sphere of visual culture (advertising). The broader audience base and shared knowledge of mass-media culture tips the balance of images' power toward the commercial, and the function of fine art in this instance is to call the assumptions produced by that shared knowledge to our attention. The act of displacement and defamiliarization that Hammons makes is a familiar trope of the avant-garde, but the late-twentieth-century context diminishes the visibility of the art image in the noise of consumer culture. The quaintly handmade, awkward, even amateur quality of the rendering of the mass-produced cereal boxes is a conspicuous feature of their having been made over into art. They register their fall from the grace of high production values to the artifactual domain of fine art in the formal transformation of design language back into personal handmade art production.

The concentrated effort on the part of many artists to insert their work into a broad public arena, well beyond the defined parameters of gallery and museum spaces, leads to certain other contradictions and problems in the dialogue of fine art and design rhetorics. When an LCD display of Jenny Holzer's *Raise Boys and Girls the Same Way* is photographed *in situ* in a sports stadium, this problem comes into sharp focus. Signage has become so naturalized and integrated an element of the public landscape that in this case the Holzer does not stand out from its surroundings by any distinguishing marks. Holzer's piece has to compete with the signs of the company whose equipment she uses for display, as well as with the full field of signs that are on the wall in which it is located. As an artwork, the Holzer image functions just as any other sign. It is not enframed as art in any formal terms, insofar as it is distinguishable as a rhetoric—which is to say, it is the rhetoric of its language as argument and the rhetoric of its existence in the world as surprise element of unexpected message that makes the sign distinct from those by which it is surrounded. It must read against and in contrast to the product signs with which it competes for attention. The very site and means by which the sign is produced raises other questions. The conspicuous presence of the Sony logos and tags of corporate identity pose the question of whether Sony is sponsoring Holzer or whether her work serves to promote the company, demonstrating its "art-friendly" status.

We encounter Pittman's 1994 *A Decorated Chronology of Insistence and Resignation* as a painting (whether in installation or reproduction). This

Lari Pittman, *Untitled #32 (A Decorated Chronology of Insistence and Resignation)* (detail)

knowledge helps grant it cultural status as an art object and thus to read its rhetoric as an act of "enframing," of setting apart and commenting upon the language of consumer advertising. In Pittman's painting, the Visa and MasterCard have a presence as signs, but they are not signs or packaging for products; rather, they function as signs of corporate identity, promoting themselves as a necessary means of maintaining a share of the credit market. There is no way to raise questions of "truth" value in relation to Visa—it is simply a fact. The identity of Visa/MasterCard *is* intimately bound up with its image and vice versa—their image is identity. A huge corporate industry has its reality as the extension of that image, but the image function implements the activities of this industry in a fundamental and necessary way. As a painting the Pittman is still a "sign" of a private voice, enclosed within the "public" domain—maintaining the fictive but real identity of that position as an element within the public sphere. The frenzied continuum with its assaultive insanity on the image

Signs of Life / Spaces of Art

works to contextualize those signs. The central image of a deathlike head, a contemporary version of Munch's *The Scream,* bespeaks the very nightmarish reality of a life driven by pressure to consume in tension with the recognition of mortality. The brevity of human life is spun out in a banner announcing the passage of Halley's Comet—whose seventy-year cycle so closely resembles a human life span. But in the Paik video of recycled media, every image takes on the appearance of a logo, a free-floating but autonomous sign that presents an identity as image without revealing any substantive information about its corporate structures or relations. The size and scale of the piece reinforce the sense that Paik's work is an aesthetic legitimization of the corporate supplier of the equipment. The work reinforces the absence of any frame of reference outside the monitors. Its repleteness and hermetic insularity, the speed at which images move through it and repeat on a loop of disconnected signs, suggests the totalizing integration that legitimates the commodification of ever more areas of our existence in order to sell them back to us as products in a visual rhetoric of autonomous signs as consumable images.

In the late-twentieth-century context, then, the work of Lari Pittman, originally compared with the work of John Sloan, can also be contrasted with other artists' use of signage in the now clearly ageographical spaces of commercial media and sign production. Nam June Paik's *Megatron* (1995), installed in the lobby of the Guggenheim Museum (downtown branch) as part of the Mediascape exhibition in 1996, is, in its physical form, indistinguishable from a trade-show display. Huge banks of monitors are piled on each other to make an enormous single screen unifying the discrete spaces of each monitor into a single integrated whole—pattern and image in continuous display. But the technological contrast between these two is not what determines their capacity to produce (or failure to produce)—a "dialogue" between the rhetorics of art and graphic-design signage. A monitor presents as much of an opportunity for interaction as a painting. We receive the images from both in the same passive, visual manner. The dialogue is what happens in response, around the edges, in the space in front of, moving away from, or commenting upon the images displayed in the monitor or on the canvas. Dialogue is a function of community, of individuals in exchange with each other, using their interactions and points of difference, contention, and common interest as a basis of social and political action. There exists a possibility for a rhetoric of disjunction, of defamiliarization, of affirmation, or articulation of something other than the product/produced seamless totalized rhetoric of commercial media and/or the infotainment industry in any medium (video, street signs, traditional painting, conventional or electronic imagery).

This loss of context is like the loss of history: It conceals structures that might provide insights into the "real" through providing some actual information, however mediated, about the determinative and causal relations of power in terms of material forces and social relations. Efficient function, the old goal of an earlier age, returns transformed into an integrated circuit. This new set of signs of equivalence and infinite-seeming interchangeability and arbitrariness baffles the eye and mind in their seamlessness and overwhelming seductive capacity. The face of the monitor gives an appearance of invulnerability, inaccessibility to interaction or dialogue—even as the hype of interactivity comes to dominate the promotions for the product line of which it is the front runner.

Paik's work is mysteriously networked; it is both the evidence of and the performance of those integrated circuits whose tropes of economic and social relations it displays. Its elaborate inner connections operate out of sight. Like the mythic structures of corporate power it sustains, it shows us only a glittering, shining illusion to which we attach more value for knowing less. In Pittman's painting, the figurative beauty of the sign—VISA/MASTERCARD—flashes brilliant in the dark night of new nightmare. It would show its vivid colors pathetically in the toxic glare of a polluted daylight, if we cared to see it that way. Or we could give in to the absorptive potential of the bright face presented to us while asking, what has happened to that discrete border, that enframing set of distinctions among rhetorics, that allowed us to distinguish one message from another, differentiate one image from the next, one aspect of the social from its integration into a synthetic, totalized, and unresponsive undialogic whole? The issue of these new works is not merely one of what dialogue they make possible, but what dialogues, disjunctions, contradictions they manage to inscribe in their actual imagery.

Obviously, culture never exists in a static state. The current moment has to be characterized by the implications of electronic modes of communication and production in all sectors of art, design, and so forth. It seems pernicious to indulge in either the apocalyptic assessments (total capital = total repression = the disappearance of all forms of public life and dialogue) or utopian ones (cyberspace as democratic ideal of classless equality with equal access and opportunity for all). On the other hand, it behooves us to be attentive to the implications of the ways new forms, by their very specificity, have an impact on the configuration of various dialogues: between graphic design and fine art, between commercial interests and the public interest, between individual perception and formulaic production. Because at every point the features of these various rhetorics both do and do not contribute to making such dialogues possible. And it is in the dialogues among people with and through the media of art and design, conventional or electronic technology, rhetorics of individual and commercial signage, that the public sphere remains alive. Dialogue is a process, not a product: It can't be packaged, commodified, experienced as a standard "brand" or sign. In an image-saturated culture, one of the functions of fine art is to keep opening spaces of such dialogue within the integrated circuitry of signs, continually pulling meaning back out of the predictable production of a rhetoric of consumption into a rhetoric of critical consideration and thought-ful exchange.

Richard Estes, *Food City* (detail)

Signs of Life / Spaces of Art

Looking into Space

Stephanie Zelman

What I really want on the Macintosh is a virtual reality interface—armholes in either side of the box so you can reach in and move logos around; a real paintbrush so that you can feel the texture of the surface underneath.
—Neville Brody[1]

[1] Diane Burns, ed., "Neville Brody," *Designers on Mac* (Tokyo: Graphic-sha Publishing Co., Ltd., 1992) 17

Although Neville Brody cannot get inside the box, the viewer of his work can. The irony of his above statement is that it was spoken by a graphic designer whose work captures the very ideal that he claims is out of reach. In stretching the boundaries of legibility and composing a layered, textured surface, for two decades graphic designers have been creating two-dimensional space with a three-dimensional effect.

Today, typefaces and their configurations contain meaning that is distinct from the words they create. Certainly, calligraphy, decorative type, and italic or bold letterforms have long served to express tone or heighten the impact of words. But the proliferation of computer technology into most areas of social experience, and especially in the field of communication design, has caused a fundamental shift

Looking into Space

in the way we decipher information. We are consumers of a complex lexicon of type and image—a viewing audience more accustomed to looking *into* space.

But computers alone do not have an effect on the way we read. All technologies incorporate a set of practices which in turn, presuppose a cultural disposition. Within the field of graphic design, there has been a shift from modern forms to computer-generated, deconstructionist ones. Underlying this trend toward digitization is a changing conception of the way we envision the world which generates new kinds of cultural meaning.

Modernism as a school of thought is supported by a model of vision that presupposes a linear path between a viewer's eye and an object of perception. In this conception, there is no "space"

Neville Brody GAM (Graphic Arts Message) poster 1992

between the eye and an image because the act of seeing is not understood to incorporate human experience. Rather, the gazing "eye of distant and infinite vision" is disembodied from the self and shielded from the outside.[2]

This way of seeing is described by Robert Romanyshyn in *Technology as Symptom and Dream*. In his discussion of Renaissance painting, Romanyshyn explains that the way artists began to represent the world in the fifteenth century caused a cultural form of vision that turned "the self into a spectator, the world into a spectacle and the body into a specimen."[3] In his view, the depiction of the world on the canvas formed our actual perception of it. We became isolated selves, detached from our own bodies and from the "outside" world, which we were left to observe from a distance.

Romanyshyn's metaphor of a closed "window" describes a barrier between us and the world which can only be penetrated by the eye,

[2] Robert Romanyshyn, *Technology as Symptom and Dream* (New York: Routledge Press, 1989) 97

[3] Ibid. 33

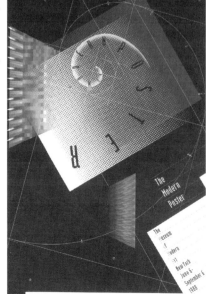

April Greiman The Modern Poster poster 1988

implying that the visual component of our being is the only bridge between "inside" and "outside." As a result, our disjointed world (the legacy of the partition of the canvas) is infinitely removed from us. And the eye, as a gazing, distant point in space, distills our soulful sensuality. He writes,

> The vanishing point, the point where the world as texture, quality, and difference has shrunk to a geometric dot, has no sound, no taste, no smell, no color, no feel, no quality. It has only measure.[4]

[4] Ibid. 89

Romanyshyn claims that linear perspective vision was an artistic view of the world that became a cultural one, as the "innate geometry of our eyes" began to perceive everything in the world on the same horizontal plane.[5]

[5] Ibid. 32 (phrase attributed to Samuel Y. Edgerton)

This model of vision corresponds to the methodology of modern graphic design, which rejects an interplay between viewer and image and affirms that our internal makeup does not alter the impressions we receive. The modern designer's objective is to control the viewer's detached visual component so that information is transmitted seamlessly. In this process, meaning is finite and the text is closed.

In declaring that their practices were "neutral" and "objective," modernists in the 1940s began designing in accordance with these underlying conceptions. It was simply accepted that the human eye—divorced from the subjective apparatus of the emotional body—would always decipher a message in the same way. In attempting to control the eye, modern design dismissed the creativity of viewing.

The notions of monocularity and the separation of the eye from the body were also addressed by Marshall McLuhan in *The Gutenberg Galaxy*. While Romanyshyn claims that the invention of linear perspective painting served to isolate the visual component of our senses and divorce the self from the world, McLuhan, on the other hand, argued that the introduction of the phonetic alphabet and the printing press caused a break between the eye and the ear, disrupting the sensory complex and impairing the social spirit. McLuhan explained that whereas an interplay of all the senses in traditional oral societies promoted a heterogeneous space of human interaction and interdependence, the invention of the printing press caused an adverse cultural transformation. He showed that printed matter was instrumental in causing the visual component to become abstracted from the other senses, inducing an internalized, static, and compartmentalized lived experience which ultimately led to a society of detached individuals.

McLuhan argued that humanity inherited a "fixed point of view" due to the abstraction of the visual factor. But unlike Romanyshyn, who believes the computer "will give flesh to this eye which in abandoning the body has dreamed of a vision of the world unmoved by the appeal of the world," McLuhan looked positively on technological innovation.[6] McLuhan affirmed that the electronic signal brings about a "stream of consciousness" and an "open field of perception" creating the possibility for a richer viewing activity.[7] He also claimed that our emerging electronic age could

[6] Ibid. 99

[7] Marshall McLuhan, *The Gutenberg Galaxy* (Toronto: University of Toronto Press, 1968) 278

Looking into Space

bring back the "mythic, collective dimension of human experience" that was experienced in oral culture.[8] For McLuhan, new information technologies cause a shift in our sense ratios, resulting in a reunification with one's self and with others:

[8] Ibid. 269

> The "simultaneous field" of electric information structures today reconstitutes the conditions and need for dialogue and participation, rather than specialism and private initiative in all levels of social experience.[9]

[9] Ibid. 141

McLuhan's writings are prophetic given that the computer's multimedia and interactive capabilities, along with its capability to layer and link moving type and images, encourage continuous and simultaneous experience. And his understanding of our relationship with new information technologies supports the conception of a new kind of visual experience that occurs when typography enters the "polymorphous digital realm."[10] He observed that the electronic age "is not mechanical but organic, and has little sympathy [for] the values achieved through typography, 'this mechanical way of writing'. . ."[11]

[10] Rick Poynor, "Type and Deconstruction in the Digital Era," *Typography Now: The New Wave* (Cincinnati, OH: North Light, 1992) 11

The canonical, fixed, authoritative text that produced a passive visual experience goes hand in hand with the linear visual system of modern design. Conversely, in a digital milieu, type becomes unfixed and so does meaning. As Jacques Derrida observed, "one cannot tamper with the form of the book without disturbing everything else in Western thought."[12]

[11] Marshall McLuhan, 135

The decline of modernist ideas of legibility was inevitable the moment graphic designers dipped their creative fingertips into the binary pool. When the Macintosh computer was introduced to the field in the 1980s, designers began to layer and dissolve type and imagery—a practice that shattered the conception of a detached, objective reader. Designers began to endorse the sort of communication that would "promote multiple rather than fixed readings" and "provoke the reader into becoming an active participant in the construction of the message."[13]

[12] Jacques Derrida, *Dissemination,* Trans. Barbara Johnson (Chicago: University of Chicago Press, 1981) 3

[13] Poynor, 9

Viewing began to be understood as a process of human involvement, which entails an "act of consciousness."[14] Ron Burnett articulates this point in *Cultures of Vision: Images, Media and the Imaginary,* where he explains that images are not just representations that enter our field of vision, but are experienced by us in a personal way. In examining our response to them, Burnett introduces the concept of "projection," which he describes as a "meeting point of desire, meaning and interpretation."[15]

[14] Ron Burnett, *Cultures of Vision: Images, Media and the Imaginary* (Bloomington, IN: Indiana University Press, 1995) 136

[15] Ibid.

This union is, metaphorically speaking, a "space" between the viewer and the viewed, where the eye, along with the rest of the body and the human state of consciousness, encounters an image and

creatively interprets it. Rather than presume that we are detached from that which is "outside" ourselves, "projection" is a way of describing how we subjectively and imaginatively engage with our world.

According to Burnett, even though we inject meaning into images—and are in that sense responsible for what we see—we do not have an observing power over the world. We may be fabricating our own viewing process when we project, but our fragile subjectivity hinges on physical, emotional, and psychological states. As Burnett explains, projections are "like filters, which retain all of the traces of communication, but are always in transition between the demands made by the image and the needs of the viewer."[16]

[16] Ibid. 136–137

Although his discussion is primarily about images, Burnett's theory of vision can be applied to the way we experience graphic design. In fact, Johanna Drucker has made a similar argument in *The Visible World: Experimental Typography and Modern Art*:

> [T]he materiality of the signifier, whether it be word or image, is linked to its capacity to either evoke or designate sensation as it transformed into perception, and that it in no case has a guaranteed truth value, only the relative accuracy within the experience of an individual subject.[17]

[17] Johanna Drucker, *The Visible World: Experimental Typography and Modern Art 1909–1923*, (Chicago: University of Chicago Press, 1994) 65

Burnett's notion of "projection" is helpful in identifying some of the features of typographic design in a digital environment, where designers have blurred the distinction between type and image. When typography is treated as imagery—that is, when it is pushed to the limits of legibility—the result is an enhanced visual involvement on the part of the viewer. As designers transform the mechanics of representation, more demands are made on the viewer to interpret messages. Designers now expect that something like "projection" will occur while reading. For example, in *The End of Print*, David Carson's art direction of magazines such as *Ray Gun* and *Beach Culture* is defended on the basis that their audience does not need visual direction. Whereas most magazines "want their readers to know what to expect, to

Christopher Vice *Beach Culture* table of contents, 1990

know where to look and how to read through a page," these publications establish "a different relationship with the reader."[18]

[18] Lewis Blackwell and David Carson, eds., *The End of Print: The Graphic Design of David Carson* (San Francisco: Chronicle Books, 1995)

As the digital medium encourages designers to treat typography as imagery, readers are simply invited to interpret messages on their own terms. In fact, designers suggest that the more often a new typeface is used, the more familiar it becomes. Simply put by one type designer, "readability is a conditioned state."[19] Apparently, since words are no longer expected to contain truth-value, the fact that they are somewhat illegible at first does not seem to present too much of a problem. As stated by type designer, Jeffery Keedy,

[19] Neville Brody, *www.type.cp.uk/snet/fuse/statesamp.html* accessed 1996

If someone interprets my work in a way that is totally new to me, I say fine. That way your work has a life of its own. You create a situation for people to do with it what they will, and you don't create an enclosed or encapsulated moment.[20]

[20] Jeffery Keedy, *Emigre* #15 (1990) 17

The less legible a typeface becomes, either on its own or in juxtaposition with other graphic elements, the more it takes on an inherent image. When this occurs, words are no longer simply read, but understood within the context of an entire visual construction. This is the visual language of deconstruction.

Deconstruction, as we learned from Jacques Derrida in *Grammatology*, is the technique of breaking down a "whole" in order to reflect critically on its parts. When using this method, the designer affirms that different interpretations will be discovered within the fabric that holds a message together. Unlike the linearity of modernism which implies a separation between the viewer and the viewed, and a "withdrawal of the self from the world,"[21] typographic deconstruction compels a viewer to take part in the interpretation of a message. This strategy of visual disorganization was embraced and legitimized by design schools such as the Cranbrook Academy of Art:

[21] Romanyshyn, 42

The Cranbrook theorist's aim, derived from French philosophy and literary theory, is to deconstruct, or break apart and expose, the manipulative visual language and different levels of meaning embodied in design.[22]

[22] Poynor, 14

This visual language conditions readers to approach text differently—to look *into* a two-dimensional space (page or screen) in order to decipher meaning. Put somewhat differently, Richard Lanham argues in *The Electronic World: Democracy, Technology and the Arts,* that we now look "at" art rather than "through" it.[23] Similarly, readers look "at" text because type designers go through pains to ensure that their fonts are not overlooked in the reading process. Consider Brody's description of his typeface, State.

[23] Richard Lanham, *The Electronic World: Democracy, Technology and the Arts* (Chicago and London: The University of Chicago Press, 1993) 45

I wanted to take the role of typography away from a purely subservient, practical role towards one that is potentially more expressive and visually dynamic. There are no special characters and presently no lowercase is planned. The font is designed to have no letter spacing, and ideally it should

[24] Neville Brody, *www.type.cp.uk/snet/fuse/statesamp.html* accessed 1996

Graphic Design & Reading

be set with no line space. I decided not to include a complete set of punctuation marks and accents, encouraging people to create their own if needed.[24]

Typographic deconstruction parallels Burnett's theory of "projection," which incorporates the view that words and images are not the sources of meaning. Like Burnett, contemporary designers argue that a seeing audience is not made up of receptors of images (and words), but capable of engaging in an interpretive "space." As well, they view typography similarly to the way Burnett regards imagery—that it "should address our capacity for intuitive insight and simultaneous perception, and stimulate our senses as well as engaging our intellect."[25] The layering, [25] Poynor, 16 texturing, and overall fluidity of typography and imagery that ensues from new media technologies now affects the way we take "in" information. The self is absorbed into the act of viewing; the eye is embodied and the window is open.

The blurring of type and image is clearly a manifestation of our cultural tendency to renegotiate boundaries that were long thought to be sacrosanct. Critical discourse in graphic design over the last two decades has highlighted some of modernism's conceptual dichotomies such as "high" vs. "low," "distinguished" vs. "vulgar," and "beautiful" vs. "ugly." In fact, oppositional binary systems underlie many of modernity's claims to knowledge. One explanation is that in the seventeenth century, when science became the new religion and objectivity the new god, Western civilization set out to create an ordered understanding of the world. A cultural value was secured to the notion of "absolute truth" and a new imperative was placed on the human race to uncover it. The belief in the existence of an objective truth brings with it a system of binary oppositions; for where there is truth, there is falsehood.

Apart from this core distinction, many other supposedly "natural" oppositions such as "mind" vs. "body," "reality" vs. "representation," and "objective" vs. "subjective" form modernity's ideological grid. This system was Modernity's way of understanding the world and our place in it. And modern design's model of linear vision that distinguished between "inside" and "outside" was no exception. By mid-century, the belief in an objective reality was so ingrained in the way Western society produced meaning, the notion of

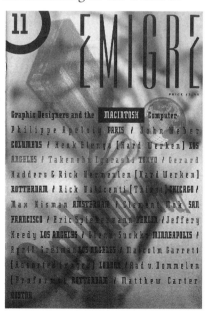

Rudy VanderLans *Emigre* 11 cover 1989

Looking into Space

57

a universal method of communication went undisputed. The fixation on logic, rationality, and closure in Western culture corresponded to an unselfconscious and linear typographic style that does not obstruct the transmission of meaning. There would be no hidden meanings, no nuances, no uncertainty. Post modern thinker Jean Baudrillard described a disenchanted world where everything must be produced, legible, real, visible, measurable, indexed, and recorded."[26]

[26] Jean Baudrillard, *Seduction* (New York: St. Martins Press, 1990) 34–35

[27] Drucker, 37

Deconstruction in design highlights yet another one of those familiar Western binary oppositions that went unchallenged by the Modern Movement—the writing/speech dichotomy. As explained by Drucker, structural linguists privilege speech over writing because of its perceived time-based immediacy and purity.[27] Unlike the truthful spontaneity of expression, writing was viewed as an inferior copy of speech, farther removed from interior consciousness and therefore seen to contain no linguistic value. It is clear by now that modernism implicitly adhered to this distinction in its drive to keep viewers looking "through" text. In a context where speech is privileged, graphic design only makes matters worse. Twice removed from the meaning of the word, the stylized letterform strays even farther from the initial thought.

The writing/speech dichotomy was understood by Derrida as encapsulating the Western drive for closure. He argued against the distinction between "live" speech and "dead" letters which structural linguists had constructed in an effort to link truth with the voice closest to the self. Derrida showed that truth is an illusion in Western thought, since both writing and speech have no final meaning. The idea that it is not the written words, per se, but the disorganization of graphic elements that can extend meaning, is a powerful manifestation of Derrida's theory.

From a modern point of view, the design methodology of deconstruction seemed meaningless and purposeless because readability was secondary to engaging the reader and eliciting an emotional response. After all, modernists thought, what is the point of communication design if the message is misunderstood? Yet it no longer seems so absurd now that we recognize that there

Graphic Design & Reading

Ed Fella wedding invitation (inside) 1994

are ways to communicate, without making "everything speak, everything babble, everything climax."[28] Type and imagery is manipulated in order to engage the viewer and beckon interpretation, ultimately blurring the distinction between "designer" and "viewer" as well.

[28] Baudrillard, 20

In our digital landscape, we do not "design and invent our world in accordance with a particular vision"[29] but reinvent our world and ourselves each time we encounter a visual message. Reading requires that we use our intellect, but deconstructed typography further encourages a "shifting movement from awareness to knowledge, to desire and its negation."[30] The eye roams, looking *into* the printed page or glowing screen, where meaning is revealed through an evaluation of the entire space. Deconstruction has not simply addressed the *look* of design but a way of LOOKING at design.

[29] Romanyshyn, 41

[30] Burnett, 135

When the theory of deconstruction penetrated the field of graphic design in the 1980s, it did not simply undermine the modern aesthetic, it chipped away at the underpinnings of Modernity. Ingrained binary oppositions such as "inside" vs. "outside," "subjective" vs. "objective," and even "humanity" vs. "technology" were renegotiated as designers tried to get inside the box. Since then, designers have brazenly blurred the line of legibility, underscoring the open text and confirming that the only knowable truth is that truth itself is an illusion.[31]

The notion of an interpretive text that appeared in the eighties and nineties was a distressing prospect for designers who came of age at a time when design was a means of ordering the world. Renowned designers who had long been working within Modernity's cultural constructions were not impressed by computer-generated solutions. Perhaps, like Romanyshyn, they wondered whether "technology has eclipsed the life of imagination more than it has been its realization."[32] For those designers who grew up in the modern tradition, the loss of a structured, understandable world was surely difficult to withstand. But to quote McLuhan, for all their lamentations, the revolution had already taken place.[33]

[31] Jean Baudrillard, *Simulacra and Simulation,* Trans. Sheila Faria Glaser (Ann Arbor, MI: University of Michigan Press, 1994)

[32] Romanyshyn, 6

[33] Marshall McLuhan, "Playboy Interview: A Candid Conversation with the High Priest of Popcult and Metaphysician of Media" *Essential McLuhan,* Eric McLuhan and Frank Zingrone, eds. (Concord, ON: Anansi, 1995) 266

Ed Fella wedding invitation (outside) 1994

Looking into Space

reading photographs

We all read photographs and images immediately, connecting what we see to what we think we know. The words included with these images recontextualize them, forcing the viewer/reader to rethink first impressions. Reading the text reveals ironies, paradoxes, and hidden stories that cannot be understood from images alone. Within these small collages there are multiple relationships between and among the images and the words. Each page has two main texts—a personal memory and a passage from an etiquette book or behavior manual. One is presented as objective information, the other completely subjective.

Selected from a larger series of prints about a young girl growing up in the 1960s, these pages invite readers to view nostalgia through a different lens.

Colette Gaiter

Reading Photographs

We should try to acquire an under-standing of the customs of each country we visit and never presume to set our own behavior up as a pattern to be followed.

p. 158, *EMILY POST'S ETIQUETTE,* 1965

I used to show this picture to friends and say, "Find my family." We were on a tour bus in Paris in the spring of 1964 and the guide took this photo. It occurs to me that the other people in the picture might also have a copy. I wonder what they thought of it then and what they think of it now. I notice that the man standing next to my father is looking away from the camera. I wonder if some of them were annoyed that they had to share their tour and bus with Negroes. I wonder which of them considered us just one of those things a person tolerates as part of being in a foreign country. Perhpas some of them thought nothing of it. I don't know if they were all Americans, which would have made a difference.

The full implications of being on that bus at that time with those people eluded me until recently. When I was a child living in Europe, on a mostly-white Army base, white people became visually benign to me. I didn't really expect to see anyone else.

THE INMAN E. PAGE LIBRARY

APR 1961

In 1962, in Jefferson City, the capital of Missouri, my sister and I wore dresses with full, starched skirts, white anklet socks, and black patent leather shoes to go downtown shopping.

I always had a problem keeping my socks on my heels and out of my shoes. It was as if the heels of my shoes ate the socks. I would see how long I could walk before the sock was all the way off my heel and scrunched around my arches and I would have to adjust it. Sometimes it didn't happen. Maybe the shoes just liked certain pairs of socks.

My mother was very particular about wearing the right kind of clothing for the occasion. In spite of that, the fact that she was the only person in her college graduation photograph who was wearing white shoes also seems just like her.

4.

Visit a store that sells chinaware and silverware. Notice the differences in costs of various kinds, and try to find out the reasons for these differences.

p. 339. TEEN GUIDE TO HOMEMAKING, 1961.

with cup and saucer

I was about eight years old and fascinated by one of my parents' sets of china. Each dish had a wide gold band around the edges with a flower and leaf pattern in a matte finish—like the pattern in jacquard fabric that is visible up close when the light hits the surface from the right angle. The pattern was a hidden surprise that you could only see if you really looked. The shape of the dishes was modern, with clean lines and simple curves. We had all the pieces—platters, serving dishes, everything. But we never used them.

I asked my mother when we were ever going to use them, because we always used another set for special occasions. "We'll use them when President Kennedy comes to dinner," she said. Even though that answer essentially meant that they were for show and would never be used, I liked entertaining the idea that the president might come to our house for dinner. We used those dishes for the first time on the Thanksgiving before my mother died, less than ten years later. No one knew at that time that it would be her last Thanksgiving. She just decided it was time to use them.

My parents are at some official military event in Germany, being received by people who were apparently important at the time. The blond woman in a black dress dates the picture by looking like Sally, Rob's writing partner from The Dick Van Dyke Show. What is striking to me, looking at this picture 35 or so years later, is not that it's another "civil rights moment"—blacks and whites together captured on film—it's that most people have seen little or none of this type of interaction that went on all the time.

The photographic evidence of these white people shaking hands with my parents and offering some perfunctory, and within that limitation, sincere greeting seems like not only a different country, but a different planet from the publicly mediated world of African Americans. These kinds of images have not been recorded in mainstream media because they would reveal our humanity, and make the business of oppression more difficult.

A lady never takes off her gloves to shake hands, no matter when or where and never apologizes for not doing so.

p. 579.
EMILY POST'S ETIQUETTE, 1965

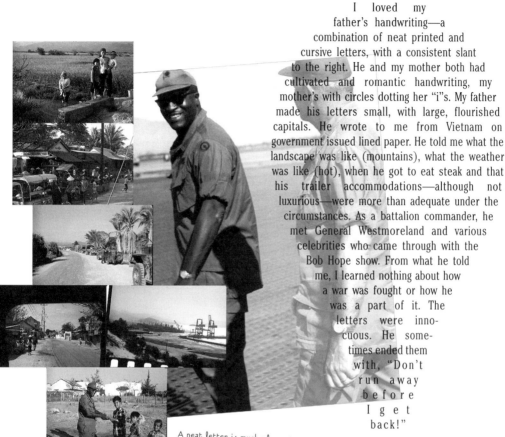

I loved my
father's handwriting—a
combination of neat printed and
cursive letters, with a consistent slant
to the right. He and my mother both had
cultivated and romantic handwriting, my
mother's with circles dotting her "i"s. My father
made his letters small, with large, flourished
capitals. He wrote to me from Vietnam on
government issued lined paper. He told me what the
landscape was like (mountains), what the weather
was like (hot), when he got to eat steak and that
his trailer accommodations—although not
luxurious—were more than adequate under the
circumstances. As a battalion commander, he
met General Westmoreland and various
celebrities who came through with the
Bob Hope show. From what he told
me, I learned nothing about how
a war was fought or how he
was a part of it. The
letters were inno-
cuous. He some-
times ended them
with, "Don't
run away
before
I get
back!"

A neat letter is much pleasanter to receive than a sloppy
one, so fold the paper squarely, put the stamp on straight
and right side up, and write the return address on the back
flap of the envelope (socially correct), or on the front
upper left corner (Post Office approved).

p. 94. MC CALL'S BOOK OF EVERYDAY ETIQUETTE, 1960

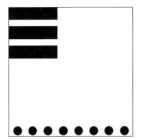

Verwenden
Sie das
Qualitätspapier
Hard-Mill
Feldmann, Dutli & Co. Zürich

Verwenden Sie das

Qualitätspapier

Feldmann,
Dutli & Co.
Zürich   Hard-Mill

Verwenden Sie
das Qualitätspapier Hard - Mill
Feldmann,
Dutli & Co.
Zürich

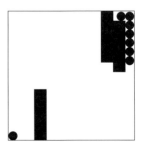

Visual Syntax

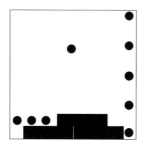

Verwenden Sie das Qualitätspapier

Hard-Mill

Feldmann Dutli & Co.Zürich

A *language* consists of a vocabulary

of signs combined according to grammatical laws. A recurring strategy of modernist design pedagogy is to repetitively arrange and rearrange a collection of marks according to given rules of combination. The compositions reproduced here, redrawn from an anonymous student exercise produced in 1930, resemble numerous later explorations of the language of vision, found in such post–avant-garde textbooks as Armin Hofmann's *Graphic Design Manual* and Emil Ruder's *Typography*[1]. The dominant task of modern design theory has been to uncover the *syntax* of the language of vision: that is, ways to organize geometric and typographic elements in relation to such formal oppositions as orthogonal/diagonal, static/dynamic, figure/ground, linear/planar, and regular/irregular.

 Switzerland emerged as the ideological center of modern design theory in the 1950s and '60s: The phrase "Swiss design" became equated with the systematic deployment of typographic elements in a gridded space, as in the studies reproduced here, from a series in Emil Ruder's *Typography* (1981). Although Swiss modernism is commonly associated with anti–individualism, intuition is a key element in such rationalist equations as this statement from Karl Gerstner's *Designing Programmes* (1963): "The more exact and complete [the] criteria are, the more creative the work becomes. The creative act is reduced to an act of selection."[2] Thus for Gerstner, a set of rules functions as a decision-making machine that submits a vast series of choices to the designer's final act of judgment—the process is rational, but only until this decisive moment of personal intuition.

[1] Armin Hofmann, *Graphic Design Manual Principles and Practice* (New York: Van Nostrand Reinhold, 1965); Emil Ruder, *Typography* (New York: Hastings House, 1981)

[2] Karl Gerstner, *Designing Programmes* (Zurich: ABC Verlag, 1963)

Visual Syntax

By the early seventies, the apparently contradictory union of rational system and intuitive choice had become a central concern for some designers working in the modernist idiom. Since 1968, Wolfgang Weingart, teaching at the Basel School of Design, has focused on the intuitive side of the modernist equation, rejecting the ideal of objectivity in favor of inventive self-expression. Yet while Weingart's design *looks* fundamentally opposed to the older rationalism, he sees it as the logical extension of the ideas of Hofmann, Gerstner, and Ruder, whose seemingly objective work was always based, in the end, on intuitive choices.[3] Weingart had a major impact on the refined formalism of the 1970s and '80s, which foregrounds the decorative potential of the modernist syntax rather than using it as a neutral envelope.

The exercise reproduced here, from Cranbrook's graphic-design program, introduces vernacular typography into Ruder's systematic grid study; its purpose is "to build a personal mythology."[4] What alternatives are there to the neomodernist project of *personalizing* modernist languages, apart from a return to the untenable ideal of universal, value-free communication? The limited formal vocabularies of de Stijl and Constructivism, the ready-made objects of Marcel Duchamp, and the political montages of John Heartfield can be seen as attempts to expose a linguistic, cultural, or psychological order that legislates the individual creative act. Rather than personalize modernism, we could foreground the power and pervasiveness of the languages we use—visual and verbal, private and public, abstract and conventional.

[3] Wolfgang Weingart, "How Can One Make Swiss Typography?" *Octavo* 87 no. 4 (1987)

[4] Katherine and Michael McCoy, *Cranbrook Design: The New Discourse* (New York: Rizzoli, 1990)

Syntax

Katie Salen

I wonder about the way in which class often overdetermines our relationship to design. —Bell Hooks

Tracing the Invisible

Beatrice Warde's 1932 incantation "The Crystal Goblet" invokes the images of transparency and lightness as purveyors of an enlightened typographic project. Utilizing a form calculated to reveal rather than hide "the beautiful thing which it was meant to contain," the typographic crystal goblet proposed by Warde was not only functional but virtuous as well, implying an inherent, although hardly unproblematic connection between form and the moral sphere. Historically, much critical discussion, particularly among typographers, has centered on the role typographic form plays in conveying meaning, as Warde's valorization of transparency as a means of semantic revelation no doubt demonstrates. Far less attention, however, has been given to an analysis of transparency and lightness as agents of invisibility for nonstandard speakers, or those who fall outside of the frame of "the beautiful thing" Warde's crystal goblet was meant to contain.

One way of thinking about this concept of invisibility is to consider the phenomena of the typographic visual "voice-over," which constitutes a national symbolic environment, as well as the organic process by which a standard "voice" is generalized across an entire range of cultural expression. *[Template Gothic, Univers, Century Schoolbook.]* The standard typographic voices we are accustomed to are utopian, belonging nowhere, regionless, without accent. *[Helvetica, Bell Gothic, Interstate.]* Seemingly transparent, these forms offer up representations of the generic, the symbolic, the superficial, and the stereotypical. *[Citizen, Democratica, Frathouse.]* In the case of the visual voice-over, language not only marks (or unmarks) identity but functions as a kind

Surrogate Multiplicities

Template Gothic

Univers

Century Schoolbook

Helvetica

Bell Gothic

Interstate

Citizen

Democratica

FRATHOUSE

of cultural border, as well. As Dick Hebdige notes, ". . . there can no longer be any absolute distinction between these two terms [form and content] and the primary recognition that the ways in which things are said—the narrative structures employed—impose quite rigid limitations on what can be said."[1] Taking Hebdige's narrative structures to include both syntactic and semantic elements of the written word, an analysis of the systems of subjectivity at play within typographic discourse can reveal the myriad ways in which visual form supports structures of cultural standardization, marking exclusionary distinctions between standard and nonstandard speakers.

In order to discuss typography as a system that marks social difference, it is important to remember that from earliest times the inscription of language by human hands involved practices in which value and meaning were assigned not to just what was written but how it was written.[2] In second century Rome, for example, three formal writing systems existed for the inscription of texts. Monumental capitals *(capitalis monumentalis)* were used for architectural inscriptions celebrating imperial accomplishments and conquests. Rustic capitals *(capitalis rustica),* an extremely condensed version used to conserve space on pages of costly papyrus and velum were used for political campaign material and outdoor advertising, while a third writing form, cursive, was used "by the people" for ephemeral, day-to-day forms of written exchange. Thus, within this complex, yet clearly politicized hierarchy, the value of the text, and hence the status of the speaker, was marked by the shape of its letterforms.

[1] Dick Hebdige, *Subculture: The Meaning of Style* (London: Routledge, 1987) 118

[2] Sojin Kim and Somi Kim, "Typecast: Meaning, Culture, and Identity in the Alphabetic Omelet," *Lift and Separate: Graphic Design and the Quote Unquote Vernacular,* Barbara Glauber, ed. (New York: The Herb Lubalin Study Center of Design and Typography, 1993) 31

This tradition of marking social difference through distinctions in typographic form continues today and is particularly apparent in the case of environmental signage where we make immediate judgments about social class, ethnicity, regional background, and a host of other social characteristics based on the sign's design. Variations in syntax —either through exaggeration or "error" —immediately place the formalized (and hence politicized) sign in opposition to a correct, or standardized, version aptly

characterized by the qualities of neutrality intrinsic to Warde's crystal cup. Forms eschewing this prized cultural transparency are labeled—by designers, most often —as forms of "visual dialect" and can frequently be found clustered together under the undifferentiated heading "vernacular."[3] Simple distinctions between "high" and "low" aside, this categorization of form is one based primarily on the concept of deviance, although linguistically speaking, dialects are not considered deviant forms of language at all, but simply different systems, with distinct subsets

Surrogate Multiplicities

[3] In *Lift and Separate: Graphic Design and the Quote UnQuote Vernacular,* Ellen Lupton writes "The term 'vernacular' has become the common parlance in the design community, referring to a natural, unschooled sensibility free from the self-censorship of modernism. . . . A 'vernacular' is simply a dialect, and every subculture has its dialects, including the subculture of 'high culture.'"

[4] Walt Wolfram, *Dialects and American English* (New York: Prentice Hall, 1991) 4

of form.[4] Yet unlike standard dialects, which are largely defined by an absence of socially stigmatizing elements, vernacular varieties seem to be characterized by the presence of these same structures. As a result, language structures that fall outside of generic, prescriptive norms offer an affront to standardized taste; vernacular forms not only represent a kind of stigmatized visual faux pas but tend to call into question the quality of the crystal from which Warde's unblemished cup was cast.

Further, because notions concerning the sanctity of language are intimately bound up with ideas of social order, typographic forms that deviate from a prescriptive discourse often incite suspicion on the part of those who wish to keep the boundaries of standardization intact. This should come as no surprise, for violations of authorized codes— in this case typographic ones— through which the social world is organized and experienced have

considerable power to provoke and disturb. As Levi-Strauss has noted, ". . . in certain primitive myths, the mispronunciation of words and the misuse of language are classified along with incest as horrendous aberrations capable of 'unleashing storm and tempest.'"[5] Perhaps the classification of nonstandard forms as "vernacular" is simply an attempt to avoid unleashing our own storm and tempest on the typographic front.

[5] Dick Hebdige, *Subculture: The Meaning of Style* (London: Routledge, 1987) 118

Agents of Standardization: Writing the Other

In street and alley what strange tongues are loud,
Accents of menace alien to our air,
Voices that once the Tower of Babel knew.
—Thomas Bailey Aldrich

Demands for linguistic standardization had been made from the earliest days of printing, which made variations more obvious by distributing them more widely. These demands became particularly insistent in the eighteenth century, when decorum of all kinds was highly prized.[6] Moreover, between the 1880s and the 1920s, urbanization and mass emigration brought together a range of languages, dialects, and idiolects previously separated through both geographic space and social difference. Linguistic criticism, spurred on by the

[6] Michael North, *The Dialect of Modernism* (New York: Oxford University Press, 1994)

publication of the *Oxford English Dictionary* (OED),[7] became a way of checking social mobility and racial progress.

Yet while linguistic borders were being fiercely defended against the forces of immigration and class mobility, visual representations of nonstandard speakers flourished. Moreover, a number of alphabets developed in the mid- to late nineteenth century were those designed and named to represent various "others" on the basis of stereotypical or non-Western forms.[8] It is not too much of a stretch to consider such culturally thematic alphabets as the visual equivalent of accented spoken English, or forms of visual dialects imbued with socially stigmatizing form.[9] Notable fonts include Chinese Wong, Japanesque, Samoa, Hobo, and Jim Crow. Typefaces such as Boston Script, Law Italic, and Society Script present the oppositional standard (in this case, white, upper-middle class) against which the typographic "otherness" of the nonstandard speakers was measured.

It is, of course, easy to dismiss these examples as historical artifacts of a time and place that had much to learn about issues of representation. In fact, Warde's model of transparency alludes to a form of visual discourse that, for all intents and purposes, erased difference through a formalized homogeneity. Yet, surprisingly, despite a radical critique of nineteenth-century practices and a cultural reevaluation of modernism, today examples of

[7] Ibid. The 1858 proposal for the OED dictionary rules out of consideration dialect words more recent than the Reformation and, in doing so, provides what the OED itself cites as the first recorded use of the phrase "standard language."

[8] Sojin Kim and Somi Kim, "Typecast: Meaning, Culture, and Identity in the Alphabetic Omelet," *Lift and Separate: Graphic Design and the Quote Unquote Vernacular*, 31

[9] "Another type of variation that the resources of English writing make possible is what has traditionally been called 'eye dialect.' This is the spelling of a familiar word in a non-standard form, while maintaining the standard pronunciation. Recurrent examples include 'wimmin,' 'sez,' 'bisnes,' and 'enuf.' Such eye dialect spellings . . . serve to hint that the overall tone of speech should be interpreted as different from the tone of conventional speech, usually in the direction of rustic and uneducated. Eye dialect spellings deliberately overstate the ignorance or illiteracy of a character. Rose-Marie Weber, "Variations in Spelling and the Special Case of Colloquial Contractions," *Visible Language* 20, no. 4 (1986)

24 Point CHINESE   H. H. Thorp, designer July 31, 1883   Cleveland

CHINESE WONG

36 Point HOBO   M. F. Benton, designer, March 30, 1915   ATF

36 HOBO CAP

36 Samoa

18 Point JAPANESQUE No. 2   Mackellar, Smiths & Jordan

18 JAPANESQUE &

24 Point JIM CROW

24 JIM CROW BADE!$

All typefaces from Morgan Press, Linotype and Ludlow Specimens. Jersey City, NJ 1917) *The introductory text reads: "In our specimen catalog you will find the modern types along with the pioneers. Here are the light-lines, black letters, shaded, extreme ornamentals, scripts, cursives, bizarre, condensed or extended letters, and the gothics all making a United Nations of types that may do some uncomfortable squirming when packed together so closely."*

Surrogate Multiplicities

12 Point LAW ITALIC on 14 Point Body

12 Law Italic LAW ITALIC fifffflffiffl

18 Point BOSTON SCRIPT   J. K. Rogers, designer, 8-15-82   Boston

18 Boston Script available from Morgan & Co.

24 Point SOCIETY SCRIPT   **SB&Co.**

24 Society Script Morga

culturally thematic alphabets abound, albeit covertly disguised through parody and pastiche. But first, a bit of history.

In the 1990s, post–Modern typographic critics reveled in the demolition of Warde's metaphor, literally turning the transparent surface of the argument inside out, in an attempt to reveal the fluidity of the relationship between form and meaning. Privileging context, or point of view, as the ultimate barometer of sense making, these critics proposed a typographic model embracing opacity and antimastery, yielding forms that denied the existence of any archetypal letter, whether crystal, gold, or glitter encrusted. Barry Deck's Template Gothic, P.

Template Gothic

Scott Makela's Dead History, and Zuzana Licko's Citizen, for example, were all attempts to imbue typography with social and narra-

tive histories. What is surprising to note, however, is that while these designers situated their practice in opposition to Warde's crys-

Dead History

Citizen

tal model by becoming involved in issues of representation—on the surface at least—their work failed to challenge the inherent quality of invisibility found in Warde's standardized model.

A heady claim, to be sure, but an examination of the typefaces sold by two popular contemporary font houses (House Industries and Emigre) not only supports the argument but strengthens it, as well. We begin with House Industries's class (un)conscious font collection Bad Neighborhood, "nine fonts from the bad side of the tracks," including Poorhouse, Condemdhouse, and the racially encrypted Crackhouse. And then there is Scrawl, another House Industries box set (with T-shirt!) that delivers Ashyhouse and Nastyhouse straight from their suburban ghetto to yours, all for the special price of $179. Sadly, the nineteenth-century representation of the pickaninny seems less than a distant cousin here.

Emigre's font catalog, on the other hand, while avoiding the questionable ghetto pastiche of House Industries, presents an exclusionary narrative of a differ-

POORHOUSE
Condemdhouse

ent sort, reveling in the mythology of the fall of Western Civilization. Read: Citizen, Dead History, Democratica, Dogma, Emperor, Missionary, Senator, Suburban, Universal. In the face of this post-Modern foundry's post-colonial positioning, the story of a united white front clouds the virtuous clarity of Warde's crystal vessel.

Thus, the opaque and highly discursive spaces created by these typographers present a model of representation equally transparent and damning in its pursuit of invisibility of the other. This practice, dramatized by contemporary type designers' love affair with

CRACKhouse

appropriation and reinscription of subcultural forms, has rendered the term "vernacular" both formally vacuous and semantically vacant. Formalized as slanglike riffs on a now familiar alternaculture, typefaces like Crackhouse merely give the appearance of inclusion, culturally irrelevant beyond the thinly veiled message of urban-suburban commodification it presents.

SHYHOUSE
AsTyHousE

Ideology in Typography: Systems of Subjectivity

Popular and prevailing usages, as surely as imposed elite usages, reflect an ideology or a manipulation of ideas and symbols for social or political gain. Overt representations of "otherness," as seen in culturally thematic alphabets like Jim Crow and Chinese Lap Song, present obvious examples of typography's claim to subjectivity. But there also exists more covert, and perhaps more powerful, instances of the written word's ability to mark ideology through typography. One such example focuses on the practice of noncapitalization to signify the historical weakness of a minority group. In standard English usage, the proper names of national and religious groups are traditionally marked with a capital letter. The rule is occasionally taken as a gesture of honor that can be bestowed or denied at the discretion of the writer or editor. Further, to deny a capital letter to the name of an ethnic group "symbolically diminishes the social status of the group . . . by the word magic of diminishing the initial letter. To deny, say, *Jew* the capital initial is clearly a slur. . . ."[10] The user concedes the pronuncia-

Democratica
Dogma
Emperor
Missionary
Senator
Suburban
Universal

[10] Irving Lewis Allen, *Unkind Words: Ethnic Labeling from Redskin to WASP* (New York: Bergin and Garvey, 1990) 69

Surrogate Multiplicities

tion and the spelling, but in print the dignity of the name is taken away.

In *Unkind Words: Ethnic Labeling from Redskin to WASP*, Irving Lewis Allen recounts the story of the most famous case of noncapitalization in American English: that of the term "Negro."

Trademarks from the early twentieth century offer an excellent example of how typographic conventions mark social difference, operating as forms of visual shorthand for specific cultural categories. What is it about the speaker's dialect that is critical in determining whether the speaker will be judged as standard or nonstandard?

All trademarks shown here are taken from the Official Gazette of the United States Patent Office, a weekly publication issued by the U.S. Department of Commerce, U.S. Patent Office, Washington, D.C.

Candy 1925

The name began its centuries-long career with a lower-case initial but after Reconstruction aspired to a capital initial. In the decades around 1900, colored competed with negro for the preferred, proper name for the group. Afro-American, first recorded in 1853, was seriously proposed in 1880, but it was not taken up, and it was to be eighty years or more before it was to gain a measure of use. Finally, negro emerged as the proper name preferred by many blacks and by white liberals. Settling on the name was not to be the end of it. Soon, a campaign began for capitalizing the initial, and the debate turned on ideology as much as anything. A side debate was over whether negro was a relative color descriptive, like fair, dark, or for that matter black and white, and hence had no claim on capitalization. Or was negro, in effect, a national name, like Englishman, German, or Spaniard, or a group name, like Jew, and so should be capitalized?[11]

[11] Ibid.

Watermelon Slices 1923

Allen points out that the struggle for capitalization signifies the changing status of historically oppressed groups and even makes a case for the dangers of typographic asymmetry, where one name, say "White," is capitalized, while the other, "black," is not. While symmetry is benign—whether or not both names are capitalized is a trivial matter—any attempt to capitalize one name and not the other implies a political gesture, or ideology in typography.[12]

[12] The Nazi resurrection of Fraktur type offers another historically important example of ideology in typography. Fraktur, a typeface initially prized by the Nazis for its "Germanness," symbolized a totalitarian politics that valued style over content. Not surprisingly, once early victories "encouraged them to look beyond Germany's borders, the Nazis, quickly recognizing the usefulness of a plainer, more 'European' style, banned Fraktur on January 3, 1941 as a 'Jewish invention.'" Robert Ray, "The ABC of Visual Theory," *Visible Language* 22, no. 4, 1989 430

Graphic Design & Reading

Bluing 1920

Borders of the Corporate Vocoder

Now let's return for a moment to the ideas of transparency and lightness discussed previously. When Warde proposed a parallel between the crystalline cup and the neutrality of the typographic surface, she was, no doubt, neatly sidestepping issues of power, agency, and mediation that are by now overly familiar. Recent typographic discourse, in fact, has recast transparency as the worst form of cultural conformity; this, despite the fact that the territory of once marginalized visual outposts has been wholly mined by a predatory design mainstream. From digital font houses such as Plazm, House Industries, or Garage Fonts to the work of M and Co., Pentagram, or Reverb, the "look" of the marginalized other is everywhere.

Textile 1926

Bluing 1918

Yet nowhere has this predilection for erasure been more apparent than in the corporate "voice-over" constituted by Levi's print ad campaign, "What's True?," where twenty-something types are pictured holding red placards on which they have been given the directive to inscribe their "own truth." With truths ranging from "I want to be happy" to "Forget Class" to "Conformity breeds mediocrity," the campaign relies on personal revelation as a form of corporate rhetoric: the language of the tribe broadcast by text and image back to the population, this time having been run through a corporate vocoder. Perhaps not surprisingly, the use of self-captioning in the context of a corporate ad campaign like this one fails to separate typographic subjectivity from the viselike grip of corporate invisibility. By failing to make a distinction between individual truth and a commodified representation of that truth, Levi's erases the very individuality it purportedly supports. In the end, the device of self-captioning does little more than provide an illusion of empowered, nonstandard speech, as it is impossible to escape the frame when Levis has positioned the speaker squarely in its center.

Potatoes

Laundry Soap 1920

Coffee 1923

Sweets 1925

Surrogate Multiplicities

THE FAR EAST

Chinese Mission Society Monthly Magazine 1929

Surfacing

Typographic representations that fail to meet the requirements of normative expression pose a challenge to the neutralizing forces of the visual voice-over, calling into question the validity of a form of discourse that marks exclusionary distinctions between standard and nonstandard speakers. Certainly any such challenge to prevailing norms of standardization can be quite startling, as forms of deviation—whether linguistic or typographic—tend to expose the arbitrary nature of the codes that underlie and shape all forms of discourse.[13] As Stuart Hall has written (here in the context of explicitly political deviance): "New. . . developments, which are both dramatic and 'meaningless' within consensually validated norms, pose a challenge to the normative world. They render problematic not only how the world is defined,

[13] Hebdige, *Subculture: The Meaning of Style*, 91

[14] Ibid.

FEZ

Men's Shirts 1923

FUJI

Canned Chow Mein Noodles 1925

but how it ought to be. They breach our expectations . . ."[14] In addition, nonstandard forms that refute normative codes *[anarchist graffiti, jodi.org, Pussy Galore]* negate the surface of cultural invisibility through a rewriting of standardized boundaries. By refusing containment within the transparent glare of the generic text, nonstandard forms claim their own space, on their own terms. Thus, within the boundaries and orientations expressed by Warde's metaphor lies the suggestion that the perfection of the crystal goblet is only an illusion, one easily shattered by a more sophisticated and discriminating palate. With some practice we can learn to draw small lessons from unsuspected sources *[type catalogs, street signage, alphabets]* as a way to breach our own expectations about typographic transparency and the boundaries of invisibility.

GLO-RAY

Silk Fabric 1926

Gold Band

Bread 1924

HOUSEHOLD
BRAND

Canned Fruit 1917

Graphic Design & Reading

IMP-O-LUCK

Medicinal 1929

Ginger Ale 1925

Fresh Lemons 1920

Lamps 1929

Laundry Lu

Laundry Soap 1920

Candy 1918

Surrogate Multiplicities

LONGWEAR

Men's Hosiery 1926

˄MERI-KAN˄

Women's Dresses 1926

Mexa-kava

Fire Extinguisher Compound 1925

OUR PRIDE

Citrous Fruit 1910/1925

˄QUEEN˄

Mops 1923

Royal White

Laundry Soap 1897/1922

SENORITA

Textile 1923

TARTAN

Paper Bags 1922

TOPSY

Peanuts 1920

Ice Cream and Frozen Dainties 1920/1922

Citrous Fruit 1905/1925 **YANKEE DOODLE**

Surrogate Multiplicities

The Crystal Goblet,

or Printing Should Be Invisible

This essay was first given as an address to the Society of Typographic Designers, formerly the British Typographers Guild, London, 1932. It was later published in Beatrice Warde: The Crystal Goblet—Sixteen Essays on Typography

Beatrice Warde: The Crystal Goblet—Sixteen Essays on Typography (Cleveland, OH and New York: World Publishing Co., 1956)

Beatrice Warde

*I*magine that you have before you a flagon of wine. You may choose your own favorite vintage for this imaginary demonstration, so that it be a deep shimmering crimson in color. You have two goblets before you. One is of solid gold, wrought in the most exquisite patterns. The other is of crystal-clear glass, thin as a bubble, and as transparent. Pour and drink; and according to your choice of goblet, I shall know whether or not you are a connoisseur of wine. For if you have no feelings about wine one way or the other, you will want the sensation of drinking the stuff out of a vessel that may have cost thousands of pounds; but if you are a member of that vanishing tribe, the amateurs of fine vintages, you will choose the crystal, because everything about it is calculated to *reveal* rather than to hide the beautiful thing which it was meant to *contain*.

Bear with me in this long-winded and fragrant metaphor, for you will find that almost all the virtues of the perfect wineglass have a parallel in typography. There is the long, thin stem that obviates fingerprints on the bowl. Why? Because no cloud must come between your eyes and the fiery heart of the liquid. Are not the margins on book pages similarly meant to obviate the necessity of fingering the type page? Again: The glass is color-less, or at the most only faintly tinged in the bowl, because the connoisseur judges wine partly by its color and is impatient of anything that alters it. There are a thousand mannerisms in typography that are as impudent and arbitrary as putting port in tumblers of red or green glass. When a goblet has a base that looks too small for security, it does not matter how cleverly it is weighted; you feel nervous lest it should tip over. There are ways of setting lines of type which may work well enough and yet keep the reader subconsciously worried by the fear of "doubling" lines, reading three words as one, and so forth.

Now the man who first chose glass instead of clay or metal to hold his wine was a "modernist" in the sense in which I am going to use that term. That is, the first thing he asked of this particular object was not "How should it look?" but "What must it do?", and to that extent all good typography is modernist.

Wine is so strange and potent a thing that it has been used in the central ritual of religion in one place and time and attacked by a virago with a hatchet in another. There is only one thing in the world that is capable of stirring and altering people's minds to the same extent, and that is the coherent expression of thought. That is the human's chief miracle, unique to us. There is no "explanation" whatever of the fact that I can make arbitrary sounds that will lead a total stranger to think my own thought. It is sheer magic that I should be able to hold a one-sided conversation by means of black marks on paper with an unknown person halfway across the world. Talking, broadcasting, writing, and printing are all quite literally forms of *thought transference,* and it is this ability and eagerness to transfer and receive the contents of the mind that is almost alone responsible for human civilization.

If you agree with this, you will agree with my one main idea, i.e., that the most important thing about printing is that it conveys thought, ideas, images from one mind to other minds. This statement is what you might call the "front door" of the science of typography. Within lie hundreds of rooms, but unless you start by assuming that *printing is meant to convey specific and coherent ideas,* it is very easy to find yourself in the wrong house altogether.

Before asking what this statement leads to, let us see what it does not necessarily lead to. If books are printed in order to be read, we must distinguish readability from what the optician would call legibility. A page set in 14 point Bold Sans is, according to the laboratory tests, more "legible" than one set in 11 point Baskerville. A public speaker is more "audible" in that sense when he bellows. But a good speaking voice is one which is inaudible *as* a voice. It is the transparent goblet again! I need not warn you that if you begin listening to the inflections and speaking rhythms of a voice from a platform, you are falling asleep. When you listen to a song in a language you do not understand, part of your mind actually does fall asleep, leaving your quite separate aesthetic sensibilities to enjoy themselves unimpeded by your reasoning faculties. The fine arts do that, but that is not the purpose of printing. Type well used is invisible *as* type, just as the perfect talking voice is the unnoticed vehicle for the transmission of words, ideas.

We may say, therefore, that printing may be delightful for many reasons, but that it is important, first and foremost, as a means of doing something. That is why it is mischievous to call any printed piece a work of art, especially fine art: because that would imply that its first purpose was to exist as an expression of beauty for its own sake and for the delectation of the senses. Calligraphy can almost

Graphic Design & Reading

be considered a fine art nowadays, because its primary economic and educational purpose has been taken away; but printing in English will not qualify as an art until the present English language no longer conveys ideas to future generations and until printing itself hands its usefulness to some yet unimagined successor.

There is no end to the maze of practices in typography, and this idea of printing as a conveyor is, at least in the minds of all the great typographers with whom I have had the privilege of talking, the one clue that can guide you through the maze. Without this essential humility of mind, I have seen ardent designers go more hopelessly wrong, make more ludicrous mistakes out of an excessive enthusiasm, than I could have thought possible. And with this clue, this purposiveness in the back of your mind, it is possible to do the most unheard of things and find that they justify you triumphantly. It is not a waste of time to go to the simple fundamentals and reason from them. In the flurry of your individual problems, I think you will not mind spending half an hour on one broad and simple set of ideas involving abstract principles.

I once was talking to a man who designed a very pleasing advertising type that undoubtedly all of you have used. I said something about what artists think about a certain problem, and he replied with a beautiful gesture: "Ah, madam, we artists do not think—we *feel!*" That same day I quoted that remark to another designer of my acquaintance, and he, being less poetically inclined, murmured: "I'm not *feeling* very well today, I *think!*" He was right, he did think; he was the thinking sort, and that is why he is not so good a painter, and to my mind ten times better as a typographer and type designer than the man who instinctively avoided anything as coherent as a reason.

I always suspect the typographic enthusiast who takes a printed page from a book and frames it to hang on the wall, for I believe that in order to gratify a sensory delight he has mutilated something infinitely more important. I remember that T. M. Cleland, the famous American typographer, once showed me a very beautiful layout for a Cadillac booklet involving decorations in color. He did not have the actual text to work with in drawing up his specimen pages, so he had set the lines in Latin. This was not only for the reason that you will all think of, if you have seen the old type foundries' famous *Quousque Tandem* copy (i.e., that Latin has few descenders and thus gives a remarkably even line). No, he told me that originally he had set up the dullest "wording" that he could find (I daresay it was from *Hansard*), and yet he discovered that the man to whom he submitted it would start reading and making comments on the text. I made some remark on the mentality of boards of directors, but Mr. Cleland said, "No, you're wrong; if the reader had not been practically forced to read—if he had not seen those words suddenly imbued with glamour and significance—then the layout would have been a failure. Setting it in Italian or Latin is only an easy way of saying, 'This is not the text as it will appear.'"

Let me start my specific conclusions with book typography, because that contains all the fundamentals, and then go on to a few points about advertising.

The Crystal Goblet

The book typographer has the job of erecting a window between the reader inside the room and that landscape which is the author's words. He may put up a stained-glass window of marvelous beauty, but a failure as a window; that is, he may use some rich, superb, typelike text gothic that is something to be looked at, not *through*. Or he may work in what I call transparent or invisible typography. I have a book at home, of which I have no visual recollection whatever as far as its typography goes; when I think of it, all I see is the Three Musketeers and their comrades swaggering up and down the streets of Paris. The third type of window is one in which the glass is broken into relatively small leaded panes; and this corresponds to what is called "fine printing" today, in that you are at least conscious that there is a window there, and that someone has enjoyed building it. That is not objectionable because of a very important fact which has to do with the psychology of the subconscious mind. This is that the mental eye focuses *through* type and not *upon* it. The type which, through any arbitrary warping of design or excess of "color," gets in the way of the mental picture to be conveyed, is a bad type. Our subconsciousness is always afraid of blunders (which illogical setting, tight spacing, and too-wide unleaded lines can trick us into), of boredom, and of officiousness. The running headline that keeps shouting at us, the line that looks like one long word, the capitals jammed together without hair spaces—these mean subconscious squinting and loss of mental focus.

And if what I have said is true of book printing, even of the most exquisite limited editions, it is fifty times more obvious in advertising, where the one and only justification for the purchase of space is that you are conveying a message—that you are implanting a desire straight into the mind of the reader. It is tragically easy to throw away half the reader interest of an advertisement by setting the simple and compelling argument in a face that is uncomfortably alien to the classic reasonableness of the book face. Get attention as you will by your headline and make any pretty type pictures you like if you are sure that the copy is useless as a means of selling goods; but if you are happy enough to have really good copy to work with, I beg you to remember that thousands of people pay hard-earned money for the privilege of reading quietly set book pages, and that only your wildest ingenuity can stop people from reading a really interesting text.

Printing demands a humility of mind, for the lack of which many of the fine arts are even now floundering in self-conscious and maudlin experiments. There is nothing simple or dull in achieving the transparent page. Vulgar ostentation is twice as easy as discipline. When you realize that ugly typography never effaces itself, you will be able to capture beauty as the wise men capture happiness by aiming at something else. The "stunt typographer" learns the fickleness of rich men who hate to read. Not for them are long breaths held over serif and kern; they will not appreciate your splitting of hair spaces. Nobody (save the other craftsmen) will appreciate half your skill. But you may spend endless years of happy experiment in devising that crystalline goblet which is worthy to hold the vintage of the human mind.

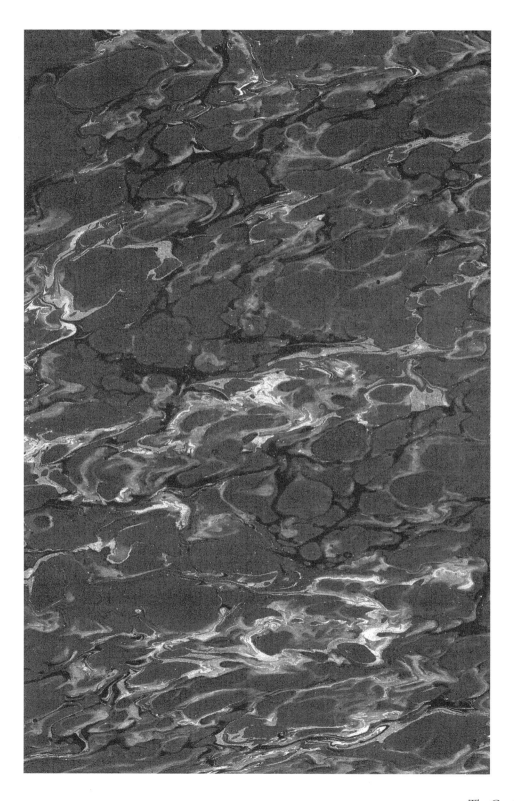

The Crystal Goblet

Legi-
bility

Rolf F. Rehe

The Need for a Functional Typography

Most of the scribes of medieval Europe were monks. For them, producing books was a work of art, an attempt to please God with beautiful lettering. Concern for communication was generally a secondary issue. When the honorable burgher of Mainz, Johannes Gutenberg, invented movable type and thus industrialized book production, he copied, in his first type designs, the hand lettering of scribes. The justified line, with its miraculously even word spacing, was achieved with the aid of a large number of ligature letters and abbreviations, marking the shortened words with a horizontal bar above the letters.

In general, the basic approach to typography has not undergone major changes since the days of Gutenberg. The stylistic stagnation resulted from the unchanging technical methods of producing type and typography. The horizontal linearity of typesetting and the methods of putting type together in a form (later to be speeded up by the invention of typesetting machines) have, in principle, remained since the craftsman of Mainz invented movable type. There were printing techniques, simple platen presses, later supplemented by the cylinder presses. At times even the new presses forced additional restrictions on typography. The Hoe Type Revolving Machine, for instance, required newspapers to have vertical rules between the columns to hold the type locked onto the cylinder. Consequently, newspaper typography was restricted to setting and arranging type in single columns with single-column headlines.

Gradually, especially in the twentieth century, a new situation evolved. The level of education has risen dramatically. Much more information is being transmitted. Reading speed and comprehension have become important factors in the communication process. Not all the print communication produced—in fact, only a small part of it—can be absorbed by the average reader. Typography emerged as a functional aspect of print communication.

Scientific Investigation of Typography Appears

At about the turn of the twentieth century, an important factor contributing to the development of a new, functional typography appeared: the scientific investigation of typographic legibility. Psychologists studied the ways by which printed type is perceived, and what arrangements and forms of type provide maximum legibility. (While psychologists made the first investigations into type legibility, today the range of investigators includes journalists, educators, computer scientists, governmental agencies, and the graphic-arts industry in general.)

The first serious investigation of legibility is thought to have begun in 1878, by Professor Emile Javal of the University of Paris. Javal tried to establish the legibility of individual letters of the alphabet by distance tests and visibility trials. In the years following, sporadic research was conducted, but concentrated research into legibility on a broader scale evolved in the years around 1920.

The areas investigated mainly concern the problem of increasing reading speed and comprehension; that is, finding the typographic arrangement that best facilitates these factors, and finding such typographic variables that please the eye and achieve reader attention and response.

The Typographer as Mass Communicator

Even today, only a few typographic designers have taken advantage of available research findings in legibility. A frequent complaint by researchers is that their findings have not been widely applied in the design of typographic communications. Part of the problem stems from the fact that most research results have been published in scientific journals, usually in a vernacular not easily understood by the typographer.

In a mass-media system, the typographer is usually a member of the encoding team. He stands between the original source of the message and the channel (for the purposes of this discussion, the printed page) that will carry the message to an audience. He has considerable control over the coding process by selecting typefaces and type sizes and by determining the typographic arrangement of the message. He should be concerned with the perception of his message, the attention it can elicit, the mood it creates, its legibility and degree of comprehension, and with maintaining the reader's attention after it has been attained initially as well as a high degree of reader recall. He is, in short, no longer a designer of aesthetic printing or simply an artist or craftsman. The typographer of today is a mass communicator, playing an important role in the mass-media system. Typographic message packaging has become an important determinant of whether a print communication is selected and read—and read completely.

Research Methods and Approach

Research into legibility of print may be one of the oldest forms of research in the communications field. The earliest legibility research may have been a count of words and ideas conducted by the Talmudists around A.D. 900, who used frequency of word occurrence as a means of distinguishing usual from unusual meaning of words.

Systematic research into legibility of print began in the late nineteenth century with Javal's pioneer study, attempting to determine the relative legibility of individual letters of the alphabet. During these pioneer stages of legibility research, emphasis was placed on investigation of individual letters and their visibility. Size and width of letters, height of type, and relative alphabet length were subjects of elaborate studies.

Around 1920, research into legibility flourished. A wide variety of factors relative to legibility was investigated by psychologists, ophthalmologists, educators, and journalists. A controversy about the value of certain systems of methodology was discussed in many journal articles. At one time, illumination (optimal light conditions) was of major interest to researchers, the intensity of the light usually measured by the number of wax candles used. Today, because of the advent of electricity, standard research into illumination has become extinct.

The most recent trend in legibility research seems to emphasize investigations that produce results directly applicable to typographic design.

How the Eye Perceives the Printed Word

To understand the bulk of legibility research conducted, it may be helpful to illustrate how the human eye perceives the printed word. When reading, the eye sweeps along the line of print in so-called saccadic jumps. It pauses quickly (for about a second) at regular intervals, and it is during that short pause or fixation that actual perception of words takes place. After the short pause, the eye proceeds with another saccadic movement, then pauses again to perceive and comprehend the words. Occasionally the eye might move back on the line to reread what might not have been comprehended adequately the first time. Return moves are termed "regressions."

One study found that the proportion of time taken by eye movements varies with comprehension demands of the reading situation.[1] Pause or perception time usually involved 92 to 94 percent of reading time.

[1] M. A. Tinker, *Bases for Effective Reading* (Minneapolis, MN: University of Minnesota Press, 1965)

The Methods of Measuring Legibility

To measure legibility, eight basic methods of measurement have been established:

Speed of perception. This is measured by short-exposure technique. Printed matter is briefly (i.e., one-tenth of a second) exposed to a subject by a tachistoscope, a special instrument designed for this purpose. This method has been applied primarily in experiments investigating the legibility of individual letters and symbols.

Perceptibility at a distance. This measures the distance from which letters and symbols may be perceived. This method, too, has been applied primarily in investigations into the legibility of individual letters and symbols and has been used to test the legibility of posters, road signs, etc.

Perceptibility at peripheral vision. This investigates the horizontal distance from which print can be perceived and the distance by which typographic matter can be thrown out of focus and still be recognized.

Visibility method. This employs a visibility meter, a set of filters through which the subject views printed material. The density of the filter provides the measurement of perception. The method has been applied primarily for studies of individual letters and symbols.

Reflex-blink technique. With this method, the reader's frequency of blinking is counted, either manually or photographic–electronically. It is assumed that poor legibility of type will result in increased blinking. The validity and readability of this method has been questioned frequently.

Rate-of-work technique. This measures reading speed, such as amount of reading within a given time limit, or time of reading for a given amount of text. Comprehension checks after the reading measure accuracy of reading in this method. It is perhaps the best method of measurement available, and it is the most frequently employed method of measuring legibility.

Measurement of eye movements. This method provides good clues to the understanding of legibility factors in typography and information such as why a certain typographic arrangement is perceived positively or negatively by showing the fixation pauses, their duration, and the regressions. Eye movements are recorded photographically or electronically. This measuring method, too, is considered an excellent one. Measuring eye movements, however, can be a very tedious task.

Fatigue in reading. This has been investigated extensively, but research has not provided significant clues to legibility. One study has shown that readers can sustain several hours of uninterrupted reading without significant signs of fatigue.[2]

[2] I. H. Anderson and C. W. Meredith, "The Reading of Projected Books with Special Reference to Rate and Visual Fatigue," *Journal of Educational Research* 41 (1948) 453–60

These methods of measurement can provide data on the legibility of print; however, it needs to be pointed out that all methods are only relatively accurate, since measurement of perception includes a variety of uncontrolled factors. The results are best seen as aiding factors in typographic design and not as automatic guarantors of maximum legibility. But applied with care, research results in the form of recommendations and proposals may aid the typographic designer in creating a more effective mode of typographic communication.

In addition to these methods, a number of unique measuring devices exist. A generally new area of typographic research, the investigation of congeniality, or atmosphere value of printing type, combine different methods of investigation.

The majority of studies consist of univariate analysis; that is, only one typographic variable was investigated at a time. But obviously, in typography, a variety of variables interact. As a rule, isolated research findings may be applied with good results, but it is suggested that research findings be combined, when possible. For instance, type size, line width, and leading should always be considered together since these variables greatly interrelate.

Legibility of Individual Letters

The width of individual letters contributes to legibility. Condensed type designs are somewhat more difficult to read than those that are moderately extended. When selected letters of "normal width" alphabet were slightly extended, their legibility generally increased.[3]

To some extent, the space around individual letters influences legibility. Additionally, the white space within letters (such as in o, e, c, etc.) influences their recognition.[4] These letters, due to their similar shape, are often misread, and the white space within and around them helps to differentiate them.

Fine strokes of individual letters, a common feature in both Modern and Old Style Roman, tend to reduce legibility of individual letters by also reducing their differentiation value. Fine strokes have low visibility, and letters with fine strokes may be easily confused with other letters of similar shape, leading to reading errors.[5] The words "light" and "fight" provide an example of possible errors based on the wrong perception of individual key letters. Letters of poor legibility have a marked tendency to be misread and confused.

this is Bodoni **Modern**

Old Style this is Bembo

The right half of individual letters, incidentally, is most significant for letter recognition. Similarly, the upper halves of letters provide better cues for recognition.[6]

In general, then, letters with specific differentiation are more easily recognized than letters without such differentiation. This finding applies to both serif and sans serif typefaces. The variables influencing legibility of individual letters, then, are the complexity of letter outline, stroke width, heaviness, weight of hairlines, space within and around the letter, and differentiating letter features.[7]

Type Size

Since one initial decision in typographic design concerns size of text type, it is not surprising that a large number of studies have investigated type sizes most beneficial to legibility.

[3] C. Berger, "Some Experiments on the Width of Symbols as Determinants of Legibility," *Acta Ophtalmologica,* 26 (1948) 517–550

[4] B. E. Roethlein, "The Relative Legibility of Different Faces of Printing Type," *American Journal of Psychology* 23 (1912) 1–36

[5] M. A. Tinker, "The Relative Legibility of the Letters, the Digits, and of Certain Mathematical Signs," *Journal of General Psychology* 1 (1928) 472–496

[6] D. G. Paterson and M. A. Tinker, *How to Make Type Readable* (New York: Harper and Brothers Publishers, 1940); P. A. Kolers, "Clues to a Letter's Recognition: Implications for the Design of Characters," *Journal of Typographic Research* 2 (1969) 145–168

[7] E. C. Poulton, "Letter Differentiation and Rate of Comprehension of Reading," *Journal of Applied Psychology* 49 (1955) 358–362

A definition of the most legible type size has been hampered by the fact that x-heights for individual typefaces differ greatly. Sizes of typefaces come from the metal body on which the letter is cast, and which always must be accurate "to the point." Heights of individual typefaces on a uniform body (measured by the lowercase *x* and therefore called "x-height") might vary considerably and will in many cases. Some 8 point typefaces may appear as large as a 10 point size of a different type design, while some 10 point type sizes may consist of a relatively small type design, giving it the appearance of a smaller type size. Even small differences, such as one point in type size, significantly influence legibility of text type. (We are here primarily concerned with text type sizes in the neighborhood of 10 point, in which case a one-point difference reflects 10 percent of the total size.)

Research findings in optimal text type sizes have to be seen in light of the x-height problem.[8] The most legible type sizes appear to be either 9, 10, 11, or 12 point. The somewhat generous range of sizes stems from the differences in x-height. One carefully designed experiment[9] avoided the x-height problem by matching typefaces under investigation in actual x-height, reducing or enlarging different typefaces so that they matched optically.

[8] D. G. Paterson and M. A. Tinker, "Eye Movements in Reading Optimal and Non-Optimal Typography," *Journal of Experimental Psychology* 34 (1944) 80–83; D. G. Paterson and M. A. Tinker, *How to Make Type Readable* (New York: Harper and Brothers Publishers, 1940)

M. A. Tinker, *Bases for Effective Reading* (Minneapolis, MN: University of Minnesota Press, 1965)

M. A. Tinker, "Perceptual and Oculomotor Efficiency in Reading Materials in Vertical and Horizontal Arrangements," *American Journal of Psychology* 68 (1955) 444–449

[9] E. C. Poulton, "Letter Differentiation and Rate of Comprehension of Reading," *Journal of Applied Psychology* 49 (1955) 358–362

Univers

60 point Univers (this caption is 12 point)

Bembo

60 point Bembo (this caption is 12 point)

The experiment provided an interesting example of the problem: To achieve the same x-height (1.6 millimeters) for two typefaces, Univers and Bembo, Univers had to be reduced to 9.5 point body size, while Bembo required a 12 point body size. In other words, a 2.5 point body-size difference existed for two typefaces of the same x-height.

Univers

60 point Univers (this caption is 9.5 point)

Bembo

60 point Bembo (this caption is 12 point)

Larger type sizes increase the number of fixations since they take up more space both vertically and horizontally. Smaller type sizes simply reduce visibility of the type and hamper all-important word recognition. Larger sizes force readers to perceive words in sections, rather than as a whole, and consequently slow down reading speed.[10] In general, readers tend to prefer moderate type sizes and small amounts of leading.[11]

Line Width

Line width is another important contributor to legibility of continuously running text. Although it will be discussed as an independent factor for the time being, it is dependent on both type size, amount of leading, and, in a marginal context, on the typeface selected.

For optimal type sizes of 9, 10, 11, and 12 point, about ten to twelve words per line seem to be most comforting to the eye. That means, in practical, terms a line width of about 18 to 24 picas, depending on the letter width of the typeface selected.

The optimum line width for 10 point type appears to be eighty millimeters, which equals about 19 picas. In general, a line width somewhere between 18 and 24 picas (for 10 point type) seems to be a safe guideline.[12] There is possibly a bias built in: Evidently, these measurements are based on book typography; they do not necessarily apply to magazine or newspaper typography, where shorter line widths are standard.

Less efficient reading will occur with very long and very short lines. Difficulties in reading short lines is attributed to an inability of the eye to make maximum use of horizontal perceptual cues. Difficult perception of very wide lines seems to come from inaccuracies and difficulties in relocating the beginning of each new line.[13] The majority of readers found the most legible line width also to be most pleasing to the eye. In general, readers prefer a moderate line width.

Although smaller type sizes are legible, they still have their optimal line widths. For 7 and 8 point, a line width of 12 picas produced greatest legibility.

9/9. Leading is the space between lines of type, named after the pieces of lead used to space lines in hand set lead type. This is 9 point Franklin Gothic Book set without leading, or "solid."

9/15. This is 9 point Franklin Gothic Book set with six extra points of leading, often called "nine on fifteen"

Leading

The third major factor contributing to legibility of text matter, the amount of leading, also has been investigated extensively.

The typeface, of course, influences the amount of the leading necessary, and different typefaces require varying amounts of leading.[14] Unleaded material is read relatively slowly, and reading rate increases with additional leading. One experiment that employed the eye blink technique found the optimal amount of leading for 10 point size to be 3 points.

The optimal size of 10 point type, 19 picas wide (optimal width), seems to benefit most by 2 point leading, which increases reading speed by 7.5 percent over type set solid (no leading at all). An increase of leading to

[10] M. A. Tinker, "Criteria for Determining the Readability of Type Faces," *Journal of Educational Psychology* 36 (1946) 453–460

[11] H. D. Hovde, "The Relative Effect of Size of Type, Leading, and Context, Part II," *Journal of Applied Psychology* 14 (1930) 63–73

[12] M. A. Tinker and D. G. Paterson, "Studies of Typographical Factors Influencing Speed of Reading: III. Length of Line," *Journal of Applied Psychology* 13 (1929) 205–219

[13] D. G. Paterson and M. A. Tinker, "Influence of Line Width on Eye Movements for Six Point Type," *Journal of Educational Psychology* 33 (1942) 552–555

[14] D. Becker, J. Heinrich, R. Von Sichowsky, and D. Wendt, "Reader Preferences for Typeface and Leading," *Journal of Typographic Research* 1 (1970) 61–66

4 points caused a 5 percent increase of reading speed compared to solid type. For optimal sizes of 9, 10, 11, and 12 point, the most beneficial amount of leading ranges from 1 to 4 points, depending on the individual typeface used.[15]

[15] D. G. Paterson and M. A. Tinker, "Studies of Typographical Factors Influencing Speed of Reading: VIII. Space Between Lines of Leading," *Journal of Applied Psychology* 16 (1932) 388–397

[16] M. Luckiesh and F. K. Moss, "Boldness as a Factor in Type-Design and Typography," *Journal of Applied Psychology* 24 (1940) 170–83

[17] M. A. Tinker and D. G. Paterson, "Studies of Typographical Factors Influencing Speed of Reading: VII. Variations in Color of Print and Background," *Journal of Applied Psychology* 15 (1931) 471–479

[18] D. O. Robinson, M. Abbamonte, and S. H. Evans, "Why Serifs Are Important: The Perception of Small Print," *Visible Language* 4 (1971) 353–359

[19] M. A. Tinker and D. G. Paterson, "Reader Preferences and Typography," *Journal of Applied Psychology* 26 (1942) 38–40

Kinds of Type

Heaviness of individual letters provides another important clue to legibility. The ideal text type should be medium, not too heavy, nor too light.[16] A typeface that is too heavy (bold) tends to tire the eye easily. On the other hand, a typeface of a very light design provides a rather poor differentiation from the paper background and reduces legibility. The "brightness contrast," the perceived blackness of type against the brightness of the paper background, constitutes an important determinant of legibility.[17]

Italic type, traditionally considered the superior mode of emphasis in text matter, is actually disliked by readers. Moreover, italics tend to slow down the reading speed. Application of italics, when compared to roman, reduced reading speed by about fourteen to sixteen words per minute. Boldface, then, is more legible than italic, but it should be applied only in limited amounts, since it tires the eye easily.

Serif or Sans Serif Type?

One of the most often asked questions concerns the comparative legibility of sans serif versus serif typeface designs. Numerous studies have investigated that problem, most always without finding a significantly valuable answer. One extensive study suggests that "the neurological structure of the human visual system benefits from serifs in the preservation of the main features of letters."[18] It seems that since words are perceived by their outline shape, single letters with serifs, which have a more distinctive outline shape over sans serif letters, may also be more easily perceptible than are sans serif letters.

Another study found that serif typefaces are marginally more legible than sans serif designs. Two highly similar trial stories were presented in both serif and sans serif type. From the trial story set in serif type, subjects were able to read between seven to ten more words per minute in comparison to the trial story set in sans serif type. The majority of the readers, almost two-thirds of them, when given a choice, preferred serif type. This coincides with earlier findings that what is most legible is preferred by readers.[19]

These findings, of course, do not signal the disappearance of sans serif typefaces. For one, the legibility differences between the two type categories, although scientifically significant, are often of a minimal nature. Secondly, the typeface design needs to relate to and support the "tone" of the message.

Justified or Unjustified Typography?

One factor of typographic arrangement, unjustified typography compared to traditional justified (blocked-out) style, has been investigated often in recent years. In unjustified fashion, lines are set with a standardized word spacing, and no attempt is made to block out lines by adjusting word space. Lines are flush left, and excess space is added at the end of the line. In traditional, justified typography, lines are blocked out to a predetermined line width by adjusting (either enlarging or reducing) word space.

In general, a number of investigators discovered that there seems to be no significant difference in legibility of either justified or unjustified typography. When three different right margins were investigated (unjustified, unjustified with a printed vertical guideline at the end, and justified), it was shown that neither level of comprehension nor reading speed differed significantly for either one of the arrangements.[20] In another case, no difference in reading speed nor reader preference for either justified or unjustified composition was found.

In a similar study, unjustified lines, unjustified lines with a vertical line printed on the right, and justified lines were compared, and no practical difference between any of the arrangements, either in reading speed or in comprehension, was found. There seemed to be a favorable attitude toward shorter lines with more uneven endings. A larger study, investigating newspaper typography, found that justification on lines did not affect how accurately or quickly newspapers are read.

A number of experiments, then, do suggest that unjustified typography compares well to justified composition. There is some support that unjustified typography is actually preferred by readers. It takes up the same space as justified type but reduces production costs: The ragged right-hand space may allow for a few more words to be added without resetting several lines, or a few words may be deleted by simply making the lines shorter, again without resetting much type, which is so often necessary in justified style.

Lowercase or Uppercase Typography

Words are perceived by their specific word-shape outline, which is unique for lowercase words. Once the outline of the words has been perceived and stored in memory, future recognition or recall of the word takes place without letter-by-letter deciphering. Words set in all caps, however, do not provide specific word-shape outlines since they produce an oblong, uniform word shape. No cues can be perceived by the eye, and a time-consuming deciphering of the word, letter by letter, is necessary. Further evidence for this process was supplied when one researcher found that more reading errors were made in reading lowercase words than of words set in all caps, indicating that all caps words are indeed read letter by letter, while lowercase words are not.[21]

Words set in all caps use up to 30 percent more space than words set in lowercase, which leads to an increase in time-consuming eye fixations;

[20] R. Fabrizio, L. Kaplan, and G. Teal, "Readability as a Function of the Straightness of Right-Hand Margins," *Journal of Typographic Research* 1 (1967) 90–95

[21] M.A. Tinker, "The Influence of Form of Type on the Perception of Words," *Journal of Applied Psychology* 16 (1932) 167–174

4.74 words per second, one study showed, can be read in all-caps type, and 5.38 words per second can be read in lowercase type.

Text set in all caps retards reading speed by about 13 percent, due to an increase in fixation time, and results in a corresponding decrease in the number of words perceived per fixation.

Numbers

A surprisingly large amount of research has gone into the legibility of numerals, mathematical symbols, and the arrangement of mathematical tables.

Numbers in Arabic form are read faster and with fewer fixations than numbers written out in word form.[22] Although numbers as such are read more slowly than individual letters, when perceived as a group they are comprehended faster than words. Arabic numerals not only have a more compact form but also favor reading speed. For instance, "2,314" is easier to perceive in numerals than "two thousand three hundred fourteen." Numerals also take up less space.

[22] M. A. Tinker, "Numerals Versus Words for Efficiency in Reading," *Journal of Applied Psychology* 12 (1928) 190–199

1234567890

"Modern" or "Lining" numerals

1234567890

"Old Style" or "Hanging" numerals

Arabic numerals, when compared to Roman numerals, are read faster in all reading conditions. This seems to be caused by both the greater differentiation of Arabic numerals and the relative familiarity of the reader with Arabic symbols.

Old Style numerals, with differentiating ascenders and descenders, are somewhat more legible than modern numerals when isolated and are considerably more legible when in groups. The greater differentiation of the Old Style numerals accounts for the difference here.

Color and Background

A related problem in typographic design concerns paper color and background. This has been investigated by a number of researchers, and relatively similar results have been reported.

The brightness contrast between print and background seems to be the most important factor when color in printing is under consideration.[23]

Black on white and black on yellow seem to provide best legibility results, both studies showed. Both investigations emphasize brightness contrast as a major factor in determining the color/paper combination for maximum legibility.

Individual differences in the surface of printing paper have been investigated by several researchers. All report that, with the possible exception of extreme "whiteness," which seems to advance legibility, paper surface has little influence on legibility.

[23] M. A. Tinker and D. G. Paterson, "Studies of Typographical Factors Influencing Speed of Reading: VII. Variations in Color of Print and Background," *Journal of Applied Psychology* 15 (1931) 471–479

Type in Reverse

Type in reverse—that is, white type on dark or black background—retards reading, several studies have proven. When 10 point text type in reverse (white on black) was tested against the normal black-on-white arrangement, the reverse arrangement retarded reading speed by 14.7 percent.[24]

In another study investigating the same problem, black-on-white printing was found to be 10.5 percent superior in reading speed to the white-on-black arrangement. It was suggested that when reversed type is used to attract attention, it should be restricted to very small amounts of copy and to type sizes of at least 10 or 12 point.

Reversed type is also least preferred by readers: 77.7 percent in our study found the black-on-white arrangement more pleasing to the eye.

[24] G. Holmes, "The Relative Legibility of Black Print and White Print," *Journal of Applied Psychology* 15 (1931) 248–251

Writing Style and Typography

One study investigated the interaction of readability (style of writing) and typographic legibility.[25] It compared a news story in four versions: 1) long sentences and few paragraphs; 2) long sentences and frequent paragraphs; 3) short sentences and few paragraphs; and 4) short sentences and frequent paragraphs. The intent was to show that readability (through application of short sentences) supported by frequent paragraphs (which increased the white space within the columns) improves the legibility of the news story. Tests supported the hypothesis. It was also demonstrated that white space around or within the text block had a higher impact than readability improvements; that is, writing style. A moderate indention at the beginning of a paragraph improves reading speed by about 7 percent.

[25] J. M. Smith and E. McCombs, "The Graphics of Prose," *Visible Language* 4 (1971) 365–369

Congeniality

The concept of congeniality or atmosphere-value of printing type has been investigated by several researchers. They have, however, restricted themselves to investigating different possibilities and values of congeniality studies. Generally, there is good reason to assume some of the methods of investigation will eventually produce valuable results in this important field of typeface "expression." Until now, however, studies conducted are primarily of an exploratory nature.

It was established that typography may communicate connotative variations.[26] It was concluded that, despite some notable problems, there seems to be substantial basis for the use of typography as a code for the communication of connotative variations.

Another study, which investigated the influence of typeface variables on the judgment of emotional meaning, found that specific typefaces tend to express specific moods. By and large, research into congeniality of typefaces is at an ini-

[26] P. H. Tannenbaum, H. K. Jacobson, and E. L. Norris, "An Experimental Investigation of Typeface Connotations," *Journal of Journalism Quarterly* 41

Legibility

tial stage. Results of investigations have only shown the value of certain methods of investigation. Eventually, however, results from careful investigations into congeniality of typefaces may become an important determinant in the selection of typefaces for typographic design.

Fatigue in Reading

For how long can the eye go on reading without any tiring effect? If there is fatigue after prolonged reading, what factors cause or influence such fatigue?

Under optimal reading conditions, and when the context of the reading material is of general interest to the reader, prolonged reading for many hours without signs of fatigue can be maintained. When reading of books and of microfilm material was compared, no evidence of fatigue for either group was found after two hours of reading.

When fatigue in reading does occur, it results in an increased number of fixations per line, slower reading rate, more regressions, reduced accuracy of perception, and weakened comprehension.[27] Typographic variables, improving legibility in general, may successfully battle reading fatigue, but the context of the material remains an equally important determinant.

[27] L. A. Demilia, "Visual Fatigue and Reading," *Journal of Education* 151 (1968) 4–24

Conclusion and Outlook

In what direction should legibility research and application of research findings go? First of all, univariate research, that is, investigation of individual typographic variables, needs to be increased and broadened. Individual research findings are the tile pieces of the mosaic of better legibility. Second, the interaction of various legibility findings needs to be investigated on a broader scale. Testing of texts that apply new research findings, compared with texts that use conventional typographic elements, may present valuable results. Third, the methods of measuring legibility remain in need of improvement. Methods of subject selection and pre-screening, and a tight experimental control of the experimental situation are major factors requiring refinement.

Furthermore, typographic legibility plays a major role in electronic media, particularly the internet. These specific typographical requirements have to be investigated.

The research presented here in the form of recommendations is, in general, supported by a number of research findings—but they are still few in numbers. A reasonable case for their application can be made. Yet individual judgments, dependent on the specific typographic situation, will be necessary.

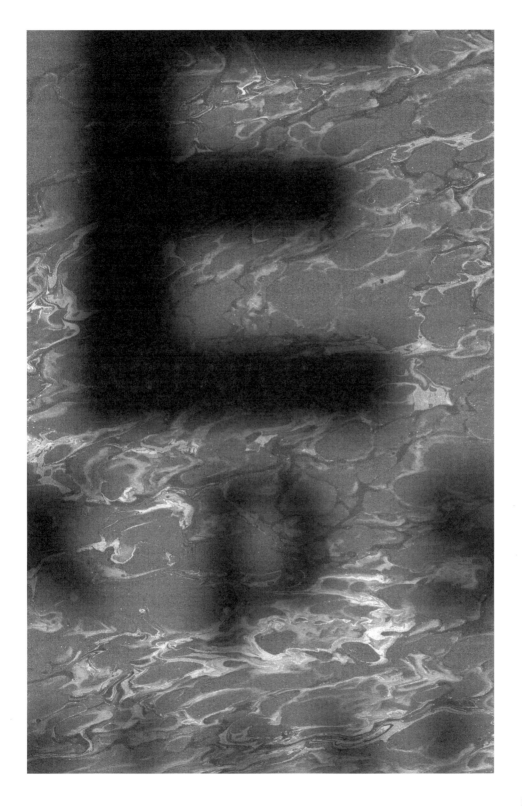

Improving the Tool

Hrant Papazian

Written communication has one primary function—to record thought on a semi-permanent medium for later retrieval. By "written communication" I really mean "visible language"—any manifestation of language (itself a formalization of thought) that can be seen. This is not restricted to the act of writing by hand. It includes cave painting, engraving, pressing ink on vellum, exposing photographic paper, shooting electrons at phosphor-coated glass, and even skywriting.

Although written communication doesn't have a handle, pointed parts, or other features that we might expect to find in a tool, it is a tool nonetheless, a fundamentally functional thing. As a tool, it's second in relevance only to the mother of all tools: the hand. Writing is an offspring of the hand. However, once a tool is born it is free to evolve and improve as needed, irrespective of its origins.

The Latin Alphabet

There are three primary methods of recording visible language: logographies, such as Chinese; syllabaries, such as Japanese Kana; and alphabets, such as Latin. Alphabetic writing is the most recent of the three and embodies the highest level of abstraction: Each elemental symbol (a letter) represents a basic sound of language. These symbols are strung together to form meaningful words. Because of this high level of abstraction, alphabetic writing only needs a small set of elemental symbols. Also, these symbols can combine as needed to form new or foreign words. These two advantages have proven to be of especially great relevance in the modern age: Alphabetic systems are more easily adapted to printing than syllabaries and especially logographies, and they are better suited to the mechanics of cultural exchange.

The Latin alphabet is one of the many writing systems of the world. It has enjoyed increasing adoption across the globe. Extensive western political expansion has laid the foundation for its dissemination. As an alphabet, it possesses a level of abstraction that facilitates borrowing. Also, its compositional simplicity and minimal symbol set have made it very easy to "quantify": to automate its use, from Gutenberg's movable type all the way to 8-bit ASCII.[1]

The Latin alphabet, just like any writing system, is a tool. As such, it is versatile but also imperfect. An alphabet is more difficult to learn than a syllabary, which is much closer to actual speech,[2] and the Latin alphabet is particularly ill-suited to the transcription of the English language.[3] In addition, it is not well-matched to the human visual physiology and the adult reading process. The purpose of this work is to arrive at an improved Latin alphabet that can be read more fluidly.

Any tool can be improved. In fact, a tool either improves or disappears, if it abruptly becomes mismatched to its environment. Tools are improved either consciously or unconsciously. Tangible tools are generally improved consciously: The scythe's pole was made to curve by the people who saw the ergonomic advantage of such a design; the beagle was bred by humans to have a white "flag" at the tip of its tail, which it holds high while running, for good visibility. Yes, the beagle is a tool, too: It's been "designed" to track down the hare and hold it at bay.[4]

Intangible tools, on the other hand, tend to improve through unconscious means, as a result of undirected forces in the environment. For example, the angularity of the majuscule Greek alphabet is a result of the need to carve it in stone, and the high resistance of that medium. Comparatively, the curlicues at the ends of strokes in Thai script were prompted

[1] ASCII is the standardized code that most computers use to assign numerical value to letters and other characters.

[2] The Korean Hangul writing system uses a hybrid scheme of alphabetic syllables that possesses the advantages of each while avoiding their drawbacks. For a description of this most admirable script, refer to Insup Taylor and M. Martin Taylor, *The Psychology of Reading*, (New York: Academic Press 1983) chapter 5

[3] "The most serious defect of the English alphabet is that only 23 letters are available to represent about 44 phonemes. (Of the 26 letters, 'c, q and x' are superfluous.)" Taylor and Taylor, 93

[4] Beagles also make wonderful companions, however.

by the use of bamboo as a writing medium. Another example is the development of the Latin lowercase forms: They are basically the uppercase forms adapted for ease of writing, but with no conscious effort, letting the hand do the talking. Until recently, ease of writing has been the strongest evolutionary force in the development of visible language.

Intangible tools can also be improved consciously; it's just rare. And whereas unconscious improvements can have detrimental effects in some aspects, conscious improvements—if well reasoned—can largely avoid such consequences. In the case of a tool, functionality is the name of the game, and this can best be improved through conscious development.

The Latin alphabet is in the public domain. There is no organization responsible for its definition, dissemination, or improvement. It's a transparent but pervasive part of society, and it can be said to evolve through the contributions of all of society. However, any conscious effort in improving something so pervasive—but without an "owner"—can be seen only as a different process than evolution: reformation. Also, reform is inherently a public event, and the public is solely responsible for its implementation.

Reform is problematic in many ways. Many valiant and valid attempts at various kinds of reform have failed miserably. One reason for this is that society is inherently conservative, and any reform is at some level an antiestablishment act. But the biggest barrier is the inertia of the general public, where day-to-day concerns understandably overpower the need for long-term improvements. None of this, however, makes it a bad idea to try.

Writing versus Reading

Until the advent of printing from movable type, handwriting was used exclusively to record written communication. The written and read letterforms were necessarily the same. However, with the spread of printing, we started to increasingly read letterforms detached from the hand. The typeset forms are made by sculpting metal, resulting in what are called "sorts," which are arranged, inked, and pressed onto paper.[5] And although this is certainly a manual task, handwritten forms per se have been gradually receding since the invention of printing.

Initially, desiring to emulate the established practice of scribal writing, printing adopted letterforms that tried to match handwriting as closely as possible. Gutenberg created a large number of alternate and ligated letterforms to better match the appearance of a manuscript. However, the foundation for a conceptual shift was in place, and, over time, type designers came into their own, realizing that their craft was not restricted to mimicking another. This was motivated by the simple fact that handwritten and typographic forms have different facilities and restrictions of creation. Handwriting is restricted mostly by the movements that the hand is attuned to executing and the writing medium's attributes.[6] Typeset forms

[5] For a meticulous description of punch cutting, consult Christian Paput, *La Gravure du Poinçon typographique* (Vendôme, France: Imprimerie des Presses Universitaires de France 1998)

[6] "The visual aspects which distinguish manuscript writing from either monumental inscriptions or print are its elasticity of form, adaptability of size, and mutability of spatial arrangement." Johanna Drucker, *The Alphabetic Labyrinth*, (New York: Thames and Hudson, 1995) 104

Improving the Tool

were mostly restricted by the nature of typesetting, such as limitations in the surface area that bounds letters, and its inherent "economy of scale"—repeatability—which allows for the creation of an unlimited number of sorts from a single design. Where handwritten letterforms are free to roam a sheet of paper, the repeatability of type —its essential feature—allows for the creation of thoughtfully crafted, minutely detailed forms.

Perhaps the most interesting result of the invention of printing was that our handwritten alphabet in effect spawned a new, distinct alphabet, one that is solely intended to be read, and is free to evolve accordingly. Over time, this freedom has become increasingly manifest, and the written/typographic alphabet duality has become more pronounced. We now have devices such as the PalmPilot that allow us to execute handwritten letterforms using a "pen," converting them in real-time to typographic forms intended for reading. In effect, this process relies on two alphabets, each attuned to a different purpose.

Evolution

The alphabet is generally regarded as an unchanging fixture of society, even though a mere cursory glance at its history reveals that it does indeed evolve. This is because things that evolve so slowly as to remain virtually unchanged over an individual's lifetime are assumed to be ever constant. And society is in effect a collection of individuals, who perpetuate their beliefs by educating the successive generations. The general impression that the alphabet is unchanging endows it with a false sense of merit and fosters a resistance to realizing that it can indeed be improved. This makes conscious reform of the alphabet an uphill battle.

In order to establish the malleable nature of the alphabet, we can look at its evolutionary methods and history. Also, it might be worthwhile to define "evolution" in this context: It doesn't fit the Darwinian model of random modifications that are subjected to natural selection, causing a change to take hold if it is indeed an improvement; it fits the Lamarckian model much better in that it is goal driven, although the goals are very rarely consciously chosen, determined instead by the requirements of the environment, such as the properties of a given writing medium.

The written alphabet has evolved considerably through the ages, depending on the material used to record it as well as stylistic trends. It has even undergone at least one case of conscious evolution: Charlemagne's standardization of the lowercase forms. (Since spawning the typographic alphabet, however, the written alphabet has evolved much more slowly.) The typographic alphabet, on the other hand, has evolved little since its inception, not least because it's much younger than its written counterpart. However, another reason that it has not evolved much is that it's been subservient to its written parent, clinging close to it like a child. If we assume typography to now be a mature, self-sufficient craft, this strong attach-

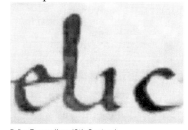

Prüm Evangeliary (9th Century)

ment is unnatural and unhealthy. Typography needs to become its own master if it is to achieve its true promise.

Let's look at how each of the two alphabets evolves and the patterns they follow. The written alphabet is affected by five major forces:

Facilitation. This is certainly the strongest evolutionary force and is a result of our instinctive desire to write faster, causing the strokes to curve, shorten, blend into one another and sometimes even disappear entirely. The derivation of the lowercase *h* from its uppercase form is a good example. The effects of facilitation are omnipresent in the alphabet, and as we saw, one major result was the very creation of the lowercase forms. However, the effects of facilitation can be negative. As Watt states, "Facilitation of the programs can easily lead to a disfacilitation of the patterns, in that the latter become harder to discriminate from each other," where "program" means the execution of a letter and "pattern" means its form.[7] For example, the facilitated Greek lowercase letters " ," " ," and " " are much more easily confused than their uppercase parents " ," " ," and " ."

Homogenization. When we write down letters, we try to bring a systematic method to the rendering of the individual forms. As a result, the various letters converge in the manner of their execution, and hence com-position. For example, the single most prominent routine of making a letter is drawing a vertical stem, then adding an "augmentation" to it; the *P* is a prime example. Almost half of all the letters have adapted to follow this basic rule.

Heterogenization. This is a conscious force, but not a very powerful one. It acts as a counterbalance against facilitation and especially homogenization, prevent-ing the letters from becoming too similar and causing confusion. For example, in cultures where the numeral *1* is written with a prominent "beak," the numeral *7* is given a horizontal bar to differentiate it.

Economy. This is also a conscious force, and a significant one, although lim-ited in scope. In cases where writing was used for the mass production of books, and financial constraints were placed on the usage of material for the writing medium, economy motivated the adoption of more compact letterforms.

Inertia. Society's general resistance to change is very strong indeed. Unless presented with compelling doubt, people tend to follow convention. For example, the crossbar of the *A* is purely an artifact of the past. Although such conventions make communication among people easier on the surface, they impede progress towards solutions that ease communication in truly significant ways, such as an alphabet that is inherently easier to read.

In tracing back the evolution of the Latin alphabet, we risk stumbling in the murky darkness of the distant past. We can instead look at the patterns of evolu-tion in terms of the conceptual stages that an alphabet generally goes through. It is interesting to note that the evolutionary progress that an alphabet makes over the ages is paralleled somewhat by an individual person's progress in learning to use the alphabet, from childhood to maturity.

In the beginning, alphabets are generally written any which way, with no

[7] Derrick de Kerckhove and Charles J. Lumsden, eds. "Canons of Alpha-betic Change," *The Alphabet and the Brain*, (New York: Springer-Verlag 1988) 133

sense of order, not even direction. The letters are flipped horizontally in haphazard fashion, and there is no visual harmony, alignment, or regularization. This stage lasts a short time, as it doesn't take us very long to try to impose order—at least superficial order—on the environment.

In the following stage, a general sense of order is implemented, in one very clear way: The letters are oriented to face the direction of writing. In the Latin uppercase alphabet, none of the letters except *J*—which is, in fact, a late addition—face leftward. In ancient Greece, there was a period when text was written in boustrophedon (lines of alternating direction), and each letter was flipped as necessary to face the direction of a given line. Also, the *L* faced opposite the direction of writing in the Phoenician alphabet but was reoriented by the Greeks.

After this stage, writing becomes practiced on a larger scale, and speed overpowers ceremony. The power of facilitation comes into full force, overriding some of the results of the previous stage and causing fundamental changes in the letterforms. Certainly the most prominent and significant outcome was the branching off of the lowercase alphabet from its uppercase parent. The lowercase forms evolved to be written faster, such that many letters no longer faced the direction of writing, and often departed dramatically from their uppercase models. This was a case where superficial visual order was partially sacrificed for functionality. However, a quick glance at some lowercase text reveals that the facilitated forms still face rightward overall.

The next evolutionary stage comes about as a result of the mass production of texts, where scribes copy voluminous works in large quantities. Under these circumstances, abbreviations become heavily relied upon, through a desire to reduce the amount of work as well as create neatly justified blocks of text. More significantly, in order to economize the use of writing material (often obtained at great expense and effort), letterforms become narrower, and generous stroke extensions are curtailed. The black-letter style—upon which Gutenberg based his type—was partly a result of this economy.

The most recent evolutionary stage was somewhat of a regression. When printing took over the chore of mass producing books—due to its much greater economy—the cramping of handwritten letterforms was no longer as necessary, so aesthetic issues regained prominence.

There is also a development that doesn't fit nicely in a chronological progression. This is the trend of making a letter more regular in terms of balance and symmetry. The Greeks and especially the Romans were great masters of such refinements. The *M,* for example, in its Phoenician origin, had a short leftmost stroke; this was elongated to create a symmetrical shape that sits comfortably on a line.

This is pretty much where the written alphabet now stands in its evolutionary journey. By default, one might think that the written alphabet has stopped evolving, especially in light of the discussion in the following section. However, this is really never the case. In fact, we can even glean the next stage: As a result of the spread of devices that recognize handwriting, but in distorted form, we

Graffiti, The Palm® writing system

will see changes in the letterforms that facilitate their recognition by machines. This means, for instance, that the *V* might acquire a small extra stroke to sufficiently differentiate it from the *U*, as in the PalmPilot.[8]

The evolutionary forces of the typographic alphabet are somewhat different from those of its written counterpart. They are also five in number:

Efficiency. Printing from movable type was invented on the basis of efficiency. Its founding purpose was lowering the cost of book production. Hence efficiency is paramount, and its repercussions many. Besides economy of media, which also applied to mass-produced handwritten works, the main results were: The confining of letters to rectangular shapes of uniform height in order to greatly simplify the task of arranging them in a frame; the reduction of the number of abbreviated, ligated, and other special sorts; and the use of counterpunches to reproduce similar shapes in letters when manufacturing the original designs.[9] The use of counterpunches has an interesting parallel in the contemporary creation of type by computer: The practice of copying and pasting modular parts of letters is a prominent technique.

Rationalization. Because type design allows for minute control over the appearance of a letter, and because imposing order is instinctive for us, the features of the letterforms are often made to behave in a classical, regularized manner: The curves become highly sculpted; everything

Didone
(Bodoni typeface)

aligns; angles, proportions, and dimensions are normalized; and the whole alphabet acquires the appearance of a stark Roman temple.[10] The Didone category of typefaces embodies the pinnacle of this design philosophy, which has had great bearing on the craft since its inception. The highly geometric typeface designs of the twentieth century are also a result of rationalization.

Heterogenization. Although even less powerful than its counterpart in the realm of handwriting, heterogenization still plays a role in the development of type, especially since rationalization tends to make some letters converge greatly in appearance. For example, the early-nineteenth-century typeface series Types de Charles X (used by the Imprimerie Nationale of France for the hand composition of books) exhibits a lowercase *l* with a tiny mark to differentiate it from the numeral *1* and the capital *I*.[11]

Imitation. Type is very good at emulating other forms of written communication, mainly because of its high level of design control. Type was in fact born as an imitation of handwriting and has never outgrown its propensity for emulation, mostly because designers themselves are partial to it, given a capable tool. Type has been used to simulate copperplate engraving, rough-hewn lapidary inscriptions, and

cartes avec
)oint¹. Il g
ait en rega
d'Illinois,

[8] On the other hand, the more sophisticated handwriting-recognition algorithms become, the less our handwriting would evolve in this direction.

[9] For a unique contemporary treatment of this topic, consult Fred Smeijers, *Counterpunch*, (London: Hyphen Press 1996)

[10] A great overview and analysis of historical attempts at rationalization can be found in Matthew Carter, "Theories of Letterform Construction," *Printing History* 26/27 (New York: American Printing History Association, 1991)

[11] Christian Paput, personal communication

Improving the Tool

117

even has exhibited affectations that are not normally associated with written communication—letters made to look like animals or nuts and bolts are not uncommon.

Inertia. Just like in the evolution of the written alphabet, society's tendency towards inertia also plays a role here. For example, mainstream text typefaces have single-sided serifs on ascenders but double-sided serifs on descenders, mainly for tangential historical reasons. In such a versatile tool as type, a high degree of lethargy is particularly unwarranted.

One thing we notice when considering the five forces previously mentioned is that they are all consciously applied, except for inertia. This might give us hope that the typographic alphabet has evolved in a relatively desirable fashion. What's disconcerting is that except for heterogenization—a very minor force at that —the other conscious forces have generally acted to reduce the functionality of the alphabet in its primary role of being read.

As far as its evolutionary path, the typographic alphabet is much easier to trace, being in relatively recent, well-documented memory. As we saw, type was originally meticulously designed to look like handwriting. It was in total slavery to the form of the manuscript.

The force of rationalization soon came into play, initially simply imposing some vertical alignment guidelines, such as for ascenders and descenders, but eventually affecting details of the letterforms, such as stroke stress and serifs. During the modernist era, rationalization was taken to its terminus: simplification. Sans serif faces came to the fore, usually exhibiting a high degree of geometry, which is also a natural extension of rationalization.

In recent times, deconstructivism has played the central role in innovating type, and although there are things to be learned from it, its effects on text typeface development have been very limited but not entirely absent.[12]

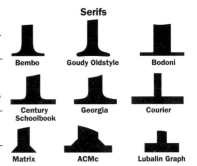

[12] Although the relationships between terms such as "deconstruction," "deconstructionist," "deconstructive," and "deconstructivist," are confused, and the correspondence of various philosophies, critical methodologies, and design practices questionable, the term serves to describe a range of formal experimentation in graphic design of the 1980s and 1990s.

The Transition

Until the widespread implementation of printing, people read handwriting exclusively. Since then, we have been reading more and more typeset text. However, until recently reading other people's handwriting was still common. Add to that type's heritage of emulating handwriting as well as the general perception that there is only one alphabet with a universal function, and it's easy to see why the typeset letterforms have maintained some handwritten features. However, it simply does not make sense for typeset forms to be easy to write.[13]

Let's take serifs as an example. Serifs are a direct result of entrance and exit strokes that the hand is prone to making when writing. Their historical relevance is clear, but their benefit to type's actual function—being read—has to be ascertained in order to justify their existence in type. It turns out that serifs are indeed beneficial to readability, but certainly not because they are a by-product of handwriting.[14]

But things have been changing. We now have affordable, easy-to-use printing technology that the personal computer has provided. As a result, these days we very rarely convey our handwriting to others, submitting printed text—or simply electronic text—instead. The principal use of handwriting is now in an internal, generally transitional capacity. This fact has given the typographic alphabet more focus and a greater freedom to evolve. Coupled with the open-mindedness in type design that deconstructivist experimentation has brought, we are now one step closer—I hope close enough—to attempt to reform the alphabet, with greater readability in our sights.

Some History

Before we embark on a journey of alphabet reform, we might benefit from looking at previous such attempts. The bulk of well-conceived reform efforts have dealt with reconciling English spelling and pronunciation, since the great discrepancy between the two causes much consternation. As such, these efforts really fall into the category of orthographic reform, although many of the schemes include the addition of new letter symbols.

There have been three notable attempts at alphabet reform from a purely visual perspective. The first one, the Carolingian standardization of the lowercase forms, was not highly innovative or ambitious but became a success, not least because it was imposed by a king. The other two occurred in the twentieth century and were more ambitious, if not as practical.

The Bauhaus school of design was obsessed with simplification and populism, and one of its principal figures—Herbert Bayer—created an alphabet based on the premise that the uppercase letterforms were relics of an autocratic past. The result was a single-case alphabet with forms derived from the conventional lowercase letters. Although ideologically significant, Bayer's Universal typeface was a result of dogma and has not had much practical consequence.

abcdefghi
jklmnopqr
stuvwxyz

Herbert Bayer, Universal alphabet

The other attempt was somewhat in the opposite direction. The famed poster artist and avant-garde type designer Cassandre wanted to discard the lowercase forms—which he rightly regarded as having a mottled heritage—in favor of the uppercase.[15] How-

[13] "The factor of easy writing, which influenced the forms of the alphabet at the time of the scribes, can have no actual significance any more; we have to reckon with the technical requirements of typography nowadays." G. W. Ovink, *Legibility, Atmosphere-Value and Forms of Printing Types* (Leiden, The Netherlands: A. W. Sijthoff 1938) 213

[14] G. W. Ovink, *Legibility, Atmosphere-Value and Forms of Printing Types,* (Leiden, The Netherlands: A. W. Sijthoff 1938) Although there is much controversy surrounding this matter, I side with Ovink's blunt statement: "No one can seriously dispute the important function of the serifs in the constitution of the word-gestalt." 78

[15] *baseline* 10 (East Malling, Kent, UK: Bradbourne Publishing, 1990) contains great insight into the unique work of Cassandre.

Improving the Tool

ever, approaching the issue with a scientific as well as an aesthetic mindframe, Cassandre conducted research that revealed the high importance of ascenders and descenders in readability. So he maintained the two cases of forms but endowed the lowercase letters with the grace and dignity of their majuscule parents. Cassandre's work—which resulted in his Peignot typeface—was truly

PEiGNOT

AaBbCcDdEeFfGgHhIi JjKkLlMmNnOoPpQq RrSsTtUuVvWwXxYyZz

lucid in its pragmatism: Design is the artful balance of compromises, and his design for the lowercase *d* (leaving it in its conventional form) is inspiring. Although the application of Cassandre's reform has been limited to Peignot, it is certainly a widely used face. And although Peignot might be termed "quirky" or "quaint," it remains readable without overtly betraying its reformist foundation. This, in fact, is very encouraging for other attempts at reform.

Necessity versus Sacrifice

Reform is compelling in its challenge and good intentions. The only true justification of reform, however, is necessity. Furthermore, the necessity of reform is "necessary but not sufficient"; reform must also be viable. Reform by definition entails sacrifice, and for any change to be viable, its necessity must handily outweigh any sacrifice.

The necessity of alphabet reform can be established relatively easily. In fact, we can instinctively state that since the alphabet is a tool, it cannot be perfect, and there is always room for improvement. To truly reinforce necessity, however, we will study the act of reading and observe the misalignment of the tool with its function.

The sacrifice involved in alphabet reform is in the relinquishment of inertia by the reading public. The gain of reforming the alphabet is admittedly unlikely to be of monumental importance, so readers can only be expected to relinquish a small amount of inertia. In fact, in creating an improved alphabet we must not expect any active effort whatsoever on the part of the reader. Ideally, all we should ask for—and not necessarily explicitly—is open-mindedness. This means that an improved alphabet must be composed of letters that remain decipherable with no conscious effort. Any conscious effort entails active learning, something we should not impose on the reader. It might seem impossible to arrive at an improved alphabet while maintaining high decipherability, but a study of human cognition and the physiology of reading reveals a very interesting avenue.

How We Read

We must start by understanding how we read. This is by far our most difficult task. Countless studies by some of the keenest minds in the field of linguistic cognition have yet to shed an unfaltering light on this convoluted thing.

> *And so to completely analyze what we do when we read would almost be the acme of a psychologist's achievements, for it would be to describe very many of the most intricate workings of the human mind, as well as to unravel the tangled story of the most remarkable specific performance that civilization has learned in all its history.[16]* —E. B. Huey, 1908

[16] E. B. Huey, *The Psychology and Pedagogy of Reading* (New York: Macmillan 1908)

We do, however, seem to have a general view of reading that most if not all scholars agree upon. We should note here that different people read in different ways, and reading conditions also have an effect.[17] One type of reading is a process of deciphering letters and using their sounds to form words. This is the case with those first learning to read; for example, children, or those acquiring a foreign language. The other type of reading is termed "silent," although this doesn't refer to the vocal chords but rather to the brain's treatment of words as concepts as opposed to compilations of sounds.[18] Silent reading comprises the bulk of adult reading, and only unfamiliar words cause us to revert to our childhood technique of vocalization. Although it would be beneficial to study vocalized reading to try to optimize it, we are here concerned with alphabet reform with respect to silent reading, which is a much more complex process.

[17] "The abilities and the condition of the reader play an important part; these differences in reading-skill are not to be neglected." Ovink, 113

[18] "Legibility of isolated letters follows other rules than legibility of cohesive texts." Ovink, 111

Until the late nineteenth century, it was thought that we read in a smooth, flowing manner along the lines of text, composing the words from the letters as we go. This might have actually been the case before the early Middle Ages, when the lack of word-delimiting spaces made reading much less efficient than it is now.[19] However, typeset text has always benefited from the clear demarcation of words, and this proves to be highly relevant.

[19] For a comprehensive treatment of this topic, consult Paul H. Saenger, *Space between Words* (Stanford CA: Stanford University Press, 1997)

Then the French scientist Javal discovered that the eyes perform a nervous dance across a page of text, jumping, pausing, and even regressing in seemingly random fashion. Javal made a lot of headway into understanding the reading process, and, in the following years, an army of scholars joined him. Although they left much to be understood, the foundation was placed: When reading, our eyes perform saccades (jumps) along a line of text, fixating on various words momentarily, and sometimes saccading backwards as well. What's particularly interesting is that we don't fixate on every word, much less every letter, implying that there's a complex process in the works.

A fortunate occurrence of this first period of discovery was that type designers and typographers paid attention to the findings of the scholars, balancing them with the considerations with which they were previously working. For instance, one of Javal's findings was that the tops of letters play a greater role in their identity than the lower parts. Accordingly, designers shortened the descenders of their type,

Improving the Tool

gaining economy with little detriment to readability.

In the 1970s and early 1980s, scientific study of reading was reawakened, and much was learned about the details of the process, including relevant characteristics of the retina and the ways in which eye movement is directed. These discoveries paved the way for a much more robust definition of the reading process. By this time, however, typographers were fully mesmerized by the aesthetic attributes of their field, and readability was considered secondary. In the design community, reading efficiency was—and still is—generally considered to be wholly determined by relative familiarity with a given layout or typeface. The progressive type foundry Emigre exemplifies this with its unofficial slogan, We Read Best What We Read Most. Although this statement is valid in a primitive way, it is in fact an oversimplification, reinforcing the dismissal of the analytical study of readability. Morse code is not as readable as the Latin alphabet for very concrete reasons. Although this is an extreme example, it illustrates the point that readability is not entirely relative, and this can be applied globally: Dogma—although a beautiful typeface—is not as readable as Mrs Eaves.

Dogma

Mrs Eaves

Before we go into the details, it would be helpful to characterize the brain and how it approaches the world. The brain is not like a sharp knife that cuts through a problem; it is like a viscous liquid that both envelops and permeates what it seeks to grasp, simultaneously grasping the generalities and the details. The brain is not precise or meticulous, but it is very powerful in its heuristics. It is what we might call "intelligent" as opposed to merely "smart." The way this applies to visual processing is that the brain benefits from all the available information that it gets from the retina, but in different ways, and in parallel. Also, it directs the movement of the eyes in a nonlinear, somewhat exploratory fashion, although the result is high efficiency.

The following description of the mechanics of silent reading is not taken from one source. In fact, there might not be a single scholar who agrees with its every detail, although most of them would agree with most of it. It is an amalgamation of scholarly conclusions of the past hundred years, taking the ideas that seem to converge the overall model, discarding those that seem errant, and sprinkling the whole with a dash of personal introspection.

Our eyes saccade from point to point on a given line of text, fixating for a fraction of a second at each point. The saccades vary in size but average about the span of ten characters. Sometimes saccades are very short, causing a fixation on the latter part of a long word. Sometimes saccades go backwards, regressing to text that has already been scanned.

During a fixation, all the information that the retina sees is used by the brain to formulate the semantic meaning of the text. All the words of the given line in the field of vision are processed, in parallel. However, the acuity of the retina varies greatly across its surface, and we can demarcate clearly between foveal vision and parafoveal vision. The former is a small, more or less circular region of high spatial resolution. It is the part of the retina that receives the image from the point of fixation, but it only spans about three characters. Parafoveal vision starts outside the foveal region and drops off quickly in spatial resolution—the farther away from the fovea, the blurrier things get. Beyond about fifteen characters from the point of fixation, visual acuity becomes too low to differentiate words; we only see large patches of light and dark.

The foveal region is the only place where we can clearly differentiate and identify the component letters of a word, and at most three. Coupled with the fact that an average saccade spans ten characters, we must conclude that parafoveal vision—which presents us with blurry, nebulous word shapes—plays a significant role in reading. So, the brain does not usually need to make out the individual letters of a word to decide what the word is.[20] The blurry image of a word is often sufficient to identify it. This phenomenon was studied extensively by the Dutch psychologist Herman Bouma, and the nebulous word images have come to be called "Bouma shapes." For the sake of convenience, we will adopt the term "bouma" to mean the shape of a word.

editor's note: these illustrations represent my owner's imagination rather than any scientific depiction of bouma and/or parafoveal vision.

A bouma is recognized by comparing it against boumas stored in the brain through previous exposure. Familiarity with a bouma is the primary way the brain decides what the word is.[21] As we saw, this often happens through parafoveal vision, because a blurry bouma is often enough to identify a word—the more words are recognized through parafoveal vision, the fewer fixations we need to perform. This is because fixations occur at points where the parafoveal boumas do not give enough information.[22] This can happen either because of an unfamiliar word (often the case with long words), or because of an ambiguous bouma. This latter case is, in fact, where we will focus our reform efforts.

When we fixate on an unfamiliar or ambiguous bouma, foveal vision goes to work in a very interesting way. We might think that since the individual letters are available to us, thanks to the high visual acuity of the fovea, they would be used to form the word in question unequivocally. But, in fact, determining a word by compiling its constituent letters is a much slower process than bouma recognition and is only relied upon as a last resort, in the case of an unfamiliar word.[23] Unfamiliar words are generally rare in most texts we read, so bouma recognition is also the strategy of

[20] *Perception and Psychophysics* 25 (Austin, TX: Psychonomic Society, 1979) "Text is a succession of words, but a word is not a succession of letters." P. A. Kolers, *Processing of Visible Language*, volume 1, p. 5.

[21] "Word recognition is a key determiner of reading central to any theory of reading processes." H. Bouma, *Processing of Visible Language*, Paul A. Kolers, Merald E. Wrolstad, Herman Bouma, eds. (New York: Plenum, 1979) vol. 1, 225

[22] Insup Taylor states that there are about sixty words in English that are short and common and are thereby very rarely fixated upon. From "Psychology of Literacy," *The Alphabet and the Brain*, 215

[23] For an in-depth analysis, consult D. Bouwhuis and H. Bouma, *Visual Word Recognition of Three-Letter Words as Derived from the Recognition of the Constituent Letters*.

[24] "We shall find this [inner speech] a powerful factor in welding together what is seen, and in keeping it together before the mind's eye until the full meaning dawns." Huey, 116

choice in foveal vision, even though all the word's letters might be clearly distinguishable.

This process of saccadic, bouma-based reading is not as well regulated as it might seem. It actually has a complex, dynamic relation with the brain's linguistic processing that is carried out in parallel.[24] Fixation points and even bouma recognition are partially directed by the linguistic content of the phrase in question, and regressions often happen if the bouma recognition results in conflict with the semantic meaning that the brain is trying to build. A small number of regressions also happen when foveal bouma recognition results in conflict with the slower letter-by-letter processing that is carried out "in the background," just in case.

So, What's the Problem?

Readability is proportional to reading speed, which in turn is a function of reading comfort. Reading comfort itself is best gauged with respect to the number of saccades a reader has to perform: The fewer the saccades, the more comfortable it is to read. Part of the reason that difficult texts—those with a high proportion of unfamiliar words—are more tiring to read is the physiologic exertion they entail.

In examining the previous description of the reading process, we can make two observations that might lead to improved readability. One thing we realize is that the Latin alphabet is too expansive horizontally. Since the letters are more or less squarish, and they form words through horizontal sequencing, words are generally wide and short. This causes two problems: Longer words don't fit in our foveal vision, often requiring two fixations since long words also tend to be less familiar; also, a string of words in a line quickly overruns the retina's acuity, putting more words than necessary outside potential parafoveal recognition.

Because our visual acuity drops off in a somewhat circular pattern, we would need less fixations to read text where the boumas are squarish: Foveal vision would be able to grasp "long" words in a single fixation, and more words would fit in parafoveal vision inside the region of adequate acuity.

To make the Latin alphabet fit this mold of squarish boumas we would have to do one of the following:

Greatly compress the letters horizontally. As studies have shown, however, this ends up reducing readability because the inherent design of the Latin letters causes them to become distorted and unrecognizable when highly condensed.

Devise a new alphabet with tall and narrow letter symbols that combine to form squarish words. This is simply too ambitious, demanding great active-learning effort on the part of the reader.

Maintain the conventional letterforms, but compose words by stacking two rows of letters. As most words—especially familiar ones—are made up of six or fewer letters, the resultant

He wan/ts to ha/ve the abil/ity to re/ad bet/ter .

boumas would generally fit nicely in foveal vision, and more words would benefit from parafoveal recognition. This is, in fact, somewhat analogous to how Hangul works. However, although such a modified script would not be too difficult to learn, it's still too much to expect in terms of reader effort.

In the end, we have to abandon the idea of making the Latin script much more horizontally economical.

Futura Shape
Gill Sans Shape

The other thing we realize when considering how the Latin script is read is that ambiguous boumas cause problems. Because we rely so heavily on boumas during silent reading, any doubt when matching a bouma to a word causes a fixation, or worse still, a regression. Although this cannot be avoided for unfamiliar words, in most cases it is caused by the potential mapping of a bouma to more than one word. The level of ambiguity varies a lot even among existing conventional type designs: Because of its high level of modularity and reliance on the basic line and circle, Futura presents us with much more uniform—therefore ambiguous—word shapes than Gill Sans. Unlike existing efforts, however, the purpose of this work is to greatly decrease bouma ambiguity by modifying the underlying abstract definitions of the letters.

The Fix

How can we make boumas less ambiguous? We need to determine what features make a bouma distinctive in the first place, and accentuate them.

The key feature of a bouma is its silhouette. The brain's primary mechanism of identifying an object is by way of its external outline. This is especially relevant for boumas seen through parafoveal vision, since their blurry appearance obscures much of the internal detail. And even in foveal vision—where all letterform details are available—the silhouette of a word is of key importance.

The most prominent features of a bouma's silhouette are its width, and the ascenders and descenders of its constituent letters. It is, in fact, the lack of such extenders that makes all-uppercase text much less readable than lowercase text. The first and last letters of a word also play an important role, as they provide the leftmost and rightmost profiles of its bouma.[25] In foveal vision, all the constituent letters of a word—being identifiable—play a role in creating a distinctive bouma. They also play the role of a fallback mechanism in case bouma recognition fails, due to unfamiliarity or more often ambiguity.

We can conclude that we need to modify the letters of the alphabet such that the boumas they compose diverge from one another as much as possible. These modifications are needed primarily in the ascenders and descenders of letters, but also in their bodies, to distinguish them as much as possible. However, the words these new letters form also need to remain decipherable in case of nonbouma (letter-by-letter) scrutiny, so we cannot stray too far in

[25] H. Bouma, *"Visual Interference in the Parafoveal Recognition of Initial and Final Letters" Vision Research* 13 (Oxford, UK: Pergamon Press, 1973)

Improving the Tool

our modifications. So, how far is too far? In devising a strategy for modifying the letterforms, the fundamental question is how much—and in what directions—can we modify a letter without sacrificing decipherability? To figure this out, we first need to understand how a letter is seen and how it is formed.

In looking at a letterform—or any other shape, for that matter—we look for its acrocratic feature,[26] meaning the part of the form that can identify the whole unequivocally. Some letters have more than one acrocratic feature. Others—like the *l*—have weak acrocracy because of their simplicity or their modularity with respect to other letters. As an example, the acrocratic feature of the lowercase *e* is its "eye." The nonacrocratic parts of a letter play a very small role in determining its identity. Another interesting observation—first documented by Javal—is that the upper parts of letters play a greater role in decipherability than the lower parts. Alternately obscuring the lower and the upper halves of a line of text reveals this clearly. These two phenomena can be used to direct our modifications of the letterforms. But what are we really modifying? If we were to take an actual existing typeface design and modify its forms, we would not only be limiting the usefulness of our work but also missing the point entirely: What we need to modify is the conceptual structure of the letters, from which new, specific instances are to be created. To better understand this process, let's look at how specific letterforms are conceptualized.

Generally, when designing a letterform of type, we have its underlying structure in mind, and we create an instance of this structure by applying certain characteristics to it, such as stroke weight, serifs of a certain shape, and anything else that would embody our aesthetic and technical goals. The basic structure, or "skeleton," is relatively firm in our mind, although it is not totally static, varying somewhat between one person and the next, even in one person over time. We might assume that a letter's skeleton is its most abstract representation and is what ensures the recognizability of the end-result glyph. In reality, this skeleton is an interpretation of something even more abstract, something highly nebulous that we would be hard pressed to visualize clearly: the "essence" of the letter.

The essence of a letter is what gives it its identity and is conceptual more than it is visual. This essence is a result of numerous intangible forces, including all the previous instances of the letter that we have seen, the ways in which we have been taught to make that letter ourselves, and also the inherent and sociocultural symbolism involving certain shapes. All of this is melted together to form the essence of letters in our mind. For example, pretty much anything with a large tail attached to its bottom is a capital *Q*. This is because the tail is that letter's acrocratic feature. If, however, we were to attach a tail to a capital *B,* we would still have a *B* because that letter is acrocratically very strong in its whole. The capital *O,* being such a primitive and common shape, serves as the weak secondary feature of the *Q,* and replacing it

[26] Term coined by Alfred Kallir in his fascinating *Sign and Design,* (Richmond, Surrey, UK: Vernum, 1961)

judiciously does not overly harm the essence of the Q. This implies that the essence of a letter is what ensures its decipherability, and its visual skeleton—which is the source of the actual drawn letterform—is simply an interpretation of the essence. One interesting note is that a letter can have more than one essence, mostly due to the Latin alphabet's upper/lowercase duality. As we will see, this duality can be of some benefit.

So, in modifying the alphabet, we need to create a new set of letter skeletons that maintains the essence of the letters and serves as the source for designing the actual glyphs. The new essence-preserving skeletons are to be designed with one primary aim: to diverge the resultant boumas, which reduces ambiguity and therefore the number of saccades. A secondary aim is to diverge the individual letterforms to aid nonbouma foveal recognition.

It's worth pointing out here that type designers have always been interested in improving readability; this reform effort is not novel in its ambition.[27] The difference, however, is that designers have generally restricted themselves to the conventional skeletons of the letters in order to avoid unorthodox forms. I believe that unconventional forms do not cause problems as long as the essence of the letters is preserved. Furthermore, it is possible to improve readability by giving type designers a new set of skeletons from which to work. Also, a well-directed reform effort is generally more thorough and rigorous than the efforts of an isolated designer. It is hoped that such reform—if justified through rational argument—can give designers the confidence to open this new door.

[27] Improving readability has even been scientifically considered in the design of type for display usage, not just text. The inimitable Roger Excoffon, for example, expended great effort in the analytical study of reading in order to create better-performing display typography.

Modules & Similars

The Nitty-Gritty

As we saw, there are two types of ambiguity that we need to reduce. The first and more important is bouma ambiguity, where letters contribute parts of themselves, and these parts are what need to be diverged. Of secondary importance is the need to reduce ambiguity among the individual letterforms. In both cases, we need to define the specific problem areas of the conventional alphabet in order to address them. The Modules & Similars diagram represents both sets of ambiguity conflicts for the lowercase alphabet. In this work, we are limiting reform to the lowercase set since the uppercase letters play a very minor role in readability. In the diagram, the "modules" are the groupings of letters into regions; these represent the components of letters that contribute ambiguity to boumas because of the similarity of their components. For example, all the letters with ascending stems are grouped, as they contribute that uniform element to boumas. The diagram also shows the relationships between individual letters, called "similars."[28] The lines indicate pairs of letters that are similar, causing confusion during decipherment. The thick lines indicate a higher degree of similarity than the thin ones, hence a greater problem.

[28] The "similars" component of the diagram is partly derived from the research results of Ovink and Bouma, "Visual Recognition of Isolated Lower-Case Letters," *Vision Research* 11 (Oxford, UK: Pergamon Press, 1971)

When considering a given letter, we can easily see the two forces of ambiguity that act on it. We can then proceed to "pull" the letter away from these forces by changing its skeleton, always remembering that preserving its essence is paramount. Note that the diagram shows simplified letterforms that represent the conceptual skeletons; the actual glyphs are derived from these forms.

Also, the diagram is based solely on visual attributes of the letter skeletons, with no regard to linguistic issues. Linguistic issues are highly significant in deciding what modifications to actually carry out in the various letters. For example, a vowel is much more likely to be interchanged and confused with another vowel than a consonant, and vice versa. Looking at the diagram, this means, for example, that the confusion between *e* and *o* might have more relevance than the confusion between *c* and *e,* even though the latter shows a thicker line. Another issue is letter frequency. A relatively rare letter such as *z* might not need too much modification, because it doesn't contribute much ambiguity. Ideally, I'd like to consider the entire lexicon and grammar of a language to determine which words—or sets of words—have ambiguous boumas and couple that data with the relative frequency of the words to arrive at decisions of how to modify the letters. This is a daunting task, which I have not attempted. Moreover, this would be highly language specific, and results for English might make things worse for German, for example.

Another thing the diagram can't show is the new conflicts that any modification might cause. As a result, when considering a change, we need to observe its repercussions. In fact, the modifications should not be thought of in a sequential manner: They form a set that has to be considered in parallel, as a whole; a set that needs to avoid causing new ambiguities.

What techniques can we use to diverge the letter skeletons? There are three basic methods:

Add or remove features that neither weaken nor replace a letter's acrocratic essence.

Modify curved features to make them angular or straight, and vice versa. Angular and curvy features play a large role in forming a distinctive bouma, and as long as changing one into the other doesn't violate the letter's essence, it helps.

Borrow from the uppercase essence of the letter, if different than that of the lowercase. Some letters, like *c*, can't benefit from this technique, but others, such as *n*, can.

Since navigating the mental labyrinth towards a complete set of modifications takes very many hours of effort, and putting a complete convoluted explanation in writing would be impractical, I will not attempt that here. However, here is one conclusion of the extensive mental machinations, at least for the lowercase forms. As an illustration, let's go through the bulk of the process for the letter *q*.

The essence of the *q* is something to the effect of a more or less circular shape with something hanging from its right side that doesn't turn leftward (to avoid being a *g*). The conventional skeleton of the *q* exhibits two modules: a descender and *o*. The first is of greater significance, since extensions play a primary role in forming a bouma's silhouette. I can't turn the descender to the left, but I would like to avoid leaving it straight, because the *p*—the most common descending consonant—has a straight stem. What I can do is borrow from the handwritten essence of the *q*, which has a rightward turn at the end of the descender. Typographic instances of the *q* rarely include such a feature, but this could very well be because of the erstwhile difficulty of implementing protrusions in metal type. There is nothing to stop me from reinstating the rightward turn at the end of the descender, considering it will help our purpose. In fact, even if the handwritten essence of the *q* didn't feature such a turned descender, I would still incorporate it, as it doesn't adversely affect its essence. The one technical issue is the possibility of inferior spacing of the letters as a result of this protrusion, considering the avoidance of letting letters touch. However, in this case I can predict that there will be no problems, since the *u* follows the *q* pretty much exclusively, and it has no left-hand descender. As for the actual form of the protrusion, this can be determined by looking at the reformed *y* (which has followed its own path to a reformed structure): To avoid similarity, I make the descender of the *q* angular instead of curved. As far as the body of the *q*, I would like to reduce its *o* modularity by adding angularity to it. I can do this first at its top, since the tops of letters bear more weight in recognition. I could stop here, but to avoid modularity with the reformed *c*, I would also flatten the bottom of the body. This can also be justified by the need to pull the *q* away from the *p*, which has a curved stroke at the bottom of its body. I have now moved to reducing "similar" ambiguities, and the only remaining issue is the *g*, which turns out to be sufficiently dissimilar by this point.

All the other letters were subjected to the same type of thought process, and the resultant reformed alphabet is hopefully a viable first step. One important observation is that the specifications for the new *q*—just as for the other letters—are pretty exacting. This might seem counterintuitive in type design in terms of restricting the actual end-result letterform instances, but it is a necessary part of the process since the reformed skeletons represent a precise, conscious effort at reducing specific ambiguities in the conventional alphabet.

q

Lucida Sans

q

restructured

Implementation and Dissemination

The actual letterforms of a typeface are derived from the structural skeletons. In conventional type design, the skeletons are somewhat loosely defined. As we saw, however, the skeletons of the reformed alphabet are necessarily of a stricter nature.

A reformed typeface should ideally take the skeleton features literally. For example, the middle part of the *w* should not reach the x-height. Even so, there is still ample room for a world of diversity through the variation of stroke contrast, stroke stress, weight, width, x-height, ascender and descender size, serif shape, and other attributes. Also, it's worth noting that a designer can choose to not follow some of the prescribed skeletons, especially if this helps avoid ungainly or uncharacteristic forms in a given design. This is obviously undesirable in terms of readability and can have significant negative consequences because the reformed skeletons are so finely tuned and carefully balanced against one another. It is an option, however.

The freedom of design mentioned above is part and parcel of the way in which this reform is to be disseminated. It is not a top-down process. No organization or entity can have authority over its implementation and adoption, simply because the alphabet is "public property." It cannot be promulgated but has to be embraced by individual typographers, with the support of individual type designers. And the authors of content are also involved—just like Bernard Shaw insisted on the use of Caslon for the setting of his work, a writer can specify the exclusive use of a reformed typeface, or perhaps a preference to that effect.

The reading public obviously plays the biggest part in this effort, but it is entirely an unconscious role. The reformed alphabet has been based on the premise of not requiring any active effort on the part of the reader, so the public does not need to—and, in fact, should not—be subjected to preaching about the benefits of a book set in a reformed typeface. Although a short blurb in the colophon pointing out the use of the unorthodox readability optimized face might be a good idea, the six o'clock news need not carry a story.

There are, however, some practical tactics that might aid dissemination. One possibility is setting a book on a related topic—for example, a work about reading or cognition—using a reformed typeface in order to get some effective preliminary exposure. Alternatively, a progressive publisher could opt to release a popular novel—perhaps a work of science fiction—using the modified alphabet, providing for immediate wide exposure. Also, to ease the transition of the reader from the expected forms to the new ones, the text could possibly migrate gradually, starting with the conventional version of a given typeface and slowly substituting the letters from the reformed version of that typeface over the span of many pages. Using such techniques, the reformed alphabet could make a home in the mind of the general reading public.

The main daunting task now is to convince the typographers of the benefits of this effort, as they are the ones who hold the power to improve the tool.

I would like to thank Peter Enneson for pointing out numerous relevant references, as well as engaging in fruitful discussion.

abcdef

ghijkl

ɯNOPQ

rstuvw

zʎx

Clarety: Drinking from the Crystal Goblet

Gunnar Swanson

Note: Beatrice Warde (1900–69) was a typographer, writer, and scholar who edited The Monotype Recorder. *Her essay "The Crystal Goblet" is perhaps the most famous English language essay on typography. In it, Warde argues against the introspection of avant-garde typography, asserting that classical typography provides a transparent vessel for the ideas of the author—if one notices the type, one is distracted from the thought, just as an ornate wineglass might distract the drinker from true appreciation of the wine.*

Beatrice Warde wrote that type is like a wineglass. The point of the simile had nothing to do with either craftsmanship or the potential for lead poisoning from handling Bembo or Waterford. Warde valued a plain crystal goblet over an ornate chalice because the latter vessel obscures the observation of the wine, which, she assumes, is the point of drinking. It is her greatest failing as a type critic that she never mentioned (or, apparently, even considered) the jelly jar.

Drinking wine from a jelly jar reveals the color of the wine and saves both money and landfill space. The shape of the jar may not be optimal for swirling the wine to show off its legs, but the point of oenological gams is lost on me. If a wine has a feature that I cannot distinguish by smell, taste, or feel, why should I care? Such observation is useful in connoisseurship, but I have little interest in that. Knowing that I've paid three times the retail price for a better wine than the one that the folks at the next table paid three times the retail price for is, for some reason I can't explain, not central to my being.

If we are to assume that Warde was not merely a shallow snob obsessed with reassuring herself that she consumed the best available drugs, perhaps it is not the glass that she should have criticized, but the wine. I do not refer to criticizing the wine in the sense of comparing its color to various gemstones, examining its body, noting the bouquet, sloshing it around in one's mouth, then spitting out both the wine and a pompous list of adjectives. I mean we should reconsider wine and wine drinking.

What is the relationship of color to consumption? Is the look of the wine an arbitrary aesthetic addition to the drinking experience? How, then, are the ruby

Bookman Swash

tones and visual indication of substance superior to a tankard encrusted with actual rubies—a vessel of more substance than any wine?

Such questions should not be dismissed as denigrating wine, as mere antio-enologism. The wine is the medium that connects the wine maker and the drinker —it is not more important than either. Did Warde equate the typographer with the truck driver who delivers the wine to the café? No, I think maybe the busboy who sets the table or the restaurant manager who chose which glasses to provide . . . but I digress. Let's get back to the main point.

Perhaps the point of knowing whether a wine has legs is not a dry functional problem but a sweet bit of fantasy. (I have, by now, come to assume that a woman as thoughtful and accomplished as Beatrice Warde would not have ignored the jelly jar. Unless we are willing to consider the possibility of a morbid fear of getting jar-lid thread marks on her lips, we must believe that the legs issue was foremost on her mind, even though her biographers have not revealed any record of discussion of the subject.) There may be some considerable satisfaction in imagining the secret pattern of the rivulets formed as one swallows.

Knowing that viscous flows of Chateau Laffite grace one's tongue while flaccid sheets of Dego Red take a lingual fall at the next table could provide a sense of separation from the evil of banality that surrounds us all. I read an interview with a man who had several rings in piercings of his penis. He said it gave him a real satisfaction to stand in a crowded elevator knowing that he had something under his suit that nobody else even imagined. An old girlfriend of mine said she liked sitting in a meeting with a group of Japanese businessmen knowing that her garter belt, lack of underpants, and shaved pubic hair set her apart from everyone else in the boardroom. Perhaps a private knowledge of vinous currents provides that same sense of personal distinction.

The corporate records at Monotype are woefully incomplete. Among other things, they offer no insights into Beatrice Warde's preferences in underwear or hairstyles, and no particularly cogent information on the role of wine choice in type design.

A dozen years ago I drank alternating gulps of Fresca and rum with someone I met in Quintana Roo (or was it Yucatan?). In retrospect, it was a bit like reading Bookman with swash variations, but since we were drinking right out of the bottles, I'm not sure whether Beatrice Warde would find this story relevant to her essay.

The Object Poster:
Word + Picture = Impact

Steven Heller

N THE BEGINNING was The Word. . . and The Word played a wondrous role in the history of humankind, for it gave breadth to both the spirit and the flesh. However, the story that I relate is not of biblical proportions. The word to which I refer is more earthly and common. It is not *The Word* that came from the mount (as in "And The Word was. . .") but rather *a* word, or words, carefully selected and strategically composed by an advertising agent for the purpose of evoking the decidedly primal urge to consume.

In the beginning (of the early nineteenth century, that is), commercial advertising and graphic design relied on words because pictures were just too costly to reproduce. Ideas and messages were communicated through words set in wood or metal typefaces, printed in multiples, and posted on any empty surfaces. Walls, fences, and hoardings were covered with bold letters announcing miraculous patent medicines, daring-do entertainers, and honest-as-the-day-is-long political candidates. In fact, there were so many words that printers, the craftsmen fundamentally responsible for producing advertisements, could garner attention only by using the most raucous of letterforms. Larger, bolder, decorated letters were akin to screaming hawkers. But amid the cacophony of Tuscans, Latins, Egyptians, and novelty faces galore, a poster or broadside had to be more than just loud, it had to have allure.

Imagery was key. Initially, wood engraving enabled printers to reproduce linear graphics. But with the advent of chromolithography—the so-called democratic art—during the late nineteenth century, a sea change in advertising and

The Object Poster

wood type poster 1854 (detail)

graphic design occurred. The reproduction of colorful tonal pictures gave birth to popular art that not only promoted and persuaded but also entertained. With this new technology, artists developed looser styles consistent with painting. The resulting posters were indeed large canvases filled with fanciful figures, mirthful metaphors, and chromatic colors, capped by artful letters. But artists, being artists, were not content to use one method alone, and so from the earliest academic renderings the visuals evolved into various graphic styles that became increasingly more complex in form, if not function.

Art Nouveau was the most elaborate of the early modern design vogues. This commercial style, manifest primarily throughout Europe and the United States around the turn of the twentieth century, was characterized by naturalistic, curvilinear ornament, such as branches, vines, tendrils, and floral patterns. Even the numerous art nouveau alphabets were designed to symbolize nature and thus prompted one critic to dub the aesthetic "floreated madness." In fact, during the few years between 1896 and 1900, Art Nouveau developed into a resolutely eccentric mannerism that dominated the commercial marketplace and prompted much mimicry by graphic, furniture, and fashion designers.

One exponent was an eighteen-year-old (although some say he was sixteen), starving German cartoonist named Lucian Bernhard who, in 1906, entered a poster competition sponsored by Berlin's Priester Match company. The prize was fifty marks, a published piece, and a possible contract to do artwork for Hollerbaum and Schmidt, Germany's leading poster printer and advertising

Alphonse Mucha
Reverie/Daydream 1896 (detail)

agency. As the story goes, Bernhard's first sketch was typically art nouveau (or *jugendstil* as it was known in Germany), including a cigar in an ashtray on a checked tablecloth with dancing nymphs formed by the intertwining tobacco smoke. Incidentally, next to the ashtray were two wooden matches. A friend complimented Bernhard on the excellent cigar advertisement, which prompted him to rethink the composition, and he eliminated the tablecloth, ashtray, cigar, smoke, and erotic nymphs one by one, leaving only the two matches. He then enlarged the matches, painted them in red with yellow tips, and left them on a dark maroon field, At the top of the image area he hand lettered Priester in block letters.

The jury summarily discarded this entry as being much too spare. Yet, as fate so often intercedes, the chief representative of Hollberbaum and Schmidt, Ernst Growald, arriving late, retrieved Bernhard's work from the trash bin and announced that this was his winning choice. A big, boisterous man, Growald held sway over the other jurors, asserting that this was the next wave of advertising. So, Bernhard was given the cash award, the poster was printed and posted around Berlin, a contract was signed for additional work, and—not inconsequentially—the *Sachplakat* (or object poster) was born.

Art Nouveau met its demise not because of Berhard's accidental "invention" of the object poster, but because the world was rapidly changing. Industrialization, the growth of cities, the increase of vehicular traffic, and the fast pace of everyday life required that advertisers compete for attention as never before. Visual complexity no longer worked. Passersby moved much too quickly to appreciate the levels of craft and symbolism in elaborate art nouveau composi-

Lucien Bernhard
Priester poster c. 1905

tions. Growald understood this, and Bernhard intuited it, too. The alternative was bright color, stark imagery, and bold words.

What constituted a bold word, however, was subject to location. In America, billboards contained terse slogans and minimal art. In Berlin it was enough simply to state the company or brand name, such as Priester, Steinway, Manoli, or Frank. At this time, before the era of multinationals and diverse subsidiaries, one company produced one product, which may or may not compete with another company producing the same product. There may have been other match companies in Germany in 1906, but once the Priester poster was hung—with the block lettering that read Priester atop two colorful matchsticks—there was no other brand in the minds of consumers. The same holds true for Steinway pianos, Manoli cigarettes, Frank coffee, and the many other products that Bernhard (and his Berliner Plakat cronies) advertised in this same manner.

The Object Poster

Hans Rudi Erdt
Opel poster 1911

The word was a mnemonic cue, and it alone forced recognition, but its close proximity to the object was necessary for full effect on the audience. The stark combination of the word and image was invincible. In fact, the object poster could be defined as a verbal/visual sentence that required the proper name and visual noun in order for the viewer to *read* it. In addition, these posters worked best when hung in multiples of three or more consecutively in a long line, which created a visually rhythmic refrain—Priester, Priester, Priester, Matches, Matches, Matches. The concept is not unlike the constant barrage on radio or TV of annoyingly memorable jingles and slogans.

It doesn't take a behavioral psychologist to know that the repetition of any single word or image will lodge itself in the conscious *and* unconscious minds. When Bernhard made object posters, the advertising industry had not yet embraced pseudo science or market research to determine what influenced the public most. The notion of subliminal intervention had not become a codified strategy. It was simply logical that after an era of visual complexity, visual simplicity would have a positive impact. It was also predictable that after a period of simplicity the novelty would wear off, and more aggressive (or at least more novel) means of mass communication would be necessary.

The object poster was dominant from 1906 to around 1914, when the Great War in Europe brought rampant commercialism there to a crashing halt. During the war, wordy slogans and complex renderings sold patriotism as well as what few products remained. After the war, advertising techniques shifted once again, and a variety of new ideas emerged in modernist hothouses. But it was clear to anyone who could read the posters on the wall that the word could not be displaced as the main ingredient of persuasion.

END PAPER

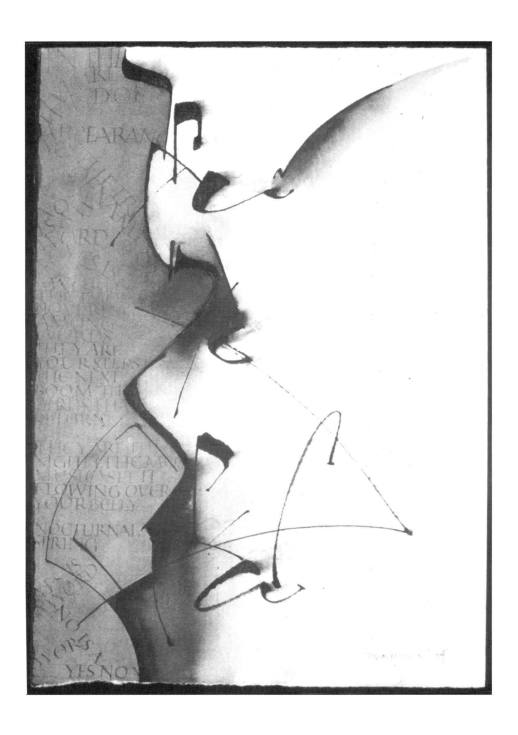

Thomas Ingmire
untitled 1994

The New Calligraphic Renaissance

Steven Skaggs

Nearly a generation ago, calligraphers on both sides of the Atlantic began to disinter Western calligraphy from the moldy tomb of "beautiful writing." Artists such as Jean Evans, Dick Beasley, Rene Schall, Paul Freeman, Karlgeorg Hoefer, and Gottfried Pott began working in freely intuitive ways, improvisationally creating compositions of great dynamic diversity. At first, highlighting its sense of drama and emotional display, this calligraphy was called "expressive" calligraphy. But what calligraphy is not expressive? Over the years, this style has become the norm.

Contemporary calligraphy is expected to be dynamic, emotional, spirited, and free. But to the outside world, where calligraphy is often regarded as kin to macramé, calligraphy means one thing: the laborious perfection of decorative historical letters.[1] Therefore, ironic as it may be to call a movement that has been gaining momentum for twenty-five years "new," it still has the cachet of novelty to many people, who, upon experiencing a piece by Ingmire or Holliday for the first time, are heard to exclaim, "That's calligraphy?"

[1] The misperception of calligraphy says a lot about calligraphy's irrelevance—indeed, nonexistence—to the larger world of art.

Is the novelty a passing fashion, or does the new calligraphy represent a more fundamental change? I believe that the new calligraphy is more than simply a stylistic fashion. Rather than merely extending or elaborating upon the historical Western calligraphic tradition, the new calligraphy overwhelms it, and represents an important shift in the core values of calligraphy, making it remarkably relevant to design. What are these new values, and what principles have arisen to replace the venerable one of making letters beautiful?

"Touch Gives Grace"

The seed of the new calligraphy was planted in the old. Speaking at mid 20th century, Alfred Fairbanks said, "Handwriting is a system of movements involving touch, and in a sense, touch gives grace."[2] Calligraphers began to reach beneath the letterform, emphasizing the graceful touch itself. More than beautiful letters, calligraphy became "disciplined freedom"[3] or "the dance of the pen." It seemed at the time to be an insignificant note a sort of passing acknowledgement that calligraphy is inherently kinesthetic and depends on a kind of soulful touch. But the new focus on touch, rather than historical letterform, defined the essential difference between calligraphy and typography and fueled important developments in sense of purpose. A fundamental split had rent the framework of calligraphy and would present a younger generation with license to challenge not only the golden idol of letterform but the master-god of legibility as well.

[2] Attributed to Fairbanks by P. W. Filby, *Two Thousand Years of Calligraphy* (1965; reprint, Taplinger Publishing, 1980) 132

[3] Ray DaBoll, from Eastern Paper Company poster, 1940s

I regret that it is not possible here to show dozens of examples of what this transformation has wrought. Look at the work mounted in the Peabody Institute Library in the mid-sixties (the catalogue of which is available as *Two Thousand Years of Calligraphy*) and compare it to the work in any recent *Letter Arts Review* (LAR). The work from the first half of the twentieth century was a clear progression of the preceding nineteen hundred years. It featured the perfection of letterforms, carefully crafted and traditionally balanced and arranged. Recent award-winning work in LAR, on the other hand, is frequently illegible, and the letterforms are sometimes virtually absent. Long before typographers were experimenting with rich layers and organic compositions, calligraphers were tumbling multicolored texts over each other. What is inevitably emphasized is the sense of the act of writing—the tactile moment.

The influence of Asian calligraphy—especially on German and American calligraphers—at mid-century is unmistakable. To the Western eye (the eye that cannot read the Asian character), its power lies in the sense of motion, the pace, pressure, and rush of brush over paper. The sensuality of the kinesthetic movement, the gentle pressure of pen on paper fibers like finger on skin, the responsiveness to fluidity and to acceleration, provide the ideal expressive vehicle. Who would not recognize this as calligraphy, even though there is no readability? There is enormous visual allure, and something else with which recent calligraphers love to play: the allusion to speech.

Like the Asian work, the new calligraphy in the West capitalizes on revealing touch. Legible or illegible, such calligraphy is unsurpassed in its power to convey emotion through the action of the hand. The calligraphic stroke is the trace that remains after movement has departed. It is a document, a snapshot of emotion. The new calligraphy puts more emphasis on the "honesty" and "integrity" of the stroke as a tactile sign, less emphasis on the purity of letterform. "Move like music,"[4] Pott teaches. The alphabet has been dethroned. The new monarch: the graceful touch.

[4] Gottfried Pott, lecture, Santa Clara, California, 1989

Eliza Holliday
Mark Book 1991–1993

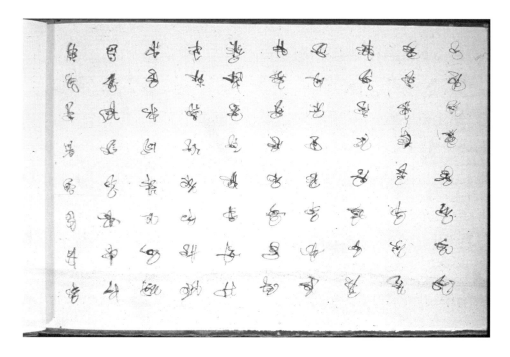

The New Calligraphic Renaissance

Eliza Holliday

Mark Book (detail)

Page after page of character marks slowly transforming themselves like Bach's Goldberg Variations.

Gesture

Motion, added to touch, produces gesture. Counter to post-Modern dogma, calligraphers trust that the unselfconscious gestural mark communicates a gracefulness that flows directly from the spiritual center of the artist. It is a kind of honest and truthful expression of what the Asians call *chi,* the creative life spirit. In doing calligraphy, the goal is to enter "the zone," in which marks are made seemingly without reflection and inevitably convey a sense of grace and authority. The marks may be rawly expressive or controlled, but inevitably they project a sense of unfussed ease. The marks breathe with life spirit. This is a higher goal than following the structure of a historical model.

Movements made in the zone, in which the whole body and mind are centered on the action itself, are believed to carry a cross–culturally available "message". The integrity and grace of such a mark can be called "beautiful." Furthermore, calligraphers tend to believe that this kind of beauty (or "integrity" if the word "beauty" is off-putting) is universal. In the face of current intellectual fashion, the new calligraphers flaunt their belief that gestural marking from the zone is as universally appreciated as the enjoyment of a Michael Jordan dunk or a Gene Kelly dance step. They point to the cross-cultural appreciation of Asian and Islamic calligraphy, and they see their work in similar light.

All of this talk of universal beauty is either incredibly reactionary or amazingly prescient of some new artistic temperament depending upon your point of view. But what is important to notice in this discussion is that the measure upon

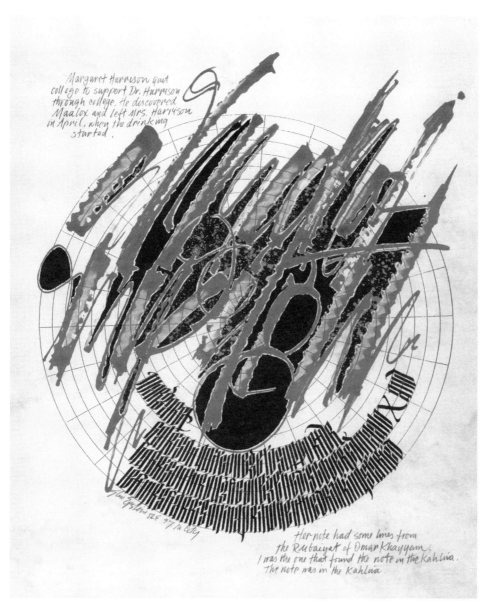

Glen Epstein
untitled 1997

which a work is accepted as calligraphic, as well as the basis for value judgements regarding its quality, has shifted from issues surrounding the perfection of letter-forms to issues concerning a special process of marking.

The New Calligraphic Renaissance

Character Marks

Marks that are written as configurational units are called character marks. They are clusters of only a few strokes that form discrete signs. Letters of the alphabet are examples of character marks. But character marks need not be actual signs from any writing system, or combined into words, and may not even be legible as a clearly identified unit. Yet they become essential for understanding calligraphy because they separate calligraphic gesture form other nonlinguistic gestural artifacts: things like crosshatching in drawings or representational gestures, or painterly washes.

Character marks are "proto-writing," a world of forms among which alphabetical forms are a small, but significant, subset. In other words, all alphabetical signs are character marks, but not every character mark is alphabetical. Calligraphy's special territory, and discriminating distinction as an art form, is this attention to character marks. Through character marks, the calligrapher powerfully communicates the expressive potential of language. They may be like scat singing, staying this side of verbal content, but they make a continuous allusion to linguistic visual form just as scatting makes a continuous allusion to linguistic aural form.

Because of this unique nature of the character mark, calligraphers "write" when they make any sequence of character marks, even when no one is able to decipher the "language." A piece of Asian calligraphy in which the character marks are unreadable to a speaker of English is equivalent in every respect to a string of character marks that derive from no writing system at all or to English words written illegibly. Each is equally privileged to be called "beautiful writing."

So here is the crucial divide between the old and the new aesthetic stances. Whereas the old calligraphy demanded that touch be in the service of recognized models of the alphabet sequenced into legible words, the new calligraphy reveres the "zoned" character mark as both beautiful and as writing, not only vastly widening the scope of calligraphy but altering the intent of the art.

This upheaval is nowhere more dramatically felt than in the issues surrounding legibility. In the new calligraphy, legibility

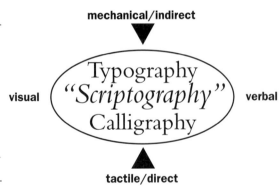

If you imagine a space called "scriptography" where language is made visible, then typography and calligraphy are two varieties of scriptographs. They are defined by the method of production. Typography is mechanical and indirect, calligraphy is tactile and directly produced (although, of course, it may be mechanically manipulated at a later stage). The "new calligraphy" enhances or exaggerates the tactile qualities and the direct method of its production. In other words, it highlights those aspects which most distinguish it from typography.

is a choice. Calligraphers accept the possibility of beautiful writing that is totally unreadable because it is the integrity of gestural character marking that is the essence of the calligrapher's work. Although the new calligraphers may see themselves as painters of language, on closer inspection it is the painting of writing signs (or "writing-like" signs) that is their subject.

Because illegibility is acceptable, calligraphers feel free to emphasize form as much as words. The visual component becomes equal to the verbal component. Calligraphers can use this tension to powerful effect—the viewer slows down when looking at this kind of work. Questions arise during this time—what will the relationship be between the visual and verbal parts? Are some words hidden, and can they be teased out? Are other words ambiguous, forcing the reader to guess at them? The act of contemplation becomes a more active process, and the new masters play with this perceptual period. They hope a viewer's extra time is rewarded with a richer experience. The increased levels of interaction within the work create an increased level of interaction between work and the reader. Interpretation is opened up, and what is lost in denotative specifics is regained in expressive and connotative fullness.

As we become more aware of the new calligraphy, we approach it with a completely different mindset than we might have a generation ago. Our expectations change, as does our relationship with the work. We realize new possibilities for calligraphy and see dozens of fine artists around the world as they push a visual art that is in collusion/collision with language.[5] The new calligraphy reawakens our interest in this more ancient companion art, and we realize that, in an unexpected way, what designers do electronically with typography has become closer to what is happening with pen and ink than at any time since Gutenberg.

[5] See "Calligraphy at the Fault Line," *Letter Art Review*, Winter 1998

Still, the new calligraphy does not invalidate the old. The well crafted, solidly legible letterform is a character mark, built upon a well-honed sense of touch and gesture. If it happens to function in service to the word, it is no less calligraphic for that. In the end, for all its revolutionary upheaval, the new calligraphy does not exclude the old, but encompasses it. It overwhelms old calligraphy's self-image but ultimately confirms its legacy. It throws open the shutters upon fresh vistas, but it does not shut the door on the past. This is one of its great strengths. For even as it shifts the focus away from beautiful letters, the new calligraphy permits the beautiful letterform to remain, unmistakably, calligraphic.

E Pluribus Unum

Paul Elliman

For Gavin Hills

"I'll tell you where I am if you tell me what your lucky number is."
"My lucky number is e."
"That's not a number. That's a letter."
"It is a number. It's a transcendental number: 2.178. . ."
—Iain Banks, *The Wasp Factory*

My brother was born on the day of the 1970 World Cup final. It was a drag at the time because it interrupted my first real World Cup experience, although I've since learned to appreciate his timing. If chance and coincidence seem overrated in situations that are supposedly "creative," they can be useful in more meaningful activities. Gambling, for example. In London last summer, you could get odds of five to one on the World Cup returning to England (although this seemed a bit optimistic to me and may not have been reflected elsewhere in the world). My daughter was born 3/9/93—a small palindrome, and it was another, potential palindrome, formed by lining up the winners since we last won the World Cup in 1966, that convinced me there was some easy money to be made:

> *1966, England*
> *1970, Brazil*
> *1974, Germany*
> *1978, Argentina*
> *1982, Italy*
> *1986, Argentina*
> *1990, Germany*
> *1994, Brazil*
> *1998, England ?*

England ?
It looks good on paper, anyway, and it begins to say something about the way numbers and dates, and signs and symbols, take on extra meaning under certain circumstances. Any "typographical" exchange between us and our world shares its origins with the everyday chance operations of astrology, the National Lottery, or betting shops. It's in these charged forms of reading, however irrational, that you feel a kind of essence—a connection to possibilities. The lost calculations of alchemy, I-Ching and the Kabbalah, all of which involve systems of correspondence between numbers, letters and geometric shapes, live on in all those lucky numbers and discarded betting slips.

The basic premise of the Kabbalah is a belief that the letters came first: before writing or language, even before the creation of the universe—to which the magic of letters is directly attributed. An example of the power of the letter is demonstrated in the famous legend of the golem, a kind of servant formed out of clay, and brought to life by certain rituals of prayer and fasting. Across its forehead is written the word "emet," which means "truth." Each day the golem grows in size and strength until it must be stopped. This can only be done by erasing the first letter **e** from the word, making "met"—"he is dead"—and the golem returns to clay or dust.

If, as some believe, a residue of ancient magic lives on in the alphabet, the **e** adds a certain alchemical luster of its own. In English and French, the alphabet's fifth letter occurs with significantly high frequency. While perhaps not altering our physical shape as it did the golem, its erasure might leave us marked by something equally exotic: a change to our language. French author Georges Perec confronted such a shift when he set out to write his **e**-less novel, *La Disparition*. Perec is remembered mainly for a technical approach that follows Kabbalistic faith in the preeminence of letters. ". . . Each letter is motivated," he once wrote, "the Book is an infinite network traversed by Meaning; the Spirit merges with the Letter; the Secret (Knowledge, Wisdom) is a hidden letter, an unspoken word: the Book is a cryptogram whose code is the Alphabet." For Perec, language represents a combination of spirit and letter, a force that may also reside in individual letters. Particularly those letters which, as vowels, have the ability to breathe life (or its spirit) into the language of writing. If no more magical than all the others, the liveliest single example of our alphabet's interaction with language is the letter **e**.

> Plutarch, in his essay on the letter E at Delphi, tells us that beside the well-known inscriptions at Delphi there was also a representation of the letter E, the fifth letter of the Greek alphabet—F.C. Babbitt, introduction to Plutarch's The E at Delphi, Moralia

According to Robert Graves the letter e was a gift from the goddess Carmenta, but its origins are thought also to be found in the Phoenician letter hé and the Semitic letter kheth. Its earliest beginnings may be an Egyptian pictograph (between 1900 and 1800 B.C.) resembling a figure with raised arms and a large round head, referred to by some historians as "the yelling man." The first alphabet, emerging around 1400 B.C., certainly had no **e**, although perhaps more to the point is that it had no vowels. While the feature distinguishing this alphabet from any of its graphic predecessors is that each of its signs represent a sound, it was still without a certain kind of sound. It lacked the subtle modifications of voiced breath.

A version of our present-day capital **E** was being used by the Phoenicians and other Semites of Syria and Palestine around 1000 B.C. It was back to front and had a short stem or tail, but it is recognizably **e**-like. It was called "hé" (pronounced hey) and served as the consonant *h*. The Greeks started using it after 900 B.C., gradually simplifying its form and reversing its orientation. They also changed the name of the sign to "**e**" and used it for the vowel **e**. Finally it was renamed epsilon (short or simple **e**), to differentiate it from "eta," the long **e**, derived from the Semitic kheth. By introducing "vocals" to the consonants, the Greeks were able to initiate the alphabet's wider potential. The early North Semitic alphabet had consisted of "roots," letters that functioned as a written structure for words only completed when voiced. Now, based on a richer inventory of sounds, the letters formed complete words and the process of reading was made technically easier to learn. Formally the Greek **e** passed unchanged via Etruscan to the Roman alphabet ("eta," the long **e**, was discarded), and the Roman monumental capital became the prototype of our modern capital **E**. The written Roman form developed into the late Roman and medieval uncial and cursive forms, replacing linear with rounded shapes, from which we get our modern lowercase letter **e**.

The fixing of the letter shapes and the beginnings of a universal literacy are achievements of Renaissance scholarship. And the majuscule forms of this time were versions of ancient Roman capitals, often refined in terms of Euclidean geometry. Describing the geometric construction of the alphabet as "the most secret science," sixteenth-century mathematician Luca Pacioli proposed that part of its mystery be interpreted through classical ideals of proportion. In *De Divina Proportione*, published in 1509, Pacioli gives enigmatic instruction on drawing the Roman capitals, including, of course, the fifth character: "The letter **E** is derived from the circle and the square. The widest arm is one ninth of the height of the square. The upper arm is half of the widest as is the lower arm. The center arm is one third the width of the widest as the center arm of the *A* and the above mentioned letter is as wide as half of the square and so it will be very perfect."

In more recent times, Edward Johnston, who developed an early and influential sans serif along classical proportions, advised simply that "**E**'s three arms are approximately equal in length in the best early forms," and that "the bar of the **E** (for optical reasons) must be slightly above the true middle line." But in some ways the shape of our modern capital E seems undesigned, a substantial form requiring little adjustment. In the words of Victor Hugo: "**E** is the foundation, the pillar and the roof—all architecture contained in a single letter." And the architect Steven Holl observes that the **E** is one of the typological forms common to the gridiron planning of American cities. "An individual building is to the continuous space of a city as a letter is to a sentence or a word," says Holl, ". . . and in the alphabetical city certain letter-like buildings recurred." He refers to **E**-shaped buildings in Seattle, Pittsburgh, Detroit, New York, and San Francisco, where the building type falls into two categories: ". . . one with courts turned away from the street, the other with courts opening to the street."

While unlikely to reinvent the alphabet's skeletal form, a critical aspect of modern typography also operates in the detail of writing's less-visual connections with the world. For the typographer this might involve following certain narrative paths, or, in the context of everyday use, responding to the way letters function as a component in the mechanics of language. Like Steven Holl's "alphabetical city," the shapes fit in ways that make them seem inevitable, and they go unnoticed. But even in the meter of ordinary conversation—a situation that might not usually be thought of as typographical—we feel the influence of specific letters. An array of impressive **e**'s appears in "Stress Words" by the word-collecting poet Charlotte Mew (from her self published book *The Distance, the Pleasure*), with its allusion to pocket phrase-books: "Employee, refugee, trainee, examinee | Engineer, pioneer, volunteer, mountaineer | Cashier, cigarette, maisonette, launderette."

After all, to speak a language is to get the sound right—although if the Roman alphabet had adopted both of the Greek **e** variants, things might have been a little easier. Certainly in the English use, there are far more vowel sounds than signs, and **e** is the busiest. The *Oxford English Dictionary* suggests about 15 different pronunciations. Gore Vidal once expressed unease with a letter that can sound like other letters: "Nothing wrong with our beautiful vast complex unknowable (by one person) language, which so significantly begins with an **E**. The fact that it should be I only adds duplicitous luster to the vowel letter, so very like a comb, unsnarling hyacinthine locks, taming Medusan curls—**E**—a cry!"

The dictionary, a kind of Platonic dialogue about language, generally begins its fifth chapter with a character profile of the letter **e**: "The second vowel and fifth letter of the English alphabet." And from a 1918 edition of Funk & Wagnell's *New Standard* that begins: "Fifth and the most frequently used. . . its modern English name is the first syllable of even." The various uses are outlined:

> *1. Open short as in met, half long as in bend; 2. Close long (with the help of "i" or "y") as in veil or they; somewhat more open in their; 3. High close as in he, equal and (with the help of silent "e") in mete; 4. As in over, moment, very weak in sudden, battle; 5. as in report.*

Finally it enters into a number of digraphs, which for the most part now denote simple sounds: as in "beat," "beet," "either," "believe," "people," "feud," "chew." And, as if this wasn't enough, a further characteristic: "An unfortunate peculiarity of English is its very frequent use of 'silent e' to denote the length or quality of a preceding vowel ('fat' and 'fate,' 'sit' and 'site,' 'cut' and 'cute'). This usage does not go back to Anglo-Saxon times but took root in Middle English under French influence." These lexicographers don't seem too impressed, but the silences of the **e**, when affecting the sounds of other vowels, cause it be referred to as the "magic **e**."

The letter **e** seems capable of conjuring itself beyond any dictionary, but even there its symbolic uses are as numerous as its orthographic permutations. **E** is for "Earth" and compass point "east," "electron" and "engineer," "English" and "European," as well as appearing at the front of other initials and acronyms (ESP, EST, ET, etc. . .). **E** can be for "excellent," although it can also be an academic grade for work that is unacceptable. As a numeral **E** represents 250. In the calendar it is the fifth of the dominical letters, and in general **E** is the fifth in order or in a series. In music it is the fifth tone in the scale of A minor, but also the third tone in the scale of C major. Recently, in certain multi-user cybernetic environments, **e** is a gender neutral pronoun, suggesting that your character is neither male or female. In dynamics **e** is the sign for elasticity, in chemistry **E** represents the element Erbium, in math **e** is used to quantify the eccentricity of a conical curve, and is also the base of a Napiers system of natural logarithms, a transcendental number having a value to eight decimal places of 2.17828183. . . In Einstein's theory of relativity, mass times the speed of light squared equals **e** for "energy."

In London (I live in the postal district E2) most supermarket products carry a large lowercase **e**, indicating the European Community standard weight (although most people think it means "estimated weight"), and food additives are represented by the infamous E-numbers, similarly named in that each additive is approved by the European Scientific Committee for Food. Where would the European diet be without quantities of E133 (Brilliant Blue), E251 (Sodium nitrate) or a little E523 (Aluminum ammonium sulfate)? Let's hope no one assumes them to be supplementary forms of vitamin E. And while I might not drive home from the supermarket in an E-type Jag, a "capital" **E** also appears on the back of London's taxis as the registration prefix for five-seater cabs. But certain signs carry more weight than others, and being the kind of world this is, signs for money carry the most. So it seems appropriate that, as I write this, a new **e** symbol is emerging. The euro glyph, sign for a new European currency.

Common forms, such as spoons, or coins, or the individual letters of our alphabet become nodal points, able to reflect the social operations by which they exist. Letters, for example, are also units of meaning with readers of their own—from Kabbalists and cryptographers to typographers, historians and scientists, as well as in the more casual reading experiences of daily life. In reading a single letter, through its historical development and its present social uses, its emergence as a sign for money seems particularly resonant. The written word and money share a closely connected history, from ancient forms of social exchange to contemporary notions of writing. In the international language of money—financial capitalism—the sign has clearly become the thing being represented. The euro seemed to exemplify this shift by being introduced as a currency for electronic transactions only. The sign looks like an **E**—for Europe—with two parallel lines cutting through it horizontally. Its form is clearly inspired by the Greek letter epsilon, an ambitious reference to the cradle of European civilization. As a kind of timeless and immaterial cipher, expressing a mythical democracy, the euro glyph is perfect—a gift from the gods.

> *In the current issue of the New Yorker, there is a short story by the novelist E. Annie Proulx—only it isn't. On the cover, in the list of contents and over the piece itself the writer's name is changed. She is now Annie Proulx. She had nothing to lose but her E and now, free as air, she's done it.*
> —A.N. Wilson, *The Observer*, June 21, 1998

The letter **E** covers a linguistic spectrum from vocal sounds to phonemes and morphemes in the grammar of language, to signs that refer to something and syntactical structure that just is something. One dictionary I checked declared it to be "something shaped like the letter E." Which may be as much as we need to know. Like all the other letters, the **E** slips through a range of meanings, which, at least in the form of ideas, have more to do with interpretation: the discovery of things that may not really be there. Myths are an extension of this, where the ordinary is made to seem exotic or extreme. The euro glyph, for example.

The Greeks knew this, of course. A classical text dealing with interpretation, and which may be one of the first examples of writing about writing, is an earlier investigation of the letter **E**. "De E Apud Delphos" ("The E at Delphi"), written by the Greek biographer and philosopher Plutarch, appears in volume five of *Moralia*. In attempting to explain the appearance of an **E** on the Oracle at Delphi —interpreted as a message from Apollo—Plutarch begins by discussing the use of the letter as the Greek word for "if," and that it can also mean "thou art." He then goes on to consider further significance through Pythagorean number symbolism: **E** denotes the number 5, "a most important number in mathematics, philosophy, and music. . . ."

Plutarch doesn't really claim to solve the mystery of the Delphic **E**; ". . . the likelihood is that it was not by chance that this was the only letter that came to occupy first place with the god and attained the rank of sacred offering and something worth seeing. . . ." In the sixteenth century, extra **e**'s mysteriously turn up again as a characteristic of "olde" spelling. Bibliographic scholar Randall McLeod has shown how, in Shakespeare's day, **e**'s might be inserted between characters whose descenders tended to cross each other. As he says: long *s* "cannot be set after *k* without causing the kern to foul. . . Is **e** part of the spelling? Part of the pronunciation? Is it not perfectly plausible that the **e** is merely a weak vowel whose body is being used by the typesetter who may care nothing for her intelligence?" A common trick used in sixteenth- and seventeenth-century typesetting—where a somewhat wild orthography prevailed—was to insert additional **e**'s, usually at the end of a word, in order to extend a line of type that may be clashing with an adjacent line. An important aspect of Shakespeare's work is that it begins to represent a fixed moment in the shifting landscapes ("quickesands") of the English language. In fact, even the modern spelling of his own name may be a result of the license given the type compositors of his time.

It isn't difficult to find authors who acknowledge McLeod's "typographically exigent" **e**. Walt Whitman once praised "the great 'e' box" of the letter-press compartments in the office of the Long Island Patriot, where he apprenticed as a printer. And the cryptographer in Edgar Allen Poe's story "The Gold Bug" explains the importance of our alphabet's fifth letter: "in English, the letter which most frequently occurs is e. Afterwards the succession runs thus: a o i d h n r s t u y c f g l m w b k p q x z. **E** however, predominates so remarkably that an individual sentence of any length is rarely seen in which it is not the prevailing character."

The most prodigious comment on the letter **e**'s importance (or lack of) to writing, is a book written entirely without it. Its author, Georges Perec, seems to share many of the typographer's concerns. His texts often emerged out of an obsession with the letters: "their presence, their absence, their repetition, their order of occurrence in words, or even their form," as a colleague of his once said. Even his novels caused one critic to deny that he was a "writer," that he merely forced "patterns out of alphabetical signs." Perec persisted in exploring the basic code of writing, through palindromes, acrostics, anagrams, and other forms of alphabet poetry. His experimental range includes an "attempted" inventory of everything he ate and drank during 1974, an operatic libretto using tonic sol-fa syllables (do re mi fa sol la ti) to generate words and melody simultaneously, and the world's longest palindrome—more than five thousand characters. Perhaps his most famous work is the "lipogrammatic" novel *La Disparition*, published in 1969. Its three hundred pages contain no **e**'s.

The word "lipogram" has its Greek origin in lipo or leipo—"to miss," and describes a literary device in which texts are constructed around the omission of one or more letters of the alphabet. In French, as well as English, the letter **e** presents the biggest challenge. According to his biographer David Bellos, Perec prepared by involving his friends in language games that required the **e** to be absent; whether ordering food in a restaurant, or simply rephrasing conversational sentences. He also produced a scholarly *History of the Lipogram*, in which he distinguished the absence of vowels as the lipogram's "vocalic tradition," and offers examples of the form found in Greek literature as early as the sixth century B.C. Unable to resist doing something with his liberated letters, Perec also wrote a short story—"Les Revenentes" ("The Ghosts"), that contained no other vowels but the **e**.

A significant context to Georges Perec's work is his close involvement with the group of writers known as Oulipo (Ouvroir de Littérature Potentielle): the "workshop" for potential literature, founded in Paris in 1960 by mathematician François Le Lionnais and writer Raymond Queneau. The Oulipo set out to explore the exchanges between language and writing by testing the formal structures of text—using mathematical procedures, algorithms and bi-squares, and reviving the fixed forms used in sonnets and haiku. These structures would be cast like a net, as a potential work that was intended to trap any secrets concealed beneath the surface. Secrets which in Oulipian terms might be thought of as the hidden resources of a language.

La Disparition (impressively translated into English as "A Void," by Gilbert Adair) begins with scenes of urban chaos: "25 Molotov cocktails go off around town. Pilots bomb Orly airport. Paris's most familiar landmarks burn down, and its inhabitants look on in horror at a blazing Alhambra, an Institute that is nothing but a sad smoking ruin, a Saint-Louis Hospital with all its windows alight and gaily flaming away. From Montsouris to Nation not a wall is intact." Apart from being written in 1968, the turmoil of this breathless world is also the outcome of a wounded alphabet. And the **e**, which usually marks the surface of a text like bubbles of air, is missing in action—although any drama to its absence is restricted to the narrative. As Perec pointed out, "A lipogram that did not advertise itself as such would have every chance of being overlooked."

And, to the delight of the Oulipo, the review of *La Disparition* that appeared in *Les Nouvelles Littéraires* during the summer of 1969 seemed not to have noticed. The book is dismissed as "raw, violent and facile fiction. . . A man disappears. . . Another man disappears. . . and—you must have guessed this—Georges Perec is too crafty to supply any conclusions. . . The mystery remains entire, but the novel is finished; that is the contemporary form of literary detective fiction. . .". The reviewer apparently missed a small detail (or rather he failed to). By the logic of the Oulipo: "a text written according to a constraint describes the constraint," and so *La Disparition* is also the story of the **e**'s disappearance. Characters vanish when confronted by situations that are literally unspeakable, and Perec's "missing link," the absence of a sign, leaves the impression of a blank region between writing and language (or between language and anything else).

Perec's Oulipian faith in the otherwise Kabbalistic evaluation of an alphabet's secret role, resounded in the lipogram. "The book is a cryptogram whose code is the alphabet," as he said, suggesting that one of its secrets might be contained in a hidden or missing letter. And the title of the work, *La Disparition* ("the disappearance") points to a more poignant reason for this **e**-less story. The document issued by the French government for persons missing or presumed dead during Nazi-occupied France bears the heading "Acte de Disparition." Perec's parents were among those lost. In French, **e** is pronounced "eu," very close in sound to "eux" (them); they have disappeared. The **e** is gone.

> *How are new words created? What's the logic behind neologisms? Turn to the fifth letter of the Roman alphabet for the combining form now most in vogue. . . E-speak.*
> —William Safire, *New York Times Magazine,* November 8, 1998

Like viruses and ghosts, our language lives amongst us, and the letters become avatars through which it continually reshapes. Here, along with the other twenty-five members of its hoodlum gang, the e returns, as if it were arriving on a continuous pulse, transmitted all the way from the Oracle at Delphi. Perec is right to say that each letter is "motivated," and not necessarily along a mystical path (although infinitely mysterious). They react, like cells or atoms, within the closed system of the alphabet—but also through a connection to the living cells of us, their writers and readers, and therefore to human realities of absence and loss.

A later work by Perec carries the simple dedication "for E." This is a book called *W* or the *Memory of Childhood*, more directly autobiographical, through which Perec confronts his tragic connection to the Holocaust. "I possess other pieces of information about my parents; I know they will not help me to say what I would like to say about them. . . I do not know if what I might have to say is unsaid because it is unsayable (the unsayable is not buried inside writing; it is what prompted it in the first place). . . I write because they left in me their indelible mark, whose trace is writing."

As demonstrated by the Oulipo, notions of absence, or recurrence, or the indefinite, can be explored in language along figurative ground similar to that broken by mathematical investigation. Jacques Roubaud, a colleague of Perec's, used the epsilon—a rounded **e** symbol—for the title of one of his collections of poetry. And the epsilon is important to set theory, as developed by mathematician Georg Cantor, where it is the sign for "belonging to a set." Cantor explored the mathematical conditions for infinity through the idea of transfinite numbers. These are also referred to as irrational or transcendental numbers, by which **e** makes one of its extra-alphabetical connections—as the "lucky" number 2.178. . . .

Perhaps the **e**, with its great range of sounds and silences—typographically assisted, in French, by various diacritical marks: accent grave, accent aigu, or accent circonflexe—has some of the transcendental qualities found in Cantor's set theory. To write, either with or without it, seems, after all, to acknowledge a linguistic value for the useless, the ambiguous and the improvised. As a Latin prefix, with the same value as "ex," it signifies out of, out, or proceeding from; for example, "emit" (from the Latin emittere, to send forth), or "evict" (from evictus, to conquer, to turn away). And its earliest alphabetical entry, as the Phoenician "sign for a breathing," possibly named for "a window," is an indication of its textual link to a living world. Whereas an alphabet might speak of closed systems—a set number of characters with fixed order and shape—its own letters seem to resist closure, encouraging us to do the same. Rimbaud, in his poem "Voyelles," says as much as anyone about the space our language occupies between precision and indeterminacy. Investing the vowels with colors, **e** is white with "the brilliance of vapors." With a taste for the infinite, the letter **e** is one of those "irrational" letters through which we experience the ordinary magic of language.

The codes by which signs are produced and used continue to evolve and change, less through direct human agency than through the socially and historically accumulated force of signs themselves. This is a theme in the work of Raymond Williams, addressed most directly in his book *Keywords*—which involves a collection of significant words, around which new meanings are shown to have emerged or attached themselves. The **e**'s in his alphabetically ordered words are distinctly organic: "ecology," "educated," "empirical," "ethnic," "evolution," "experience. . ." In ways that also mark the logic of Williams' project, several "new" words have recently drifted into our social vocabulary on the back of the letter **e**.

The most common recent e-words involve **e** as a prefix for electronic—for almost anything. A web site called mySAP.com claims to be the first city on the internet: "the City of e. . . a never-before place where more than 10,000 companies and millions of people are seamlessly connected." Its e-citizens presumably e-speak in seamless electronic neologism. e-chiao? "W hav this gr at n w s lling t chniqu "is how IBM launched their online

E Pluribus Unum

service, "e-business" (cheating a bit with the lipogram): "It's time to add {e} to your busin ss." At least if **e**, in an abecadarian sense, is electrical, then our alphabet begins to suggest another great writing system. The table of chemical elements was opened up brilliantly by Primo Levi, in his book *The Periodic Table*, as a poetry in itself: ". . . the missing link, between the world of words and the world of things . . .".

The simplest e-word of all is **e** for "ecstasy." It's really called methyline dioxymethamphetamine, but it may not have achieved its status if that was how—along with two pints of lager and a packet of crisps—you had to ask for it. "MDMA" seems a reasonable name, but somehow, in this age of product identification, it was always destined to be called "**e**"; apparently it was known as "empathy" before being named, probably by a dealer, the more vital sounding "ecstasy," and becoming commonly referred to as "**e**."

A final, darker e-word is "E. coli," one of those odd-sounding medical words that seem threatening, coded and technical but, of course, stand for one of our own little human pieces. The E. coli is one of many bacteria that are with us from the moment we are born. "E. coli" is the abbreviated name of the bacterium in the family enterobacteriaceae named escherichia (genus) coli (species). "E. coli O157:H7" is the dangerous strain, its genetic information having been altered by a bacterial virus DNA. Which suggests how we might finally be taken apart "typographically," just like that poetically engineered giant, the golem, destroyed, as Hebrew scholar Gerschom Scholem puts it: ". . . by the reversal of the magical combination of letters through which he was called into life."

End

P.S. I didn't make any money on my brother's birthday last summer, but an e-mail going round after the World Cup suggested a mysterious conspiracy preventing England from winning the competition:

```
>>
>>hey, i thought you might find some humor in this....
>>(Conclusive evidence that England were cheated out of
a place!)
>>
>>------------------------------------------------------------
>>-
>>Date: Thu, 16 Jul 1998 15:56:38 -0400
>>To:
>>From:
>>Subject: FW: WHY ENGLAND DIDN'T WIN THE WORLD CUP
```

```
>>Mime-Version: 1.0
>>Sender:
>>Precedence: bulk
>>
>>is there a conspiracy??
>>>
>>>
>>> The Quarter-Finalists for the 1998 World Cup:
>>>
>>>
>>> A rgentina
>>>
>>>
>>> B razil
>>>
>>>
>>> C roatia
>>>
>>>
>>> D enmark
>>>
>>>
>>>
>>>
>>>
>>> F rance
>>>
>>>
>>> G ermany
>>>
>>>
>>> H olland
>>>
>>>
>>> I taly
>>>
>>>
```

There is no language common to different languages. There is no silence common to different languages.
—Pascal Quignard, "L'e," from *Petit traites I*

On the Democratization of Typography

Gunnar Swanson

> *The clerk snapped at Degarmo's back like a terrier.*
> *"One moment, please. Whom did you wish to see?"*
> *Degarmo spun on his heel and looked at me wonderingly. "Did he say 'whom'?"*
> *"Yeah, but don't hit him," I said. "There is such a word."*
> *Degarmo licked his lips. "I knew there was," he said. "I often wondered where they kept it."*
> —Raymond Chandler, *Lady in the Lake*

The English language has changed over the last few hundred years. It used to be highly inflected (with nouns changing depending on what part they played in a sentence) like German, Latin, or its closer relative, Old Icelandic. The remaining inflections (such as "who"/"whom") seem to be passing rapidly. Our less-inflected language isn't as good for writing Skaldic poetry as Old Icelandic, but it's more convenient for other kinds of communication. We don't think of it as debased; it's just different.

The problem with rules of language use is defining right and wrong during a transition. Usage that may be proper in the future is considered wrong today. The common pattern is that a usage is dead wrong, then an irritatingly common mistake, then common usage that indicates how everything is going to hell in a hand basket, then normal, then absolutely right. A similar situation applies to the visual presentation of language. Spelling, punctuation, and the aesthetics of reading have, like spoken language, changed due to the communication needs of language users.

It would be easy enough to write about the ill effects of the "democratization" of type. There is no doubt that we have seen the standards of typography eroded by nontypographers' use of computers and, before that, rub-on type. In the long run, we will not think of this as debasement; it will just be different.

Language changes because it is used by people. People are imperfect. They make mistakes. Sometimes they find out that the mistake didn't matter. Sometimes they never know they made a mistake. Sometimes they learn from people who make mistakes. People also have different communication needs. What works in an academic journal fails in a basketball game or a singles' bar. People (philosophy professors, street-gang members, or graphic designers) adapt language to their particular needs. Typographic usage has, until recent years, been relatively conservative. Type was, after all, created and used by a much narrower range of people than was spoken language. That range is widening; one can only expect change in usage to accelerate.

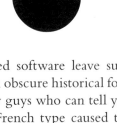

What will be the result of that change? Like other language shifts, some of it will be good, some bad, and, in the long run, it will all be just different. Will common usage make tick marks replace "real" quotation marks, or will more sophisticated software leave such typewriter traditions as an obscure historical footnote only remembered by guys who can tell you exactly when imported French type caused the thorn to be replaced by a *Y* in English typography? Will a range of tones similar to speech replace the relatively flat look of set type? Will the interrobang have its day? Will those obnoxious little happy faces that appear in e-mail to aid the humor-impaired show up in books and journals? Whomever this last idea disgusts—and I'm one of them—may have to get used to it.

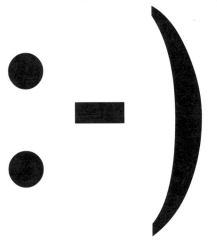

"*Did he use an em dash?*"
"*Don't hit him--there is such a punctuation mark.*" ;-)
"*I knew there was. I often wondered where they kept it.*" :-(

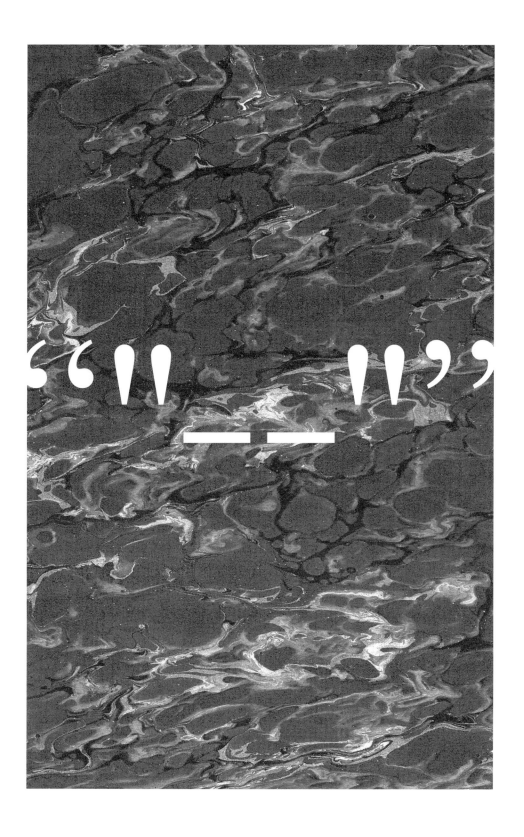

165

The Written Word:

The Designer as Mediator

William Drenttel

With all the discussion about literacy in America, the truth is that much of our country is losing its taste—perhaps even its appetite—for the written word. The issue is not what you read so much as whether you read; if the illiterate can't read, the literate increasingly don't read. If the illiterate don't know where Burma is, many of the literate don't know that Burma is now called Myanmar. In either case, the new atlases read like Latin to most of us; who, after all, can remember the new countries that comprise the Commonwealth of Independent States (the former USSR without Georgia and the Baltics) or the various nations that make up the former Ottoman Empire? In this context, it is no surprise that few understand the historical complexity of the crisis in Bosnia or that public discourse on economic matters is at best shallow.

If our reliance on the written word seems to be at an all-time low, there are many contributing factors: the influence of television, the rise of the sound byte and the corresponding loss of in-depth news coverage, the expansion and complexity of new forms of media, the decline in educational substance and quality, the prolifera-tion of languages in a multicultural society, and our growing propensity to engage in other forms of leisure activity. Of greatest concern is the facile way in which these excuses are invoked to explain away the issue. Sadly, the very acceptance of these rationales has become a self-fulfilling prophecy.

This state of the written word has a profound effect on graphic designers. The fodder of graphic design is, after all, words and pictures. Yet how many times have you heard, "Well, people just don't read anymore" offered as a rationale for de-emphasizing the role or amount of writing (copy, text, language) in a design project? Some designers seem to acquiesce to the logic of this statement. Other designers view this as one of the principal challenges of being a designer today. Still others seem more cynical, taking this situation as license to render words fundamentally illegible, engaging in dense and self-referential work under the guise of faux avant-garde typography. (Here, I am not making a conservative argument against design research or experimentation: I am questioning textual presentations that are merely stylistic.)

In commerce, these changes are equally extreme, affecting the nature and form of business communication. How do designers willingly produce promotional materials for their clients, yet trash most of what they themselves receive? When was the last time you saw someone actually read CD liner notes or an employee handbook? When magazine editors or publishers say they want their magazines to be easier to read, more scannable, they should be taken literally: They are praying that readers actually do scan it.

Many people, of course, still do read, especially books, magazines, and newspapers. I believe the reason is simple, and that hidden within this reason is a way for graphic designers to approach this issue. These books and publications were meant to be read. They were written, designed, and published to be sold, taken home, and read. Often, the better they're written, the more they're read. If some of them become decoration on the coffee table, that's okay, too. A book has a way of taking on a life of its own: Someone else picks it up off the coffee table, and a new reader is found. (It is this glow of an afterlife that makes a good bookstore interesting and a large urban magazine shop exciting.) While we perceive them on one level as objects of commerce, they are also objects of desire.

The crux of this equation is their good intent: that they were meant to be read. Some literary critics have suggested that there is an implicit contract between the writer and reader—that despite the image of the solitary artist, there is always a reader in the mind of the writer. Designers seem to have an image of "viewers" in mind, even as they design the text in printed materials. The catch is that the idea of "viewers" has become a generic category, a composite consumer in a media audience. The same can be said of "the public," perhaps even of "readers." As the novelist Paul Auster recently observed, "I don't think of 'the public.' 'The public' doesn't exist, because books are not a communal experience. They're a private experience. Every book is read by one person. No matter how many people read it totally, it's always one person reading the book. So I don't think of the physical mass of the reading public." Designers, too, would do well to imagine a single reader and design things that are intended to be read. It is here that something like a contract can begin to take shape, and where the designer assumes responsibility for mediating between text and reader.

Instead, graphic designers too often define their task as having something to do with "communication," another term more generic than specific. If one designs something and never really expects it to be read, then what kind of communication is being created? Why does so much award-winning design include language that was never meant to be read? These are trends—and traps—for contemporary graphic design. The overuse (and misuse) of the word "communication" is often used as a camouflage for delivering sales messages without an idea on the page. Look through a design annual and try to read the words: Most of the time it seems all surface, all facade. It is as if designers have grown fearful of language and are, like some audiences, only capable of thinking in visual (pictorial) terms. As one designer told me, "We may argue endlessly over the copy, but when it's done the comment is always just that it 'looks good.'" If editors sometimes play the role of the visually illiterate, then there is something out there like the "dumb designer" syndrome, the desire to hide behind the right side of the brain. This, in some cases, flows directly from the typically inferior positions designers have historically held to counterparts such as magazine editors and advertising copywriters.

In the business world, writing incorporated by designers in corporate communications projects is seldom well written, much less communicative. The usual recipes include idyllic fluff (flowery metaphors that say nothing), bullet points (snippets of services, features, and capabilities that would numb any reader), or strategic hard sell (barely rewording client strategies and pretending this is the way people speak).

Yet, designers frequently control the editorial content of their projects. They become, in effect, the editor, determining the "story," hiring the writer, assigning the artwork. It is sometimes instructive to define a project in these terms, to think of the strategy as that which requires a story. For a good editor, the story is the key, with writing and visualization both equally important. Designers, on the other hand, often consider photographers and illustrators to be more important than writers. When designers describe their favorite writers, the compliment used most often is "professional"; i.e., the manuscript is delivered on time, ideally on a disk, and the writer has a flexible attitude about changes necessary to fit the design. This is writing on demand, filler that fits.

For most of us, there is much to learn from the editorial world. Respect for editors leads to an understanding of what makes a good story, a tightly written argument, and a concise headline. Like designers, writers thrive with a good brief and a lot of freedom. Designers who work frequently with writers are also more comfortable with longer texts and more difficult, complicated arguments. Some designers find that occasionally trying their own hand at writing is a way to get closer to words; it also helps to integrate writing and design into one process. These are among many such efforts that can be made by designers to elevate the role of writing in design projects and to grow more accustomed to working with writers and with writing itself.

In the end, writing that gets read must be intended to be read. If one imagines a contract between client and audience, then perhaps there is also an implicit contractual obligation for the designer to mediate between text and reader. This is perhaps where we can begin to speak about the responsibility of designers to take seriously the role of the written word. It is here that communication starts to happen, when a reader knows that you mean it.

The Myth of Conten

Encyclopedestrianization

nd the

of Communication

James Souttar

Ideas make a strange progress through history If graphic design were a more reflective profession, we might better appreciate some of the twists and ironies of this progress. But for the most part it goes unnoticed. Nowhere is this more evident than with the advent of new technologies and new media.

Such is the uncritical hyperbole about the Internet, for instance, that one might be forgiven for thinking that it represents a wholly new approach to communication. We're presented with the dizzy vista of a "wild frontier" where pioneers —provided they've freed themselves from the burdensome legacies of outmoded thinking—can create a new world, with novel forms of commerce, entertainment, even education. It's an exciting prospect. If only it were true.

The more one looks into the ideas fueling the explosion of the Internet, one realizes that, far from being a new paradigm, it represents some very old thinking indeed. Its energy is less that of a vigorous new idea than that of an embattled philosophy that has rallied itself and made one last desperate push for victory. And I make no apologies for that simile. For reasons I intend to elucidate, it's the same seventeenth-century philosophy of modernism, which has been behind most of the dominant ideologies of the last three hundred years, that is staging its last ferocious counterattack on the battlefield of digital media.

We have, I suppose, become used to the idea that we're living in the "post-Modern" era—and to some extent this may be the case. This makes it both hard to accept, and to understand, that what seems to be the biggest idea of our time is wholly "modern" (here actually meaning quite ancient) in its conception. But so it

The Myth of Content

171

is. To really grasp this, however, requires us to understand where modernism came from—and what it is. And to do this we need to divest ourselves of the view that modernism is just a stylistic movement of the mid-twentieth century.

In an extraordinarily erudite work, *Cosmopolis,* philosopher of science Stephen Toulmin traces the origins of modernism to the middle of the seventeenth century. We need to return briefly to that time to fully appreciate the context out of which this extraordinarily influential view of the world emerged. Toulmin explains how, following the assassination in 1610 of the tolerant King Henri IV of France, Europe began a forty-year-long descent into religious bigotry and conflict of the most brutal kind. Against this backdrop, a group of highly influential thinkers—led by Descartes—sought to establish a philosophy that would once and for all resolve the questions that had been the subject of such violent contention. But in the process, Toulmin shows how they turned their backs on the humanistic tradition—characterized by a recognition that "circumstances alter cases," and the belief that the validity of any kind of knowledge depends upon the context in which it is applied. The new knowledge required certainties that were universal and timeless—which in practice meant abstracted and decontextualized from the messy ambiguities of the world.

I'll return to Toulmin's distinctions between modernism and humanism, since they have an uncanny echo in the (almost invisible) philosophies driving the Internet. But for the moment, I'd like to follow through with Toulmin's history of modernism.

After Descartes came Newton and Locke, who both managed to define many of the principal characteristics of the "modern" point of view—Newton with his mathematical approach to science, which showed how natural phenomena could be understood (and more importantly, manipulated) by representing them through abstract numerical relations; and Locke, who asserted that the "qualities" of things were secondary, subjective aspects, and that only their quantitative aspect was real. These points of view defined, of course, what later became known as the "scientific method"—but they had equally important ramifications for beliefs about culture and society. Newton's universe was set in motion by the Creator and ran to clockwork precision, which meant that not only the motions of the planets, but also the social orders, existed by divine decree. A century later, Adam Smith used a similar model to describe how the "invisible

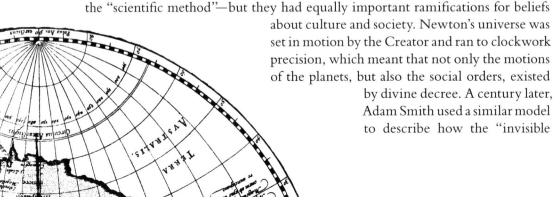

hand" of the market determined economic affairs—a view that remains remarkably persuasive to this day.

Yet within a hundred years of Newton's death, "modernism" had begun to unravel—a process that continues well into our times. Thinkers such as Herder and Goethe were beginning to ask questions about whether "science" could really be seen as independent of the social and historical context in which it took place (questions that would take two centuries to incubate before exploding into public consciousness with Thomas Kuhn's 1962 *The Structure of Scientific Revolutions*). Elsewhere, new disciplines began to spring up—such as psychology and anthropology —that recognized the impossibility of a "value free" interpretation of their chosen areas of interest.

So from about 1750 to about 1910, modernism was in a slow decline. But like many declining ideologies, it became stronger in its fundamentalist heartlands —such as technology, economics, and politics. Even so, Toulmin suggests that by the end of the first decade of the twentieth century there was a real possibility that it might be overcome. From the 1890s onward the "new physics" of Einstein, Planck, and Thomson—with its concepts of relativity and uncertainty—challenged the very basis of a mechanical universe. Freud's theories were opening up the possibility of a distinctly contextual exploration of the human psyche. And Darwinism was focusing scientific attention on the question of origins. But in 1914 another assassination plunged the world back into conflagration and genocide— reinstating the search for certainty to the top of the agenda. For most of the first half of the twentieth century, ideological conflict, economic depression, and the breakdown of a world order mirrored the conditions of the seventeenth century that had given birth to modernity. And, predictably, these conditions produced a resurgence of modernism—from the sterile, rationalist philosophy of Russell, (the young) Wittgenstein, and the Vienna Circle to the sterile, rationalist design of the Bauhaus.

The social revolution that might have happened in the first quarter of the twentieth century ended up being postponed until the 1960s, when a buoyant economy and the military deadlock of the Cold War could once again produce conditions in which it was possible to challenge the ideological behemoth. Kuhn's book coincided with numerous other seminal texts pouring from the presses of Europe and America, which presented a largely bemused citizenry with the beginnings of a critique of modernism. This is not to say that they were in any sense really "post-Modern," since they still represented a point of view that had been profoundly, and unconsciously, informed by the bases of modernism. And, in fact, it would be their avid readers, the generation of sixties "counterculturals," who —in their subsequent incarnation as nineties "digerati"— would unwittingly deliver the apotheosis of modernism in the guise of the "Information Revolution."

The Myth of Content

But to come back, briefly, to design. One might reasonably want to distinguish between the way I've used "modernism"—following Toulmin—and the way it has been used to designate a dominant design movement of the twentieth century. It's interesting, in this respect, to hear what Toulmin has to say about the influence of modernism in its "global" aspect on the more narrowly focused principles of the Modern movement:

In Mies' principles, we see the man who dominated architectural design in Europe and North America right up to the 1950s rejecting the diversity of history and geography, and the specific needs of particular activities, in favour of universal, timeless principles. This is the step that Descartes and the 17th-century rationalists took, when they ignored the varied practices and the ambiguous, uncertain opinions that were endemic to 16th-century humanism, in favour of pursuing theories and proofs that could command consensus. Between the two World Wars, other fine arts went the same way, wiping the slate clean and making a fresh start, as witness the paintings of Josef Albers; and, in due course, the renewed theme of a "clean slate" became a central theme of culture entre deux guerres. To that extent, the movement we now know as "modernism" in the arts echoed the founding themes of 17th-century Modernity as surely as did the philosophical program for a formally structured unified science: so understood, the "modernism" of architecture and fine arts in the 1920s shared more with the "modernity" of rationalist philosophy and physics than we might otherwise suppose.[1]

[1] Stephen Toulmin, *Cosmopolis: The Hidden Agenda of Modernity* (Chicago: The University of Chicago Press, 1992) 156

Two striking points emerge from Toulmin's analysis. First, that stylistic modernism closely echoed the beliefs and priorities of philosophical modernism without necessarily being aware of its intellectual debt. This is an observation that is particularly relevant in consideration of new media, since the ideologies that are driving it are not always apparent, even to its most vocal exponents. Second, the idea of "starting from zero" is by no means a new development—even if the way that it is framed in relationship to the brave new world of the Internet is particularly ingenious. Modernism has been "starting from zero" ever since Descartes climbed inside his oven, but never more self-consciously than in the series of early- and mid-twentieth-century experiments in design.

At this point, I'd like to move from the historical background to an examination of the principles that are driving the form and function of electronic communications. Having followed the Web from its humble beginnings as a document management system for—significantly—a scientific research institution, I've been interested to note how quickly a consensus has been reached on what makes for effective communication in this medium. In less than a decade a pattern has crystallized with uncanny rapidity. This would be truly remarkable if what we were dealing with was an authentically new paradigm; but, in fact, many of the features of this emergent consensus show a recognizable provenance, traceable to the very roots of modernism.

Arguably, the most extraordinary of these development is the idea of "content." "Content" is such a specious concept that it is surprising that it has attracted so little critical attention. However, since the idea of content embodies the whole philosophical basis of modernism as "new media"—in all its seductiveness and flakiness.

In the simplest terms, the idea of content is that the information component of a message can be distinguished from the form in which it appears and manipulated quite apart from it. With all previous media, "content" and "form" could not be conceptually separated in this way—one had to commit to form as part of the very act of authoring. To write, or type, a message, one had to put one's thoughts directly into permanent marks. Likewise, even to speak on the phone involved the creation of electronic signals that could neither be withdrawn nor easily converted into any other form of communication. "Repurposing," where it was possible, involved laboriously transcribing words and images from one medium to another.

But computer technologies appear deceptively different—authors capture key and mouse strokes, which can then be "flowed" with apparent impunity into different layouts and styles (even converted into synthesized voice). Content, therefore, becomes a way of conceiving of the abstract essence of a communication—the part that is "pure information"—as something quite distinct from form. Seeing it in this way, so its adherents believe, promises to liberate us from the "tyranny" of formal presentation. Form, in this view, is a morass for information—a clinging, dead quagmire from which the vital content cannot easily be retrieved—and not the creative embodiment of an idea, the "word made flesh."

Taken further, the persuasive myth of content promises to decouple the "from" and "to" components of communication. It allows information to be collated from any source and presented to any audience—without the need for dialogue between the two. One major consequence of this for graphic design is that designers can now be required to create layouts into which as yet unspecified content is to be arbitrarily imported—as already happens with some Web pages, which use information retrieved "on demand" from databases.

I urge you to pause and think about this for a moment. Imagine a world in which "content" exists quite apart from any particular form in which it could appear, and in which design exists quite independently of any "content" that it might "contain." It is a world in which a writer cannot visualize how his or her words might appear—one could not picture them on a book spread, a newspaper layout, or as a magazine article, since they will exist only as an abstract commodity to be presented at a future date in any one of a myriad of possible forms and combinations. It will not be possible to conceive of how they might move a particular audience, or how they might be interpreted in a particular context, since these factors cannot be determined at the time of writing. What kind of words would these be? Could they be words addressed by *somebody* to *somebody,* risking a point of view, or will they inevitably be slippery generalities like the sound bites of politicians?

But the prospect for the designer is worse yet, since the idea of "content" abstracted from form threatens the whole idea of the designer as interpreter of a given text. How can there be a sympathy between writer and designer if the design is simply a container for many possible kinds of content—a kind of all-purpose drinking vessel that is as likely to be filled with steaming coffee as vintage wine? This is a dangerous development, since from at least one perspective it is only as an interpreter, or translator, that the designer can be said to engage with the real nature of human communication. In his masterwork, *Truth and Method,* the hermeneutic philosopher Hans-Georg Gadamer argues, "The translation process fundamentally contains the whole secret of how human beings come to an understanding of the world and communicate with each other. Translation is an indissoluble unity of implicit acts of anticipating, of grasping meaning as a whole beforehand, and explicitly laying down what was thus grasped in advance. All speaking has something of this kind of laying hold in advance and laying down."[2]

[2] Hans-Georg Gadamer, *Truth and Method* (London: Sheed and Ward, 1996) 548

The myth of content allows no room for "implicit acts of anticipation," since it is impossible for the "translator" to know what her or his work will interpret, let alone to grasp meaning "as a whole beforehand." And while "all speaking" may possess these qualities, one's "interaction" with a "content-rich" site is more likely to participate in none of them.

There are already some recognizable, and uncomfortable, parallels here with Toulmin's distinction between humanism and modernism. Humanism, with its emphasis on the circumstantial, would insist that the only proper way to interpret a text is as a translator on a case-by-case basis—and indeed this would seem to be the approach that most affirms our humanity, in all its delightful but messy materiality. Modernism, on the other hand, would recognize in the almost Platonic abstraction of content from form an equivalence to its own (Newtonian/Lockean) view of nature, where the physical phenomenon is seen only a transient placeholder for timeless, universal principles.

It is important, however, to bear in mind that there can be no real separation of content and form—just as Newton's separation of mathematical model from optical or lunar observations was only an intellectual conceit. Mathematics gives us tremendous power over the natural world because it allows us to predict what will happen if any of the "variables" changes. But there are no numbers in nature. Likewise, although my computer may store these words as a series of magnetic orientations on a disk (conceived of as "bits"), they must be committed to a fixed form before anyone—myself included—can read them. Just because changes to the font or the size or the color on the screen *appears* to cause a "reflowing" of imaginary content does not make it so. In fact, such changes made to type within a document window are as much a completely fresh physical interpretation as copying it out longhand. "Content" is only a mental model, if a beguiling and dangerous one.

If the "myth of content" only affected the way we explained digital media to ourselves, it might not be such a bad thing. But, as I hope I've demonstrated, conceiving "content" in this way inevitably determines the way we communicate. Text that is drawn from a database can't anticipate the context in which it will appear. It can't, therefore, form a part of a coherent narrative or argument since there is no guarantee that it will appear as a contiguous whole. At best, it can only appear as one of a series of "bite-size" encyclopedia entries, grouped together because of a similarity of subject. (This has, incidentally, led some people to eulogize the supposedly "simultaneous" and "nonhierarchical" nature of the electronic medium—turning an obvious limitation into an apparent strength.)

One might suppose that this "encyclopedestrianization" of communication is a specific, practical consequence of the use of database technology. Not so. In fact, the opposite appears to be the case—the idea of atomizing knowledge into data and categorizing the resultant particles in a database is a concrete expression of a preexisting mode of thought. Indeed, the whole idea of the "encyclopedia" —the presentation of knowledge divorced from context and grouped according to an abstract structure—is one of the deliberate legacies of the early Modernists. The first encyclopedia was produced in 1751 by Diderot, d'Alembert, and Baron Holbách as a deliberate attempt to extend the Newtonian perspective to an abstract, decontextualized systematization of knowledge.

Unfortunately, the encyclopedic approach to knowledge is in direct conflict with the nature of human knowledge and learning. We do not hold our knowledge in a systematic fashion, nor do we categorize our memories in a logical, alphabetic scheme. Instead, our knowledge consists of a series of stories—narratives —and stories within stories. This can be easily seen in a beautiful demonstration developed by Professor Bruce Brown of Brighton University. Brown asks us to state the number of doors in our house or apartment—something that usually nobody is able to recall. He then asks us to imagine ourselves walking through our home, counting the doors.

Within a few moments, everybody can provide the exact number. In similar vein, we often struggle to recall dry factual information—sometimes relying on colorful mnemonics—yet most of us can describe the detailed plot of a feature film we've seen only once before, after only a few minutes of watching it again, despite having watched many hundreds of such films.

I'd like to suggest, therefore, that the organization of information in databases does not reflect the inevitable requirements of the technology so much as the inevitable consequences of a particular, discredited approach to knowledge—the modernist/encyclopedist one. I say "discredited" advisedly, since in so many ways we have already rejected the modernist legacy. Across the spectrum of the "human sciences"—and, of course, the humanities—there is now widespread understanding of the role of narrative, as well as a growing sense of the importance of seeing things as wholes. And, as if evidence was required of the fitness of narrative form to human constitution, we have only to look at its continued, universal popularity as a form of culture, entertainment, and teaching.

To understand what is happening on the Web, we need to ask why modernism so deliberately turned its back on the narrative form and embraced the encyclopedia. Toulmin provides part of the story, showing how the encyclopedists wanted to demonstrate how their knowledge existed quite apart from its circumstances—providing an entry about their hero, Descartes, that quite ignored the circumstantial facts of his life and concentrated instead on the supposedly "timeless" truths he uncovered. The "information revolution" of the 1990s took their project to its ultimate conclusion by creating a new commodity out of "information" that is entirely independent of its context as part of a narrative or argument—indeed, it must have a "granular," decontextualized nature if it is to function as a commodity product. Unfortunately, although many people can conceive of this kind of content, it proves to be far more elusive to create and vend. This, no doubt, goes a long way to explain why the World Wide Web is failing to deliver on its promise of a "universal encyclopedia"—and consists, at the time of writing, of little more than marketing collateral.

The fact that content is proving to be problematic shouldn't suggest that the project will necessarily fail—or, that if it fails, it will fail gracefully and without casualties (the sheer extent of leverage of Internet-based companies means that such a failure would have severe economic consequences). Modernism has provided the philosophical underpinnings of some of the most intransigent and stubborn ideologies—ideologies where "efficiency" had been prioritized above "meaning." And there is an interesting—if not exactly comforting—reason why this is so.

Toulmin characterizes modernism as being obsessed with certainties, of placing the universal over the particular, the timeless over the timely, the abstract over the tangible. Remarkably, in a popular book, *Learned Optimism,* clinical psychologist Martin Seligman identifies precisely these same qualities as characterizing the "explanatory style" of a depressive, or pessimistic, personality. In times of rapid change and uncertainty, these characteristics are exacerbated—as they were in the early seventeenth century, the early twentieth century, and again, for quite different reasons, in the period of corporate "restructuring" at the beginning of the 1990s. In such times people look for certainties, and the "information revolution" is busily peddling old certainties that are creatively repackaged. Depressed people make up the majority of cult followers, and we live in a period where depressive illness is epidemic—overshadowed by what Theodore Roszak has aptly described as "The Cult of Information."

I have elsewhere argued that modernism lives on in graphic design as "information design"—a discipline that has seemingly created itself to provide just the systematized, generic approach required by the separation of form and content (and information designers—or "information architects" as many like to be called—have enthusiastically taken up technologies such as SGML that are intended precisely for the "multi-purposing" of content.) Modernist graphics, I should remind you, made use of a restricted palette of graphic elements that could be applied to every conceivable circumstance. Yet the pioneers of the 1920s and 1930s could not have known how appropriate the idea of an affectless typographic "voice," or the fitting of any kind of material into a rigorously gridded, consistent layout, would be in the age of digital communications.

If this prognosis seems gloomy—of a sustained modernist "counterreformation" that reverses some of the very positive, humanistic gains of the last two centuries—there is also hope. Whereas Toulmin diagnoses the conditions of modernism, Seligman offers some of the clues for a recovery program. Just as the depressed person in cognitive treatment is asked to confront the idea that "this always happens to me," "therapy never works," or "I'm no good," so anyone who confronts the permanent, pervasive, and internal aspects of their "explanatory style" works to undo the bases of modernism in themselves. Designers who do this will find themselves chal-

lenging the idea that there are
"timeless" and "universal" principles that are fundamental to
"my style." Instead, they are more
likely to approach each job as
a unique challenge requiring its
own approaches—knowing that the validity of design principles depends on the
circumstances, and that the human being can work in any number of "styles" without losing her, or his, integrity. Such people are unlikely to find stimulation in
creating "one-size-fits-all" layouts for "content providers"—preferring to
find their fulfillment in work that requires delicate interpretation of its
specificity, context, and uniqueness. As such, whether they know it or not,
they will be drawing close to the spirit of the Humanists.

New media may be in the fervent ideological grip of late
modernism, but it need not be so. There is no reason why Web
communications can't display the exquisite integration of words,
images, and layout characteristic of, say, a William Blake. Ironi-
cally, computer technology has meant that there need be none
of the traditional demarcations between writers and designers—
I can frame my words directly into type, seeing their resonances

immediately reflected in the choice of font, size, and arrangement. This is the antithesis—the antidote—of the "myth of content," as well as a great vista of opportunity for all who love the word made visible. Nor is narrative an inevitable victim: The Web could be like Salman Rushdie's lovely image of a "Sea of Stories."

In itself, the belief that technological imperatives are "inevitable" is just another symptom of the same depressive, pessimistic "explanatory style" that gave rise to—and has continued to fuel—the modernist world view. Armed with new perspectives to understand and challenge this mindset, we are—as never before—empowered to create a different future.

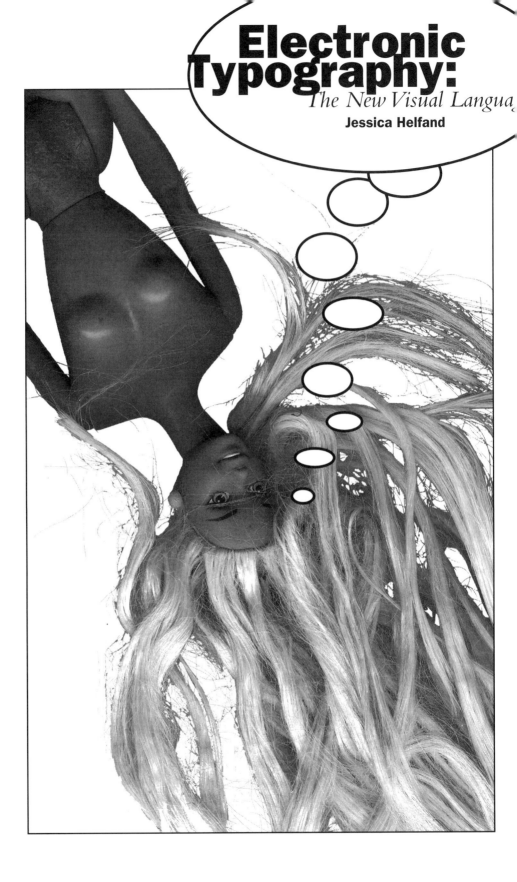

Electronic Typography:
The New Visual Langua

Jessica Helfand

In 1968, Mattel introduced Talking Barbie. I like to think of this as my first computer. I remember saving up my allowance for what seemed an eternity to buy one. To make her talk, you pulled a little string; upon its release, slave-to-fashion Barbie would utter delightful little conversational quips like, "I think miniskirts are smashing," and "Let's have a costume party." If you held the string back slightly as she was talking, her voice would drop a few octaves, transforming her from a chirpy soprano into a slurpy baritone. What came out then sounded a lot more like, "Let's have a cocktail party."

I loved that part.

What I loved was playing director—casting her in a new role, assigning her a new (albeit ludicrous) personality. What I loved was controlling the tone of her voice, altering the rhythm of her words, modulating her oh-so-minimal (and moronic) vocabulary. What I loved was the power to shape her language— something I would later investigate typographically as I struggled to understand the role of the printed word as an emissary of spoken communication.

More than thirty years later, my Mac sounds a lot like my Barbie did then —the same monotone, genderless, robotic drawl. But here in the digital age, the relationship between design and sound—and in particular, between the spoken word and the written word—goes far beyond pulling a string. Don't be fooled by voice-recognition software: The truth is that the computer's internal sound capabilities enable us to design with sound, not just in imitation of it. Like it or not, the changes brought about by recent advances in technology (and here I am referring

Electronic Typography

to multimedia) indicate the need for designers to broaden their understanding of what it is to work effectively with typography. It is no longer enough to design for readability, to "suggest" a sentiment or reinforce a concept through the selection of a particular font. Today, we can make type talk: in any language, at any volume, with musical underscoring or sci-fi sound effects or overlapping violins. We can sequence and dissolve, pan and tilt, fade to black and spec type in sensurround. As we "set" type, we encounter a decision-making process unprecedented in two-dimensional design. Unlike the kinetic experience of turning a printed page to sequence information, time becomes a powerful and persuasive design element. Today, we can visualize concepts in four action-packed, digital dimensions.

Multimedia has introduced a new visual language, one that is no longer bound to traditional definitions of "word," "image," "form," and "place." Typography, in an environment that offers such diverse riches, must redefine its goals, its purpose, its very identity. It must reinvent itself—and soon.

Visual language, or the interpretation of spoken words through typographic expression, has long been a source of inspiration to designers, artists, and writers. Examples abound, from concrete poetry in the twenties to "happenings" in the sixties, and in graphic design, dating as far back as the incunabula. Visual wordplay proliferates, in the twentieth century in particular, from F. T. Marinetti's "Parole in Libertà" to George Maciunas's Fluxus installations to the latest MTA posters adorning the New York subway walls. Kurt Schwitters, Guillaume Appolinaire, Piet Zwart, Robert Brownjohn—the list is long, the examples inexhaustible. For designers there has always been an overwhelming interest in formalism, in analyzing the role of type as medium (structure), message (syntax), and muse (sensibility). Throughout, there has been an attempt to reconcile the relationship between words both spoken and seen—a source of exhilaration to some and ennui to others. Lamenting the expressive limitations of the Western alphabet, Adolf Loos explained it simply: "One cannot speak a capital letter." Denouncing its structural failings, Stanley Morrison was equally at odds with a tradition that designated hierarchies in the form of uppercase and lowercase letterforms. Preferring to shape language as he deemed appropriate, Morrison referred to full capitals as "a necessary evil."

Academic debate over the relationship between language and form enjoyed renewed popularity in recent years, as designers borrowed from linguistic models in an attempt to codify and clarify their own typographic explorations. Deconstruction's design devotees eagerly appropriated its terminology and theory, hoping to introduce a new vocabulary for design: it was the vocabulary of signifiers and signifieds, of Jacques Derrida and Ferdinand de Saussure, of Michel Foucault and Umberto Eco.

As a comprehensive model for evaluating typographic expression, deconstruction proved both heady and limited. Today, as advances in technology introduce greater and more complex creative challenges, it is simply arcane. We need to look at screen-based typography as a new language—with its own grammar, its own syntax, its own rules. What we need are new models, better models, models that go beyond language or typography per se—models that reinforce rather than restrict our understanding of what it is to design with electronic media. "What we need," says design and new-media consultant Wendy Richmond, "are extreme and unusual metaphors."

Learning a new language is one thing, fluency quite another. We've come to equate fluency with literacy—another outdated model for evaluation. "Literacy should not mean the ability to decode strings of alphabetic letters," says Seymour Papert, director of the Epistemology and Learning Group at MIT's Media Lab, who refers to such a definition as "letteracy." Language, even to linguists, proves creatively limiting as a paradigm. "New media promise the opportunity to offer a smoother transition to what really deserves to be called literacy," says Papert. Typography, as the physical embodiment of such thinking, has quite a way to go.

The will to decipher the formal properties of language, a topic of great consequence for communication designers in general, has its philosophical antecedents in ancient Greece. "Spoken words," wrote Aristotle in *Logic,* "are the symbols of mental experience. Written words are the symbols of spoken words." Today, centuries later, the equation has added a new link: What happens when written words can speak? When they can move? When they can be imbued with sound, tone, nuance, decibel, harmony, and voice? As designers who probe the creative parameters of this new technology, our goal may be less to digitize than to dramatize. Indeed, there is a theatrical component that I am convinced is essential to this new thinking. Of what value are bold and italics when words can dance across the screen, dissolve, or disappear altogether?

In this dynamic landscape, our static definitions of typography appear increasingly imperiled. Will the beauty of traditional letterforms be compromised by the evils of this new technology? Will punctuation be stripped of its functional contributions, or ligatures their aesthetic ones? Will type really matter?

Of course it will.

In the meantime, however, typography's early appearance on the digital frontier doesn't speak too well for design. Take e-mail, for example. Gone are the days of good handwriting, of the Palmer Method and the penmanship primer. In its place, electronic mail—which, despite its futuristic tone, has paradoxically revived the Victorian art of letter writing. Sending electronic mail is easy, effortless, and quick. For those of us who spend a good deal of our professional lives on the telephone, e-mail offers a welcome respite from talking (although it bears a closer stylistic resemblance to conversational speech than to written language). However, for those of us with even the most modest design sense, e-mail eliminates the distinctiveness that typography has traditionally brought to our written communiqués. Though its supporters endorse the democratic nature of such homogeneity, the truth is, it's boring. In the land of e-mail, we all "sound" alike: Everyone writes in Monaco.

Oddly, it is laden with contradictions: ubiquitous in form yet highly diverse in content, at once ephemeral and archival, transmitted in real time yet physically intangible. E-mail is a kind of aesthetic flatland, informationally dense and visually unimaginative. Here, hierarchies are preordained and nonnegotiable: passwords, menus, commands, help. Networks like America Online require that we title our mail, a leftover model from the days of interoffice correspondence, which makes even the most casual letter sound like a corporate memo. As a result, electronic missives all have headlines, but titling our letters makes us better editors, not better designers. As a fitting metaphor for the distilled quality of things digital, the focus in e-mail is on the abridged, the acronym, the quick read. E-mail is functionally serviceable and visually forgettable, not unlike fast food. It's drive-through design: get in, get out, move on.

And it's everywhere. Here is the biggest contribution to communication technology to come out of the last decade, a global network linking an estimated fifty million people worldwide, and designers—communication designers, no less —are no where in sight.

Typography, in this environment, desperately needs direction. Where do we start? Comparisons with printed matter inevitably fail since words in the digital domain are processed with a speed unprecedented in the world of paper. Here they are incorporated into databases or interactive programs, where they are transmitted and accessed in random, nonhierarchical sequences. "Hypertext," or the ability to program text with interactivity (meaning that a word, when clicked upon or pointed to, will actually do something), takes it all a step further: by introducing alternate paths, information lacks the closure of the traditional printed narrative. "Hypertextual story space is now multidimensional," explains novelist Robert Coover in a recent issue of *Artforum,* "and theoretically infinite."

If graphic design can be largely characterized by its attention to understanding the hierarchy of information (and using type in accordance with such understanding), then how are we to determine its use in a nonlinear context such as this? On a purely visual level, we are limited by what the pixel will render: The screen matrix simulates curves with surprising sophistication, but hairlines and idiosyncratic serifs will, to the typophile, appear inevitably compromised. On a more objective level, type in this context is both silent and static and must compete with sound and motion—not an easy task, even in the best of circumstances. (Conversely, in the era of the TV remote, where the user can mute at will, the visual impact of written typography is not to be discounted.)

To better analyze the role(s) of electronic typography, we might begin by looking outside—not to remote classifications imported from linguistic textbooks, or even to traditional design theories conveniently repackaged—but to our own innate intelligence, our own distinctive powers of creative thought. To cultivate and adequately develop this new typography (because if we don't, no one else will), we might do well to rethink language altogether, to consider new and alternative perspectives. "If language is indeed the limit of our world," writes literary critic William Gass in *Habitations of the Word,* "then we must find another, larger, stronger, more inventive language which will burst those limits."

In his book *Seeing Voices,* author and neurologist Oliver Sacks reflects on sign language and looks at the cognitive understanding of spatial grammar in a language that exists without sound. He cites the example of a deaf child learning to sign and describes in detail the remarkable quality of her visual awareness and descriptive, spatial capabilities. "By the age of four, indeed, Charlotte had advanced so far into visual thinking and language that she was able to provide new ways of thinking—revelations—to her parents." As a consequence of learning sign language as adults, this child's parents not only learned a new language but discovered new ways of thinking as well—visual thinking. Imagine the potential for multimedia if designers were to approach electronic typography with this kind of ingenuity and open-mindedness.

William Stokoe, a Chaucer scholar who taught Shakespeare at Gallaudet College in the 1950s, summarized it this way: "In a signed language, narrative is no longer linear and prosaic. Instead, the essence of sign language is to cut from a normal view to a close-up to a distant shot to a close-up again, and so on, even including flashback and fast-forward scenes, exactly as a movie editor works." Here, perhaps, is another model for visual thinking: a new way of shaping meaning based on multiple points of view, which sees language as part of a more comprehensive communication platform—time-sensitive, interactive, and highly visual. Much like multimedia.

Epilogue

In gathering research for this article, I posted a query on Applelink's typography board. I received the following response:

```
As a type designer, I am sort of surprised to find myself NOT VERY
CONCERNED with how type is used in the fluid context of multimedia.
In a way, type is as flexible as photography or illustration in
a mm [multimedia] context, i.e., it's a whole new ballgame for
everyone.
```

Though my link-pal claimed not to be concerned, he did take the time to respond. As I read his reply, I realized how important it will be for all of us to be concerned: not merely to translate the printed word to the screen, but to transcend it.

Then I found myself wondering: What would Stanley Morrison have thought of all those CAPS?

Rethinking the Book

David Small

Navigation and Wayfinding

The use of three-dimensional typography has fundamentally changed the way we think about the use of space in graphic design and how the surface of the computer screen is understood by the designer. When the design of three-dimensional typography is cast as a landscape design problem, we understand that it has more to do with creating compelling views than with the strict arrangement of elements. As a garden design will lead one through a series of vantage points that hide, reveal, and accentuate a series of features,[1] a journey through an information landscape should provide a meaningful context for the information elements.

[1] Charles W. Moore, William J. Mitchell, and William Turnbull, Jr., *The Poetics of Gardens* (Cambridge, MA: MIT Press, 1988)

Just as one reads the physical landscape in order to navigate the world, so too must people be able to find their way about information spaces. The designer should be careful, however, not to confuse the abstract spaces of typographic information with the roads, subways, and buildings of our built environment. In the visual design of information spaces it is much more important to understand relative and ultimately fluid relationships between shifting and mutating information chunks than the fixed elements of the real world.

For example, in navigating the urban environment, we make use of fixed signs and landmarks, transportation systems, and place-based addressing schemes such as street addresses in the United States or *chome* (postal neighborhoods) in Japan. In information systems, the data itself can have an inherent address (e.g., Exodus 4:12 or *Romeo and Juliet,* act 3, scene 1). Since we can move instantaneously from one location to another, getting the "lay of the land" may be less important than having a clear view of your current location and meaningful jump points from there.

The tools for getting from one location to another are unclear, but we can understand what is required for a usable interface. It is always easier to find your way to something that you can already see. Through use of scalable text that can be layered, we can keep much more information simultaneously visible than was previously possible. Nonetheless, we still require clear indications of where we are within a space and what lies just out of our view.

We must also consider that any journey through space is also one through time. No movement is ever truly instantaneous, and the way in which we move and how the journey unfolds through time can be of great help in revealing the underlying structure of a landscape.

The correspondence between narrative space and architectural space or the landscape is a natural one. There are many examples, from the friezes in which the story is organized along the lines of the architec-

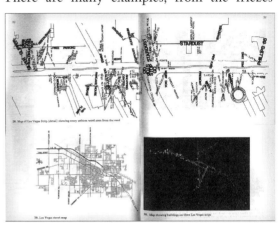

tural structure[2] to the songlines of the Australian aboriginal people.[3] In his book *Learning from Las Vegas,* Robert Venturi describes the strip as a textual event.[4] In her design of the book, Muriel Cooper visually demonstrated the sign map of the strip.

Spread from *Learning from Las Vegas*

[2] Richard Brilliant, *Visual Narratives: Storytelling in Etruscan and Roman Art* (Ithaca, NY: Cornell University Press, 1984)

[3] Bruce Chatwin, *The Songlines* (New York: Penguin Books, 1987)

[4] Robert Venturi, *Learning from Las Vegas* (Cambridge, MA: MIT Press, 1972)

Layering, Juxtaposition, and Scale

The primary problem designers encounter when moving to the digital medium is that the resolution they are accustomed to in print is completely lacking on the computer screen. Often, it is desirable to show more information at one time than can reasonably fit onto the display. We can take advantage of the computer's ability to create multiple dynamic layers of information and to rapidly change the scale of information elements to overcome that constraint and to go beyond anything that was possible in the realm of ink on paper.

The context within which we find information often tells us as much as the information itself. Although markup languages, such as HTML, allow designers to link many pieces of information together, the information elements are still viewed as isolated, fragmentary bits. It is now possible to control the focus and transparency of information objects—as well as color, typeface, and other variables—dynamically. This gives us the opportunity to concurrently display multiple threads of information and dynamically shift visual focus from one to another.

Graphic Design & Reading

Through the use of transparency and focus we can effectively layer multiple threads of text. One layer can recede into a blurry cloud while another will suddenly "pop" into focus and float above the other layers. If the computer can deduce which layer is of current interest, this focus shifting can be, at least partially, automatic. Scale has always been implicit in design because one designed real, physical objects that had a certain size and relationship to the human form. Objects are designed to fit the body, such as a book that one can hold in one's lap. Architectural design is likewise intimately connected with the human form. This extends even to the more abstract realm of graphic design. Typefaces are made to be read from a certain distance and occupy a certain size on the retina. In the virtual space of the computer screen, we are free to explore a vast range of scales. In particular, I am interested in how to design for both the reading scale, where a display can hold five hundred or a thousand words, and a contextual scale, where a million or more words can be in some way visible. While we understand a great deal about how people read characters that occupy a hundred or so pixels, it is unclear how to abstract text for display at single-pixel or subpixel resolutions.

The Talmud Project

The Talmud project, one of a series of electronic book experiments I conducted at MIT's Media Lab, directly addresses the issue of working with multiple texts simultaneously. Because it was necessary to show several texts and the relationships between them in the same space, the Talmud, in its complexity, helped clarify the visual and interaction problems involved.

The Talmud is a collection of sacred writings on the Torah, or Old Testament. This project was built around an essay by the philosopher Emmanuel Levinas,[5,6] whose commentary on a tract of the Talmud, which itself is a complex, nested series of references to the Torah, forms an intricate web of text and references. This style of writing is called "hermeneutics," the reference of scripture to support an argument.

The primary goal of the Talmud project was to create a workspace in which the relevant texts could coexist and interact. The fact that these texts are themselves complex and carry a long history of study brings the issues into a sharp relief. The system should be fast and responsive—after all, it only takes a moment to flip through a book and find a particular passage. It should give the sense that all of the material is close by and accessible. It should also reward further study, meaning that even though a novice should be able to quickly orient himself in the texts, an expert should be able to "perform" with a degree of precision that is evidence of his or her knowledge and experience.

The chosen texts deal with the subject of the Cities of Refuge. When one has caused the accidental death of another, the law recognizes that this is not the same as murder. For example, if a man is chopping wood in his yard, and the axe head flies loose and strikes dead a person walking down the street, the law

[5] Emmanuel Levinas, *Beyond the Verse: Talmudic Readings and Lectures* (Bloomington, IN: Indiana University Press, 1994)

[6] Emmanuel Levinas, *L'Au-Dela Du Verset: Lectures et Discours Talmudiques* (Paris: Les Éditions de Minuit, 1982)

recognizes that there was no intent and the manslaughterer is "subjectively innocent." Nonetheless, the family of the slain man has the right of blood vengeance. This paradox, of existing in a state of both guilt and innocence, forms the basis for the reading. Levinas, in his approach to the Talmud, brings this paradox into the context of twentieth-century life and tries to give the text the widest possible reading.

A visual representation of these interconnected texts should construct a space for discussion and argument in which scholars can pull and push the words as they dissect the intellectual issues posed by the text. Some of the initial designs for this project used graphic controls for navigating and controlling the three layers of text (the Levinas text, the Talmud, and the Torah). This proved to be unsatisfactory for a variety of reasons. First, the controls existed in the same visual space as the data being manipulated, and it was often difficult to keep one from visually conflicting with the other. Also, because graphic widgets rely on the computer mouse for control, it was difficult for more than one person to have control at any one time. Finally, there simply wasn't a good feel to the controls—they lacked the tactile quality of leafing through an actual book.

[7] Judith Abrams, *Learn Talmud: How to Use the Talmud, The Steinsaltz Edition* (Northvale, NJ: Jason Aronson, Inc., 1995)

From *Learn Talmud* by Judith Abrams: ". . . Get used to having many volumes of books out at one time. By the end of a study session you could have several books spread out on the table: the volume you are studying, a Bible to look up the verses that are cited in the Talmud, the Reference Guide for this set of Talmud, volumes of the Encyclopaedia Judaica to provide additional historical background information, various Hebrew or Aramaic dictionaries, and other volumes of rabbinic literature. This isn't messiness. This is the traditional mode of study and it really feels great. . . ."[7] The Talmud is studied in a particular manner, which although not unlike the method in which most would approach a scholarly work, has been made explicit over many centuries of study. The Talmud should be studied with another person (hevruta) and one of the two should be more experienced than the other. The act of reading should be punctuated with argument and discussion of the issues raised by the text. In a typically Talmudic expression, this is described with the prescription—there should be crumbs that fall into the binding of the Talmud because the scholars will be so engrossed in discussion that their lunch will find its way into the book.

The solution to these problems was to create physical controls that exist in the space immediately surrounding the display. I concentrated on the visual problems posed by the requirement that the various texts, under the immediate physical control of one or more readers, can visually coexist in a smooth and natural manner.

The primary problem faced by the designer in electronic media is the lack of resolution and space afforded by paper. The average computer display has about one million pixels and can display perhaps one thousand words. The resolution of paper allows for a larger number of words in the same space, and, because the resolution and contrast of ink on paper is much higher, the type itself is of higher quality. And, because paper is thin and inexpensive, many sheets can be bound into a book, which can easily contain more than one million words.

Despite these limitations, electronic media have some distinct advantages over paper, which we can exploit. The electronic display is a dynamic surface, which can change and adapt over time. More important, however, is the fact that the computer processor can manipulate and understand the underlying model of the information. Unlike paper, which knows not what is printed on it, the computer can be programmed to intelligently react to changing inputs and models of both information and the user.

Layering with Focus Control

"Layering" is defined as the simultaneous display of two or more information objects within the same two-dimensional space of the projected display surface. This can occur when two objects are in fact occupying the same space or when a particular view into a three-dimensional landscape of information causes one layer to occlude, or pass in front of, another.

Even though you may want to display several information objects at the same time and in the same space, the reader's attention will only be focused on one at a time. If we know which layer is of interest at the moment, we can adjust the display so that the various layers appear to either "pop" out to the front or recede into the background. This is accomplished through a combination of focus and

transparency controls. Different colors can also be used in this way, although it may not be desirable to constantly shift the color of an object. The goal is to make the minimum amount of change to allow the selected layer to be easily read, without giving the impression that any of the layers have really changed.

We can see this in the treatment of the three basic information layers of Levinas, Talmud, and Torah. Although all three reside in the same space, only one is ever fully in focus at any moment. So, for example, you might be reading a passage from the Torah while the referring page from the Talmud appears to hang behind the Torah and just enough out of focus so as to maximize the legibility of the Torah. This goal of "just enough" is quite difficult to achieve. The optical size of the two texts, their orientation to each other, and their color and transparency all have an effect on legibility.

Although a fully rigorous study was not done, a couple of general observations can be made: First, the smaller the text, the less of an effect blurring will have. Once text gets below a few pixels in width, it is too small to see the blur. In general, the smaller the text, the more you want to increase the transparency to give the same overall density to blurred text. Second, the more that the texts align with each other, the greater the blur needed to keep them separated. So, if two texts are at the same point size and the lines appear to be nearly on top of each other, the background text will tend to impair the legibility of the foreground text. If they are at different angles or significantly different point sizes, there will be less interference, and, consequently, less blur may be needed to keep the foreground text legible.

By using changes in both blur and transparency, it was possible to create dynamic shifts between the three information layers, which provided clear, legible text in the foreground layer. Because this could be done without otherwise changing the position or scale of any of the layers, there was far less chance of confusion about where specific areas of text were on the screen, even those that were temporarily illegible. Before going on to discuss juxtaposition, let's talk in more detail about the method used to create smooth transitions of focus.

A Method for Real-Time Focus Control

To blur an image such as the letter *A,* you multiply it against a filter. This process, known as convolution, requires a multiply and add for each element of the filter at each pixel. The greater the blur, the larger the kernel, and the number of computations increase by the square of the filter width. Early experiments by Laura Scholl and Grace Colby with Media Lab's Connection Machine supercomputer took advantage of parallel processing for these computations, but each image took minutes to blur and display.[8] Even with today's fast processors, it is not possible to filter images in real time. So, to create text that could smoothly change from perfectly sharp to bleary-eyed blurry, a new technique had to be developed.

Of course, we are not dealing with an infinite number of images. We only need to consider the hundred or so characters commonly used in

[8] Laura Scholl, "The Transitional Image" (master's thesis, Massachusetts Institute of Technology, 1991)

each typeface. So, the idea of precomputing the required blurry characters and caching the results is compelling. Still, there is a limit to the amount of memory that can be allocated for all of the copies of each typeface, especially when you consider that the most efficient rendering can only occur when the images are cached in the graphics pipeline.

Even if you cache ten or more images per character, the reader will be able to see discrete changes in focus. In order to provide truly smooth gradations and to limit the number of images to be cached, a weighted average of just two images is used. This is done by drawing two versions of the character directly atop each other and varying the transparency of each. You can think of this as a process of compression, where the image of the letter is broken into discrete spatial frequencies and then reassembled. The sharp image corresponds to the highest spatial frequencies, and the blurred image has only lower spatial frequencies. Surprisingly, this method produced results indistinguishable from individually filtered text. It was decided to use just three master images—the original, a 3×3 Gaussian filtered image, and a 9×9 Gaussian. If an even blurrier image was needed, a 27×27 filter would be used. To display an image corresponding to any filter in between, the two neighboring filters are weighted and combined.

Dynamic Juxtaposition

In traditional graphic design, the space of the paper is used as a kind of map to the underlying information. Elements that are related are located on the page in proximity to each other. These spatial relationships are fixed once the page is printed. In the dynamic context of the computer, the elements are in a continuous state of change. In order to maintain a specific relationship between two typographic elements, they have to constantly adjust to changing conditions.

Let's look at two examples from the Talmud project. Each devises a solution to the problem of keeping related texts next to each other. In the first, two versions of the same text must be compared line by line. In the second, blocks of text maintain proximity despite changes in size, position, and orientation.

Levinas's writing only reveals itself after long and careful study. Even after several readings, a passage may not be entirely clear. As with any translated work, the next step is to reread the text in its original language. This can be difficult when using printed books: The two versions are often in separate books, and it is difficult to go back and forth without losing the essence of the passage. The pages do not correspond to each other, and as the books usually will have different publishers, the type design is different. To combat this problem, an approach in which different languages run in different columns through the pages of the book can be used. Otl Aicher's *Typographie* is a good example of this technique.[9]

A recently published Dutch monograph by designer Harry Ruhé takes a different approach. The Dutch and English texts are directly superimposed in transparent inks—red for Dutch and green for English. A pair of colored gels provided with the book selectively reveals each layer. This

[9] Otl Aicher, *Typographie* (Berlin: Ernst and Sohn, 1988)

has the advantage of putting the control directly into the hands of the reader as well as conserving space. Still, it is difficult to go back and forth between the languages, and colored text is not nearly as easy on the eye as black text.

The goal in providing both English and French versions of the Levinas text was to allow the reader direct control over which language was primary and to show both languages when needed. A simple dial moves the display from one language to the other and various levels in between. At first the texts were superimposed, and transparency was varied to fade one language into another. One could read the English, turn the dial, and then read the corresponding French. This proved unsatisfactory when you wanted to see both texts at the same time—it wasn't enough to hold the image of one in the mind and switch quickly between them. The image of the one text tended to obliterate the memory of the other. (This effect is called masking.)

To address this, I tried to put the French text in the spaces between the English lines (leading). It wasn't legible unless the leading was increased dramatically, which was undesirable. Finally, I tried increasing the leading dynamically as one text faded into the other. In this way, each text seen solo was set nice and tight, but when the dial was halfway between, the French text sat just above each line of English with some leading in between each pair of lines. The two languages were different colors, so

it was easy to track either one from line to line or to glance at both simultaneously. Since the French text contained accents above characters, it was placed above the English. This increased the legibility of the French without compromising the English. This dynamic juxtaposition of the two texts gives particular affordances to the task of reading Levinas in the original and in translation.

The second example has to do with the relationship between the Levinas essay and the tractate of the Talmud, to which his essay refers. The goal is to be able to jump back and forth between the two texts easily as well as scale each larger or smaller. Each chapter of the Levinas text corresponds to a group of lines from the Talmud. To keep them separated, the Levinas text hugs the left edge of the display and the Talmud tends to the right. A control shifts the boundary between the two texts. In the original design, this was seen as a dynamic margin—it could move so that one text had the majority of the screen space and the other shrank to fit into the remaining margin. By adjusting the scale of each text to fit the available space, it ensured that each text was always visible, even if it shrank to minuscule proportions.

As the prototype developed, this simple scheme became difficult to maintain. The Talmudic text could rotate to reveal either the *mishnah* (oral text circa 200 B.C.) or the *gemara* (commentaries circa A.D. 150). Also, the overall scale of the Talmud (several volumes) dwarfed the scale of the Levinas essay. And it became clear that each chapter of the Levinas essay should be in proximity to those few lines of the Talmud to which it referred. This juxtaposition is accomplished by connecting the texts with springs that maintain the spatial relationships despite any rotation or scaling of either text and keep the Levinas text always to the immediate left of the Talmud. Although the texts exist in three-dimensional space, the visual relationship refers to the two-dimensional projection of the texts. This was accomplished by creating special spring anchors that were outside of the normal object hierarchy, at the intersection of a plane parallel to the view plane and a ray from the viewpoint to the anchor point of the text. So, as the Talmud was scaled larger or smaller, or rotated or scrolled up and down, each Levinas chapter would dynamically adjust to maintain a specific juxtaposition—aligned to the top of the referring section, its right edge to the right of the Talmud, and its left edge to the left edge of the display. Using a spring model for the constraint added a slight dynamic to the adjustment—following any user input that changed an element, the other elements would "catch up."

In each of the two preceding examples, we see how a dynamic constraint can maintain a useful juxtaposition between multiple texts. The visual relationships that are clearly apparent to the reader must match the structural relationships of the information. Moreover, we must be aware of the ways in which a reader's eyes weave about the display and design accordingly.

Scale

I would like to concentrate on problems associated with presenting several texts of different scales simultaneously. One of my early design goals was to keep all of the elements visible at all times, in keeping with one of the great advantages that books have over electronic displays: their persistence. If I have three books laid out on my desk, and I start reading one of them, the other two do not "disappear" off the desktop or behind an opaque window. They remain in the background but available.

Although computer window systems allow you to keep several views open at a time, only the information in the topmost window is visible. This places the burden on the user to remember what was on the various other windows. Furthermore, there is no smooth transition from one view to the next. So, it is difficult for the user to maintain a consistent mental model of the relationships between the different information objects. By allowing the various texts to scale between reading size and down to postage-stamp size, it is possible to keep everything in the current visual space and still have enough room to work. As well, the smooth transitions allow readers to track where they are going within a text and what the relationships are between texts.

One difficulty encountered in the smooth scaling of columns of text is that a reader would often move close to a specific passage only to find that the neighboring columns would be equally strong typographically, despite the fact that they may be inconsequential. It is analogous to reading a story in a newspaper and accidentally jumping over a column into an unrelated story. When seen at a small scale, columns of text form a meaningful image that can "read" as the underlying information structure. You can tell at a glance how the stories on the front page of a newspaper are constructed and plan a path through them.[10] You may pick up a paper, read its structure, and then bring it closer to a comfortable reading distance as you work your way through and around the page. You adjust the scale simply by moving the paper relative to your body.

[10] Louis Silverstein, *Newspaper Design for the Times* (New York: Van Nostrand Reinhold, 1990)

In the case of the Talmud project, it was possible to scale the text to many more orders of magnitude than our newspaper example. Different elements had to respond differently at different sizes in order to maintain a legible focus on the section in question. In order to clearly indicate which was the column of interest, the neighboring columns would be rendered in a kind of sketchy way to show that they were there but were not the primary focus. At a far distance, all the columns would still look like quite the same. There are many other ways in which different elements of a text could respond to scaling: In the case of the Talmud, it might be sensible to scale the *gemara,* which comprises a smaller fraction of the total text, at a different rate than the *mishnah,* with which it is interwoven.

In addition to the problem of showing texts at the same scale in different ways in order to guide the reader's attention, the Talmud project, with its multiple texts, had to allow the reader to work between texts that may be at different scales. For example, a notation sketched by the user over the Levinas text may also direct the reader to a particular phrase in the Talmud or the Torah. As the three texts vary in scale, the notation may lose any visual sense. Future work in this area could examine what types of structure add distinctiveness to scaled text so that small images of large works could present a more complete picture from a distance.

While this project primarily focused on the disposition of space in the information display, the sequential presentation of typography over time is, in a sense, another method of layering.

Almost all the animation in the Talmud project was under the direct control of the user. This sort of motion is very easy for the user to read, as long as the interaction loop between the controls and the graphics are fast and responsive. The user would turn a dial, for example, and an element would rotate in response. Because the feedback is immediate and the user can always return the dial, and therefore the information, back to its original position, there is little training required. Moreover, the user feels in control of the interaction because he can effect change in the display when and how he wants. Unfortunately, if you make a control for every possible movement of each and every object, you soon will have a control system that overwhelms the information itself. By building dynamic constraints between information objects and limiting controls to those dimensions that are meaningful, we can keep the interaction manageable without overly restricting the user.

Simple constraints were easy to implement because of the message-passing system used in the software. Each object can both send and receive messages. So, for example, if an object receives a message from a control to change scale, it can, on the receipt of that message, send a message to another object to change its position.

Any of the messages can also include a duration, which will direct the recipient to smoothly animate from its current state to a new state in a specific amount of time. Because these animations were built into the system at such a low level and were very easy to use, it meant that the designer could choose to animate any change (e.g., color, focus, position, etc.) without any extra work. While these simple animations meant that transitions were smooth and continuous, there was need for more complex motion.

The Talmud project used a physical spring model for maintaining spatial relationships during interaction. The goal was to keep certain texts next to each other, even as they changed in scale and position. As the user interacted, they would introduce energy into the system, and the springs, acting in a damping field, would move to reduce the energy. The user could, through the motion, literally see the underlying constraints and how they were solved. Initial designs damped the springs only slightly, so it would take a considerable amount of time (ten or more seconds) for the system to reach equilibrium. This motion was felt to be far too distracting, so the damping was increased to nearly cancel out the stiffness of

the springs. The system would now reach equilibrium in about a second. This brief motion was still enough to reveal to the reader the underlying constraints.

Animation was also used when the reader followed a link in the text to a particular verse of the Torah. If you think about how links work in most Web applications, clicking a link wipes the current Web page from the screen and then (slowly) paints the new Web page. The starting location is gone, and there is no indication of how it might be related to the end result. To find a verse in the Torah, the text would smoothly slide from the current verse to the new book, chapter, and verse. This worked best when the view allowed both the start and end points to be visible so that the path from one to the other could be easily traced. If the camera was close in and the verses far apart, the animation blurred into a meaningless smear, like the view out a window of a speeding car. In his thesis, Tinsley Galyean proposed a method for planning a path through virtual spaces, such as a museum.[11] While some of these techniques are applicable to a more abstract and purely typographic space, future work might examine how to plan paths through information spaces that are most meaningful and keyed to the legibility of typography.

[11] Tinsley Galyean, "Narrative Guidance of Interactivity" (Ph.D. thesis, Massachusetts Institute of Technology, 1995)

In making information accessible to people, we need to go beyond historical models. The computer screen is not a piece of paper and should not be treated as one. By taking advantage of the ability of the computer to display dynamic, flexible, and adaptive typography, we can invent new ways for people to read, interact with, and assimilate the written word. Like a well-designed landscape, information should be legible, inviting, and comfortable, and its exploration can and should be a true delight.

The Authors:

William Drenttel is a designer and publisher who works in partnership with Jessica Helfand in Falls Village, Connecticut. He is president emeritus of the American Institute of Graphic Arts and a board member of the Cooper-Hewitt National Design Museum. From 1985 to 1996, he was a partner at Drenttel Doyle Partners. Among its over 300 awards, Drenttel Doyle Partners was named to the ID 40 list of design innovators in 1994. Drenttel has written on design for *ID, Communication Arts,* and the *AIGA Journal of Graphic Design,* and has edited five books on graphic design. He also publishes literary works and design criticism under the imprint William Drenttel Editions.

"The Written Word: Designer as Mediator" originally appeared in Rethinking Design: The AIGA 50 Books Catalog, 1997.

Johanna Drucker is the Robertson Professor of Media Studies at the University of Virginia where she is professor in the department of English and director of media studies. She has published and lectured extensively on topics related to the history of typography, artists' books, and visual art. Her books include *Theorizing Modernism, The Visible Word: Experimental Typography and Modern Art, The Alphabetic Labyrinth, The Century of Artists' Books,* and her collected essays, *Figuring the Word.* Her work as a book artist and experimental, visual poet has been exhibited and collected in special collections in libraries and museums including the Getty Center for the Humanities, the Whitney Museum of American Art in New York, the Marvin and Ruth Sackner Archive of Visual and Concrete Poetry, the New York Public Library, Houghton Library at Harvard University, and many others.

Paul Elliman is an assistant professor in the Yale School of Art, and a project tutor at the Jan Van Eyck Academy, in the Netherlands. Much of his work is collaborative and includes a dance performance with British choreographer Rosemary Butcher, visual material with cycling activists Critical Mass, and projects with other kinds of designers including architects and product designers. His work is included in the British Arts Council travelling collection "Lost and Found: critical voices in contemporary British design."

A version of "E Pluribus Unum" was first published in Eye *33.*

Kenneth FitzGerald's writing on design has appeared in *Emigre* and *Eye* magazines. He is producer of the magazine *The News of the Whirled,* which has been honored by AIGA/MN. Other self-published works are in The Museum of Modern Art/Franklin Furnace/Artist Book collection. As an educator, he has taught graphic design and design history at the University of Minnesota Duluth and in the Foundation program at Montserrat College of Art.

Colette Gaiter teaches at the New Media Institute at the University of Minnesota Twin Cities' School of Journalism and Mass Communication. She previously taught at the Minneapolis College of Art and Design. Her interactive multimedia work encourages viewers to experience paradox and ambiguity as natural parts of human existence in a complex world. "SPACE | R A C E," an interactive CD ROM about the 1960s U.S. Civil Rights Movement and space program, and other interactive multimedia computer installations have been exhibited widely. She is the recipient of several grants and fellowships, including the McKnight Visual Arts Fellowship.

The images in this book are from "Modern Life Stories," a folio of prints.

Jessica Helfand is partner with William Drenttel in Jessica Helfand | William Drenttel, a design consultancy that concentrates on editorial design and the development of new models for old and new media. Clients include: *Newsweek, Business Week,* Lingua Franca, America OnLine, and Champion International Corporation. Helfand is media columnist for *Eye* magazine, a contributing editor of *ID*, and the author of *Six (+2) Essays on Design and New Media*. She is visiting lecturer in graphic design at Yale University School of Art.

"Electronic Typography: The New Visual Language" was first published in the May/June 1994 issue of Print.

Steven Heller is art director of the *New York Times Book Review* and co-chair of the School of Visual Arts MFA/Design program. He is the author of over seventy books on graphic design, illustration, and political art including *The Swastika: A Symbol Beyond Redemption, Sex Appeal: The Art of Allure in Advertising* and *Graphic Design, and Letterforms: Bawdy, Bad, and Beautiful*. He is the recipient of the 1999 AIGA Medal.

Ellen Lupton is a curator, writer, and graphic designer. As curator of contemporary design at Cooper-Hewitt, National Design Museum, she has organized a series of major books and exhibitions, including *Graphic Design in the Mechanical Age: Selections from the Merrill C. Berman Collection, Mixing Messages: Graphic Design in Contemporary Culture, The Avant-Garde Letterhead, Mechanical Brides: Women and Machines from Home to Office,* and *National Design Triennial: Design Culture Now.* She is co-chair of the graphic design department at the Maryland Institute, College of Art in Baltimore with J. Abbott Miller.

"Visual Syntax" originally appeared in the book The ABC of ●■▲: The Bauhaus and Design Theory.

Hrant Papazian is obsessed with functionality but is equally infatuated with shape, symbolism and language. An Armenian native of Lebanon, his view of written communication was formed at the crossroads of three competing visual cultures. He is dedicated to exploring the untrodden avenues to pragmatic solutions; his lack of formal education in graphic design tends to make this easier. As a multimedia designer at UCLA, Hrant creates online educational software, but his true love is the black-and-white, but colorful world of non-Latin type design. He has received commissions from Agfa, Unitype, and the Narod Cultural Institute. His typefaces include Linotype Maral, Roupen, and Arasan (which was selected for inclusion in the Big Crit '99 awards). He also spends much time dissecting the Latin alphabet, tapping into the essence of this most popular writing system.

Rolf F. Rehe is director of Design Research International, a firm specializing in newspaper and online design. He has worked with newspapers and news organizations in thirty-five countries and has redesigned some sixty newspapers. His work has won national and international awards. A frequent contributor to professional publications, he lectures and conducts workshops on typography and news design. Rehe is the author of *Typography: how to make it most legible* and *Typography and design for newspapers.* Rehe was trained as typographer in Germany and studied psychology, graphic design, and journalism at Indiana University, where he earned a Master of Arts degree. He taught typography at the Herron School of Art for ten years.

Katie Salen is an assistant professor of design at the University of Texas at Austin as well as the designer and editor of the design journal *Zed.* She spends an unhealthy amount of time playing Quake and collaborates on projects connecting design, theory, and popular culture.

Mike Schmidt is a graphic designer, educator, filmmaker, curator, and budding screenwriter. He is an assistant professor of graphic design at The University of Memphis where he also serves as coordinator of graduate studies in the department of art. He teaches a wide range of courses from the experimental to the technical and historical at both the undergraduate and graduate levels. Schmidt's design for print and independent films consistently receive awards and recognition through screenings, exhibitions, competitions, and publications, including the UCDA's top honor. His primary research and creative activities explore the ramifications of ideological biases for visual and verbal communicators from the mainstream and beyond.

Steven Skaggs is professor of design at the Allen R. Hite Art Institute at the University of Louisville. He is the author of *Logos: The Development of Visual Symbols.* His articles on design theory and semiotics have appeared in a variety of publications including the *AIGA Journal of Graphic Design, Zed, The Journal of American Semiotics,* and *Letter Arts Review* as well as chapters in *Hi-Fives: A Trip To Semiotics* and *The Education of the Graphic Designer.* His calligraphic art explores the tension between the visual and verbal word. It has been widely exhibited in the United States as well as in Italy, Canada, Switzerland, Israel, and East Germany. His work is part of the permanent collections of the Newberry Library and the Sackner Archive of Concrete and Visual Poetry. He is still following his dream of playing basketball in the NBA.

David Small's "Rethinking the Book" was adapted from his PhD dissertation of the same name. The dissertation chronicles his research on the display and manipulation of complex visual information at the MIT Media Laboratory. He began his studies of dynamic typography in three-dimensional landscapes as a student of Muriel Cooper, founder of the Visible Language Workshop and later joined the Aesthetics and Computation Group under the direction of John Maeda. The Talmud Project was featured in the National Design Triennial at the Cooper-Hewitt museum. His work has appeared in *Newsweek, Scientific American, Print, Communication Arts,* the *Atlantic Monthly, ID* magazine's 42nd Annual Design Review and the book *Information Architects.* A typographic animation designed for the Brain Opera in collaboration with Yin Yin Wong premiered in New York's Lincoln Center. He has designed interactive information environments for such companies as BMW, IBM, LEGO and Nike, Inc.

James Souttar grew up in the sixties, was a teenager in the seventies, started working as a graphic designer in the eighties, and spent his journeyman years in the nineties. Thus, he survived Compacta Black, Bookman Swash, ITC Berkeley, Template Gothic, and now the Univers revival, yet somehow he has managed to remain an optimist. Most of his career has been spent working in corporate identity, some of it for the big London houses such as Wolff Olins, some of it as an independent. Corporations are the medieval courts of our time—mostly barbaric, but not without a desire to become civilized—and the corporate designer is little more than a jester. But there has to be hope for these organizations, for without it there's not much hope for the rest of us. To which end Souttar formed a business with his good friend Maziar Raien and other friends and colleagues to try to humanize this area of design. Looking to the new thinking emerging from the social and cognitive sciences, they want to bring ideas back into graphic design.

Gunnar Swanson is a graphic designer, media designer, and the director of the multimedia program at California Lutheran University. Swanson has won over fifty awards and publications for trademark, publication, type, packaging, and graphic design from AIGA, *Graphis, How,* the *American Corporate Identity* series, and other graphic design organizations, books, and magazines. He has had over a dozen articles on graphic design subjects published by *How, Design Issues,* the *AIGA Journal of Graphic Design,* Virginia Commonwealth University, and others. His writing is included in three graphic design anthologies, translated into Spanish, and published in Mexico. He was co-editor with Katie Salen of *Zed.3.*

"Clarety: Drinking from the Crystal Goblet" appeared in the first issue of Serif. *"On the Democratization of Typography" was published in the Fall 1996 issue of the* AIGA Journal of Graphic Design.

Beatrice Warde (1900–1969) was born in the US but spent much of her life as a central figure of the British type world as a typographer, writer, editor, and scholar. She wrote and designed the Monotype broadsheet "This Is a Printing Office."

Stephanie Zelman followed her degree in philosophy/political theory with work as a graphic designer in Tokyo, another degree (this one in communication design), and the design and art direction of a range of conceptual projects in New York, Montreal, and Boston. Her passion for new ideas and concepts led her to found Uturn Design, a Boston design firm that manipulates words and images to create unexpected meanings.

"Looking into Space" was adapted from Zelman's McGill University Masters Degree in Communications thesis.

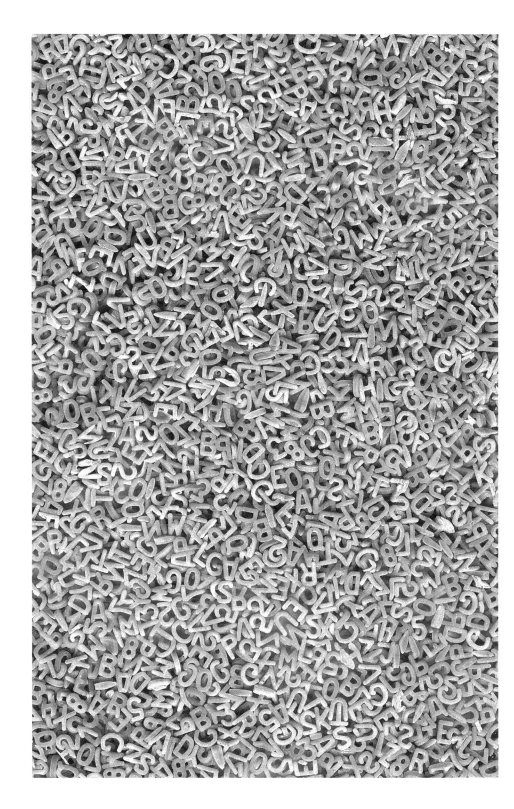

Index

FRANKLIN GOTHIC

Franklin Gothic was
designed in 1902 by
Morris Fuller Benton
and released in 1905
by the American Type
Founders company.
The son of Lynn Boyd
Benton, the inventor
of the Benton punch
cutting machine and

Colophon

The principle typeface used in *Graphic Design & Reading* is Bembo set 11/13 (eleven point size with two extra points of leading). The face is a revival by the Monotype Corporation, a design project supervised by Stanley Morison (1889-1961) in 1929. Although there is no universally agreed upon type classification system, the design of Bembo is often called a Garalde Oldstyle. Bembo was modeled on a typeface cut by Francesco Griffo for Aldus Manutius' printing of *De Aetna* in 1495 in Venice. The book by classicist Pietro Cardinal Bembo was about his visit to Mount Etna. The italic for Bembo was based on the handwriting of the Renaissance scribe Giovanni Tagliente.

Bembo was digitized as a Type 1 PostScript font by Monotype in their UK office and edited for Adobe by Alan Sanders and Ernie March before its 1990–1992 release. Most of the Bembo and Bembo Italic numerals used in this book are oldstyle (also called hanging) numerals from Adobe's Bembo Expert and Bembo Italic OsF fonts.

Side notes, captions, and incidental material is in ITC Franklin Gothic Book. ITC Franklin Gothic Demi is used for authors' names and other emphasis and the Heavy weight is featured in some drop caps and titles.

Franklin Gothic was designed in 1902 by Morris Fuller Benton (1872–1948) and released in 1905 by the American Type Founders company. The son of Linn Boyd Benton, the inventor of the Benton punch cutting machine and ATF's technical director, M.F. Benton designed typefaces and managed the typographic design program at ATF from 1892 until 1937.

Franklin Gothic was originally issued in only one weight and later expanded to include five more weights. No light or intermediate weights were developed by ATF. The International Typeface Corporation had Victor Caruso design four new weights in roman and italic — Book, Medium, Demi, and Heavy — in 1979. Typical of ITC in the '70s, the faces featured an enlarged x-height (the height of the lowercase letters). ITC Franklin Gothic was digitized by URW for ITC in the early 1980s and reworked for Adobe by Alan Sanders in 1995.

(A chart on Montoype's web site indicates that Bembo and Franklin Gothic are not particularly compatible typefaces.)

The following typefaces were shown courtesy of Emigre:
On pages 78 and 82: CITIZEN (designed by Zuzana Licko in 1986) and TEMPLATE GOTHIC (designed by Barry Deck in 1990)
On pages 78 and 83: DEMOCRATICA (designed by Miles Newlyn in 1991)
On page 82: DEAD HISTORY (designed by P. Scott Makela in 1990)
On page 83: EMPEROR and UNIVERSAL (designed by Zuzana Licko in 1985), MISSIONARY (designed by Miles Newlyn in 1991), SENATOR (designed by Zuzana Licko in 1988), and SUBURBAN (designed by Rudy VanderLans in 1993)
On pages 83 and 122: DOGMA (designed by Zuzana Licko in 1994)
On page 122: MRS EAVES (designed by Zuzana Licko in 1996)

INTERSTATE (designed by Tobias Frere-Jones in 1993–1999) shown on page 78 was provided by the Font Bureau.

STATE (designed by Neville Brody in 1991) shown on page 57 thanks to FontShop.

House Industries provided FRATHOUSE (designed by Ken Barber in 1993) shown on page 78 and POORHOUSE, CONDEMNDHOUSE, CRACKHOUSE, ASHYHOUSE, AND NASTYHOUSE (all designed by Jeremy Dean in 1996) shown on page 83.

ELDER FUTHARK (designed by Curtis Clark in 1995) shown on page 5 courtesy of Mockingbird Font Works.

BOOKMAN SWASH (based on a mid 19th century Scottish typeface) shown on page 134 is from URW.

The "I" on page 137 is part of the GOUDY INITIALS (called CLOISTER INITIALS by ATF) designed by Frederic Goudy in 1918. It was digitized by Lanston Type Co., Ltd. in 1989.

The following typefaces are from Adobe:
On page 4: FETTE FRAKTUR is a 19th century design.
On page 78: CENTURY SCHOOLBOOK (designed by Morris Fuller Benton in 1920), HELVETICA (designed by Eduord Hoffman and Max Miedenger in 1961), and BELL GOTHIC (designed by Chauncey H. Griffith in 1937)
On pages 78 and 102: UNIVERS (designed by Adrian Frutiger in 1954)
On pages 101 and 117: BODONI is an early 20th century adaption of the late 18th century faces of Giambattista Bodoni.
On page 120: PEIGNOT (designed by A.M. Cassandre in 1937)
On page 125: FUTURA (designed by Paul Renner in 1929) and GILL SANS (designed by Eric Gill in 1928)

The title type on page 111 was designed in 2000 by Hrant Papazian based on FRANKLIN GOTHIC DEMI. The alphabet shown on page 131 was designed by Hrant Papazian in 1999 based on Charles Bigelow and Kris Holmes' Lucida Sans. The TRAJIC NOTROMAN Q on page 126 was designed by Hrant Papazian in 1998.

Old type samples shown on pages 81 and 82, including Morris Fuller Benton's HOBO, are from the 1917 *Morgan Press, Linotype, and Ludlow specimens.*

Go to the *Graphic Design & Reading* section of *www.gunnarswanson.com* for links to the type foundries.

Graphic Design & Reading was designed and typeset by Gunnar Swanson using Adobe InDesign 1.5. Cover design by Gunnar Swanson using Adobe Illustrator 6.0 and 8.0 The book was printed and perfect bound by Transcontinental Printing and Graphics in Louiseville Québec on 60# Cougar Opaque.

Images on pages 63–71: ©1999 Colette Gaiter
Photo on page 79: ©1999 Lauren Sanders
Photo on page 80: ©1999 Patricia Ramos
Photo on page 112: ©1994 Mignon Naegeli
Diagram on page 127: ©1998 Hrant Papazian
Photo on page 134: ©1982/2000 Gunnar Swanson
Photos on page 160: ©2000 Paul Elliman
Photo on page 162: ©1996 Gunnar Swanson
Photo on page 182: ©2000 Gunnar Swanson
Images on pages 193, 196, and 199: ©1998 David Small
Photo on page 202: ©2000 Gunnar Swanson
Photo on page 216: ©2000 Gunnar Swanson

Thanks to Nancy Bernard, Frank Boross, Ed Fella, Nancy Harby, Garland Kirkpatrick, David Lemon, Zuzana Licko, Hrant Papazian, Barry Stock, Rosemary Swanson, Massimo Vignelli, and to everyone at Allworth Press.

Books from Allworth Press

Sex Appeal: The Art of Allure in Graphic and Advertising Design
edited by Steven Heller (softcover, 6 ¾ x 10, 288 pages, $18.95)

The Swastika: Symbol Beyond Redemption?
by Steven Heller (hardcover, 6 x 9, 256 pages, $21.95)

The Education of a Graphic Designer
edited by Steven Heller (softcover, 6 ¾ x 10, 272 pages, $18.95)

Design Dialogues
by Steven Heller and Elinor Pettit (softcover, 6 ¾ x 10, 256 pages, $18.95)

Design Literacy: Understanding Graphic Design
edited by Steven Heller and Marie Finamore
(softcover, 6 ¾ x 10, 320 pages, $19.95)

Design Literacy (continued)
by Steven Heller (softcover, 6 ¾ x 10, 288 pages, $19.95)

Looking Closer: Critical Writings on Graphic Design
edited by Michael Bierut, William Drenttel, Steven Heller, DK Holland
(softcover, 6 ¾ x 10, 256 pages, $18.95)

Looking Closer 2: Critical Writings on Graphic Design
edited by Michael Bierut, William Drenttel, Steven Heller, DK Holland
(softcover, 6 ¾ x 10, 288 pages, $18.95)

Looking Closer 3: Classic Writings on Graphic Design
edited by Michael Bierut, Jessica Helfand, Steven Heller, and Rick Poynor
(softcover, 6 ¾ x 10, 256 pages, $18.95)

Design Culture: An Anthology of Writing from the AIGA Journal of Graphic Design
by Steven Heller and Karen Pomeroy (softcover, 6 ¾ x 10, 288 pages, $19.95)

AIGA Professional Practices in Graphic Design
The American Institute of Graphic Arts
edited by Tad Crawford (softcover, 6 ¾ x 10, 320 pages, $24.95)

Please write to request our free catalog. To order by credit card, call 1-800-491-2808 or send a check or money order to Allworth Press, 10 East 23rd Street, Suite 210, New York, NY 10010. Include $5 for shipping and handling for the first book ordered and $1 for each additional book. Ten dollars plus $1 for each additional book if ordering from Canada. New York State residents must add sales tax.

If you would like to see our complete catalog on the World Wide Web, you can find us at www.allworth.com.